THE MISTAKE HAS A NAME

Inspired by a true story

Anne Weihsmann

Xulon Press
2301 Lucien Way #415
Maitland, FL 32751
407.339.4217

Printed in the United States of America
ISBN 9798642498279

ACKNOWLEDGEMENTS

To Kathy Firestone: Your definition of creative non-fiction gave me a framework for this story – a blending of real and imagined people and events into a narrative greater than the sum of its parts. When I understood that the real names, places, and many events could be changed without diminishing the power of the story, I was ready to swing for the fences.

To my loving husband Steve: Thank you for encouraging me to chase my dream.

To Therese Black: Your tough questions stretched my writing muscles to find the best words for each part of the story.

To Virginia Andre´: Your editing skills were invaluable; you are 'too' good!

To Carly, my older daughter: Your meticulous attention to grammar and details was priceless.

To my church family: You are the great cloud of witnesses who encouraged, prayed, and cheered me on to the finish line.

The seven-year writing journey would not have been possible without all of you.

PREFACE

Late afternoon is a sensual feast. Reds and oranges break into a kaleidoscope of color, dancing through the trees in unpredictable rhythm. The sweet smell of burning wood rises serenely from countless backyards, blending with the sound of waves rearranging the sandy beach under a cloudless sky. Heaven's refracted light slides under earth's door. Contentment is at home in my soul.

Gravel crunches under my feet along the path hugging the shore at Strand Lake Bible Camp. The women's fall retreat gives me space to make new friends and to find deeper levels of connection with women I know only from an emotional distance at church. The weekend will offer both motive and opportunity to be challenged, encouraged, and renewed by kindred spirits.

Julie is a church acquaintance; we share first names and a love of books. These next two days will become a game-changer as I push out the edges of casual friendship to reveal a woman refreshingly forthcoming; delightfully honest; and an engaging storyteller. My long-dormant desire to write a book awakens and rises to the surface; Julie's astonishing life is a story demanding to be told. It is an idea one part exciting and two parts terrifying.

I am deeply humbled by Julie's willingness to open windows into her troubling past. She shares her story without the end game of shock value and revenge. She does not indulge a negative self-esteem or justify years of accumulated wrongs. Julie seems, instead, to be about *soul*-esteem as her life reveals the work of a loving and gracious Heavenly Father – a Father who tears down walls of deceit and rebuilds a home of forgiveness, a home where memories are a constant healing-in-progress, and where the goodness of God trumps the unfairness of life.

YOUR SHED BLOOD

Your shed blood of Grace is an ocean
Breaking over me in ceaseless waves.
My weary spirit returns only tears
Lovingly collected in Your bottle.
Blood is the water of renewal.
Tears are the water of praise.
Tears fill a well of rejoicing.
Blood flows into a River of Life.
My weary spirit offers tears
Collected in Your bottle of remembrance.
Your shed Blood of Grace is a sea
Sweeping over me in waves of forgiveness.

PROLOGUE
April 1, 2001

Julie awakens to a hazy sky on her forty-fifth birthday. Spring crept into Michigan overnight, coaxing tired clumps of dirty snow into their melting fate. Thin sheets of wax paper ice cover ponds bubbling with life. Lengthening days encourage the pale sun to pry loose winter's pale-knuckled grip.

Dressed for church in simple khakis and a blue button-down shirt, Julie stares into the full-length mirror in her spacious bedroom. The beginnings of crow's-feet crinkle the corners of intensely brown eyes, deep-set and compassionate, framed under carefully arched eyebrows. A small chin sits squarely in her oval-shaped face, highlighted by a radiant smile showcasing bright white teeth as straight as piano keys. Normally fastidious about her short, stylish, auburn hair, she does not fuss with it today. It will soon be drenched and plastered to her head.

A newly washed, bright burgundy, ninety-eight Olds Silhouette minivan idles in the driveway, a duty-bound chariot waiting to take Julie and her husband to First Evangelical Free Church.

The fifteen-minute ride gives Julie time to think back on the years fueled by a primal need to survive; years on auto pilot, shielding her from suffocating hopelessness. When the gas finally ran out and all earthly resources were used up, Julie found God waiting to reclaim her life and give it back to her.

A fresh start tugs at her heart in the words of

Psalm thirty-four, verse eight: "The Lord is near to the brokenhearted and saves those who are crushed in spirit."

The parking lot is already overflowing a half-hour before the eleven o'clock service. Inside the sanctuary, Julie and her husband meet their extended family and search for seats in a small space compacted by the removal of the first two rows of padded chairs to accommodate the portable baptismal tank. The three-by-six-foot tank is covered in a dark wainscoting, making a dignified backdrop for the carefully placed lilies.

I spent so many years wishing the people who hurt me would get what they deserved; my awesome God chose not to give me what I deserved! Julie smiles at the musicians playing contemporary worship music during the gathering time and hopes she can settle her nerves when Pastor Tim calls her name as a candidate for baptism.

Part of this day seems like another of Julie's many dreams; yet she knows this is real. Her dreams were often full of hideous demons wearing masks; today the disguises are gone, exposing the ugliness of a past that no longer has power over her. Julie and Pastor Tim face the congregation as he recites a verse from First Corinthians and Julie whispers it in her heart: "Blessed be the God and Father of our Lord Jesus Christ, the Father of mercies and God of all comfort, who comforts us in all our afflictions so that we will be able to comfort those who are in any affliction with the comfort with which we ourselves are comforted by God." *Can God use me as a wounded healer for someone drowning in rage-filled anguish and despair?*

Pastor Tim helps Julie climb into the blue fiberglass-lined tank and lowers her under the water. Julie longs for it to wash away a lifetime of blame and shame …

CHAPTER 1
"NINETY-NINE BOTTLES OF BEER ON THE WALL"

Julie Sandford wanted a doll to dress. Not just any doll. The perfect one. The one in the Sears-Roebuck catalogue. The one on the picture she tore out and taped to the faded pink wall above her rollaway bed. At night, alone in her room, Julie whispered goodnight to the doll and imagined it life-sized, with skinny arms and legs like hers, but with jet-black hair not anything like her not-quite-blonde-not-quite-brown hair. Julie pretended she looked like one of those Breck shampoo models on TV with the beautiful, wavy, auburn hair.

The fairy tale ended at the beginning of each month on a rickety metal stool in their drab kitchen, where Momma chopped her hair into a pixie cut. Julie always sat and stared silently at the walls of the kitchen, wondering how they could be the same color as her hair – a color she could not find in her small box of broken crayons.

The doll needed a dress. The Sears catalogue did not have any, but in Julie's mind, the dress was puffy, yellow seersucker and made a swishing sound when twirled. Julie had another secret: That someday the two of them would have matching dresses.

Used-up dresses hanging from a rusty metal rod in a dark corner had long since faded from bright colors to apologetic shades of something. *At least the dresses with no color match my hair.*

Second grade was starting in six days. Julie

assumed the position on the stool and slumped her shoulders under another hair massacre. When the damage was done, she picked up the cracked hand mirror, looked at her reflection, and laid it back on the green countertop.

"Please, oh please, Momma, can I have a new dress for school? Maybe a yellow seersucker one?" Julie wasn't sure what begging for a dress would do; she had never seen Momma wearing one. Maybe she didn't have one or didn't want one. Still, she thought Momma looked like a movie star. With her slim waist and dark, wavy hair, she looked like Dorothy in "The Wizard of Oz," except that her clouded eyes made her look old and sad, like the sun had left the sky a long time ago.

Arlene Sandford ground her half-smoked cigarette into the bottom of a glass ashtray, swirled the towel away from Julie's neck, scrunched it, and dropped it on the floor.

"Okay, let's see what you got for dresses."

Julie leaped off the stool and skipped to her bedroom, hands smacking the walls of the narrow hallway, hoping for victory. She burst through the door and dove onto her bed, sagging springs moaning in protest.

Arlene was right behind Julie. She stopped in the doorway, kicked off her high heels, leaned against the door frame, and lifted one foot at a time, checking for runs in her nylons.

"We won't be able to buy you a new dress if you break your bed." Arlene pushed against the frame, stood up, and straightened the belt around the waist of her long, green tunic top hanging loosely over white pants.

Julie sat on the edge of her bed. Staying in the

middle would mean sinking into the trough formed by who-knew-how-many-bodies that had done who-knew-what in her bed before she got it.

"Yes, Ma'am," she whispered, breathing very quietly.

Arlene walked to the pretend closet and rifled through the dresses, each hanger scraping along the rod, noisily protesting the coming judgment. Her hand suddenly stopped as she stared up at a spot on the ceiling. Julie had seen her mom do this before in other rooms of the house. It was like she vanished into another world. *Maybe this time, Momma is thinking back to when she was a little girl and wore pretty dresses.*

Dropping her gaze back to the rod, Arlene grabbed a hanger, turned around, and held up a mousy brown jumper with small ink stains dotting the front.

"This'll do," she declared. "This'll do fine. What do you need a new dress for anyway? School ain't no big deal."

The dresses were ugly. After her mom rehung the jumper, walked back to the doorway, stooped over to pick up her shoes, and disappeared down the hall, Julie fell back into the bed trough. She stared at the doll picture through teary eyes. Wiping them on her sleeve, she yelled, "That's it! When I get the doll, I'll name her Thistledew – sounds like 'this'll do.'" She giggled at her joke and her world righted itself again. Now she just needed rescuing from the trough.

Julie never thought about begging Dad to fight her dress battle. She didn't know if he paid any attention to what she wore. But Julie noticed everything about her handsome father. He had bigger muscles than any man she ever saw except the ones on TV commercials. One time, she overheard her parents arguing in their bedroom. "Hey, Mr. Bigshot," Mom yelled, "If you could train for the Mr. Olympia title, how about throwing your weight into a decent job?" The next thing she heard was their bedroom door slamming. She smelled her dad's Old Spice even before he walked into the living room. He came in while she sprawled on the brown carpet in front of the TV, sat on the green plaid sofa, put on his Wellington boots, placed his welder's cap carefully over his wavy hair, checked the crease on his jeans, ran his hands over his well-trimmed beard, got up and walked out the front door without stopping to check his reflection in the hall mirror. *Did he know I was in the room?*

Julie figured she was like that mirror: neither of them ever got a sideways glance. Both were invisible to Danny Sandford. She wanted him to see her. Sometimes, though, she admitted that she was glad he ignored her, especially when he drank out of the brown bottles from the back of the refrigerator. That's when he got angry and yelled. It was scary, but funny, because he sounded like he had marbles rolling around in his mouth. But then there were times when he spit out horrible words at Momma. Julie didn't know what the words meant, but Momma spit them back until it sounded like they were playing a gross volleyball game. That's when Julie stayed away from them, so she didn't get caught in the net.

The Sandford family kept moving during Julie's first eight years. She never made friends with the classmates she left behind. Momma and Daddy never let her invite any girls over. *And even if they did, my friends would hear them fighting and would not want to come back again.* She never got invited to other girls' houses and thought maybe it was because those girls lived in houses like the Cleaver house, not like hers. The house they had now had two missing front window screens like missing teeth. The inside smelled like old shoes, fried onions, and cigarettes. The odor stayed on the torn sofa, the stained, beige drapes, and her clothes, and she could never get away from it.

Julie's best friends were discarded library books, stuffed animals from second-hand stores, and her imagination. She wished that her six-year-old brother Dan was one of her friends, but he was mainly a pest. Someday, she wanted Thistledew as her special friend. And maybe Momma would buy her an Easy-Bake Oven with the little pan big enough for a cake for two. She and Thistledew would share secrets about what they wanted to be when they grew up.

Grandma Leona Hagstrom, Danny's mom, was coming to live with the Sandfords. Julie skipped around the house, short hair lifting and dropping around her head like dandelion fluff, untied saddle-shoe laces slapping against the black-checkered linoleum kitchen floor.

"Grandma's coming! Grandma's coming!" Julie's secret spilled out. "Maybe she'll buy me a doll, and an Easy-Bake Oven, and some little boxes of cake mix, and a little tea set." *Wasn't having a grandma living with you the best of all?*

"What're you talking about?" Arlene washed dishes with her back turned toward Julie.

Julie guarded the rest of her dreams. "Momma,

why isn't Grandma's last name Sandford like ours?"
She had a hard time figuring out this family stuff.

"You ask too many questions." Arlene turned
and stared at her daughter, eyebrows creased in intense
thought, mind filtering memories. "Because ... I think
Grandma remarried after your grandpa died—"

"I don't get it—"

"And his name was Roy Hagstrom. He also died
a few years ago. Maybe."

Julie never asked why Grandma was coming to
live with them. *Does she need money? Will she bring us
money or food? I do not care – I just want her here!*

September was as hot as July had been. Julie sat
outside on the front steps, looked up at the sky and tried
to remember what she had learned about the Milky
Way. *There must be a million stars up there! I hope I
see a shooting one.* A Yellow Cab pulled up in front of
their house, interrupting her daydreams with a squeaky
door and an old woman unfolding herself from the back
seat. The cab driver walked around to the trunk, hoisted
it open, and pulled out a tan, dented suitcase. He handed
it to the woman, who carried a bulging plastic bag. The
woman grumbled, "Why'd you bring me here,
anyway?" She turned around and headed towards Julie.

This must be Grandma Hagstrom! When she
had asked Momma when Grandma was coming, she
barked, "When the spirit moves her." The woman
walked up the steps and around Julie into their house
without knocking first. Julie got up and followed her in.

Arlene came out from the kitchen, wiped her
hands on her apron, walked over to Leona and said,
"Hiya, Lee," motioning for Julie to come closer. "This

is your grandkid, Julie. Julie, kiss your grandma." She stared. *Grandma's hair looks like the water in the kitchen sink after Momma does all the dishes. And it looks like my hair, too, short and stick straight.*

Julie closed the gap to her grandma, standing on tiptoes and trying to reach her orange powdered cheek. She mostly kissed the air. Leona didn't let go of her suitcase or bag and stood as still as a statue. Finally, she declared, "Well, hi, then." Grandma Hagstrom didn't seem too excited to be in their house. Julie stepped back and tried to hide her curiosity about her grandma's clothes. *She's wearing a dress, but it doesn't have any lace, or fancy buttons, and it is not even pretty.* Leona's lime green dress was too loose around her top, and too tight around her waist. The color was faded around the bottom, and a button was missing near the top.

Leona dropped her suitcase and bag and walked to the sofa. Rubbing her hand across a cushion, she collapsed on her stomach, turning her head towards the back of the sofa. Arlene grabbed Julie's elbow and dragged her silently out of the room.

By the end of the first month with Grandma Hagstrom, Julie couldn't hide her disappointment. Grandma didn't know anything about dolls, dresses, or little girls. When she tried to get her to play paper dolls, her grandma took the scissors and cut them into shreds before Julie found Momma and begged her to take Grandma away. She wished her grandma would wear the glasses hanging from a chain around her neck. Maybe they would hide eyes too blurry to tell what color they were.

Julie showed Grandma how to play Go Fish. She

was having fun until Grandma asked her four times in a row if she had any eights. Julie carefully gathered the cards into a pile, told her grandma she was tired, and turned on the TV. Grandma fell asleep sitting up, head tipped to one side, still gripping her cards.

Leona Hagstrom drank and smoked with Julie's Momma and Daddy late at night around the kitchen table. Long after she had been sent to bed, Julie would sneak back down to the living room and hear the adults talking loudly. Soon they were arguing. Then they would use words she had heard before from her parents. She would also hear caps pop and knew they were drinking from the brown bottles. When all the noise stopped, Julie would scrunch her nightgown into one hand and quickly run back up the stairs, closing her door right before heavy footsteps followed her. From the other side of the door, it would sound like people were dragging or carrying someone, and she thought she knew who it was.

On the school bus, Julie heard the word alcoholic from some of the older kids. She looked up the word in the tattered school dictionary and thought maybe Grandma Hagstrom was an alcoholic. She never heard the word at home but started saying it when she talked about her grandma at school. It did not make Grandma Hagstrom sound very nice, but what else could she say about her?

Connect-the-dots was one of Julie's favorite rainy-day games. She sprawled on her bedroom floor with her bright pink pencil, concentrating on using just the right pressure on the paper, until the dot picture was almost done. *It looks like a giraffe. I love it. I wish*

Daddy and Momma would take me to the Seattle Zoo sometime. My teacher says it is only thirteen miles from Bremerton, but that must be a long way away, because whenever I ask Momma, she says, "We don't have time for that."

When Julie finished the last page of her book, she doodled on the inside back cover, drawing pictures of her parents, brother, and grandma, and then a big dot under each person. *If I connect all these dots, what kind of picture do I get? Daddy doesn't know I'm here. Momma and Grandma do things I don't understand. Everyone yells more than they talk. If they really want to be heard, they use bad words. When that doesn't work, they slam doors.* She wanted her connect-the-dot family to be a picture of the Cleavers, but she knew that couldn't happen. *Besides, June Cleaver always vacuums in a dress.*

CHAPTER 2
SCHOOL DAZE

Lilac bushes perfumed the air. Julie loved spring. *I wonder what happened to my bike after we moved last year.* She needed something to do on this long, boring Saturday afternoon. Kneeling on the sofa facing the back with her arms propped up on the frayed top, she looked out the window at the pretty yellow and red and blue birds landing on the feeder in the neighbor's yard and swatted at the flies coming in through the torn screens.

A noise from behind made Julie turn around. Grandma stood in the living room, slightly hunched over, holding the same suitcase and stuffed plastic bag, and wearing the same lime green dress she had worn the night she moved in with them back in September. Arlene's voice carried from the kitchen.

"Julie, kiss your grandma goodbye." Julie wanted to kiss her grandma but still wasn't any taller. She ran to the hall closet, got out the hair-cutting stool, dragged it to the living room right next to Grandma, climbed up on it and kissed her on the cheek.

"Bye, little girl." Leona walked to the door, set her plastic bag down, opened the door, walked out, and left the bag behind.

A week before Grandma left, Julie overheard her telling Momma and Daddy that this grandma thing was not for her; and that she was moving in with a friend in Seattle.

"Besides," Leona said, "You people keep taking my purse and my glasses and my toothbrush. If Ida knowed you needed stuff, I would've brung it to you." Julie hadn't heard any more of the conversation. *Why didn't anyone tell me Grandma was leaving?*

Leona was gone. The house returned to something familiar to Julie. As she sat in front of the TV watching Saturday morning cartoons, Momma lugged in an old, scratched, blue suitcase to the living room.

"Pack all your clothes, books, and other junk in this." She walked away before Julie could ask where they were going.

The family was moving across the country. Julie had heard Kankakee was somewhere in a place called the Midwest but couldn't find it on the map. She was glad to leave Grandma in Washington, and excited about living somewhere new, and even about going to a new school. But it would probably be the same old thing: her parents would not let her have any girlfriends over or go to their houses. She wouldn't get too close to other kids but also wouldn't have part of her heart torn away when she had to move. Again.

Maybe now that Grandma Hagstrom was gone, her parents would drink less, and talk nicer to each other.

Third grade started the Tuesday after Labor Day. Julie and four girls from her new neighborhood waited at the bus stop at eight forty-five, along with her brother Dan and another first-grader. Julie hoped her instant oatmeal would stay down, and that she would feel calm enough to eat her lunch.

I hope Momma made my favorite peanut butter and grape jelly sandwich, and that she packed a box of Animal Crackers. I wonder what we're having at snack time. The yellow school bus turned the corner and headed down the street. Julie took off her pink cardigan sweater, tied it around the waist of her robin's-egg blue dress, picked up her bag with her school supplies, and climbed the steep steps onto the bus. The fifteen-minute ride to school was the longest in her life, even longer than when they had driven across the country to this new place. *I can't wait to get there!*

Hubert Elementary was a red brick, two-story, plain building, surrounded by a gravel parking lot, a paved playground, a baseball field, and a row of stately maples, standing as a proud tribute to functionality and stability. Teachers started and ended their careers there. Seniors from the neighboring high school returned to thank former teachers for expecting more than they, the students, could give. Parents attended conferences, affirmed the work of those same teachers, and hung out in the hallways, sharing the easy camaraderie of people who have known each other since kindergarten.

The school had the universal elementary hallway smell of floor wax, stale milk, Elmer's Glue, Lysol, and fish sticks. Julie felt like she was back in Washington, and she knew she would be okay here. Teachers' aides directed the students to the appropriate classrooms as they poured out of the busses like ants from an anthill. Julie followed the rest of the third graders, while boys punched each other, girls straightened hair ribbons, and everyone's energy level was on high alert.

Once in their rooms, the kids staked out desks

and marked their territory with pencil pouches and boxes of crayons. Some kids had metal lunchboxes. A few of the better-dressed kids showed off their sixty-four boxes of Crayola crayons. Julie looked at her Woolworth's ten-crayon box and hoped no one would make fun of her. She felt lucky to have a new box.

A woman marched into the room. The kids instantly folded their hands on their desks and looked straight ahead. Julie noticed the woman's powerful-looking arm muscles and bet she could take on her dad! The boys whispered about who she might whoop, while Julie wondered how this woman – probably their new teacher – ignored the dress code by wearing black pants and a plain, white, short-sleeved blouse. Julie was used to her mom's dark, shoulder length hair, styled in soft waves, and her dad's neatly combed, collar length hair. Miss Whoever-She-Is had short, reddish hair that stuck straight up. The light shone right through it to a place on the chalkboard behind her. Her square-looking face was pale, eyes squinted in little slits. Her spread-legged stance protected her ground in King of the Classroom.

"Class, I am Miss Meyer." She cleared her throat like a growling dog. "You will pay attention at all times. There is to be no talking when I am standing here unless I call on you. There will be no gum chewing. You will raise your hands at all times."

For the next ten minutes, Miss Meyer read the rules in her low voice even deeper than Julie's dad's when he was mad. Julie's excitement turned to fear. When she climbed back on the bus that afternoon, the school gossip was that Miss Meyer was kicked out of the Marines. Julie did not know what that meant but was already scared of saying or doing something wrong in class. *I am invisible to my father. With any luck, Miss Meyer won't notice me, either.*

By the end of the second day, even the bravest-looking kids kept their hands folded in their laps or tightly gripping their number two pencils during teaching time. No hands waved for attention. No one whispered or passed notes. Miss Meyer looked like someone who would not just take prisoners out to the hallway and have them sit on the floor, like Julie's last teacher did with some of the naughty kids. She might do something else, and Julie did not want to find out what that something else would be.

"Where does oil come from?" barked Miss Meyer one rainy morning during the third week of school. The students had learned that their teacher was full of trick questions, and they didn't know whether this was one of them. "It's not necessary to raise your hands – just shout out answers." Miss Meyer had never changed her rule about hand raising. None of the kids knew what was coming.

Silence.

"Come on, let's have fun! Show me what you know!"

"Rocks!" one boy fearfully shouted. Everyone giggled.

And from near the front, "The ocean!"

More silence.

The kids looked around. Julie was nervous and sweaty.

Miss Meyer walked over. "Sandford?" she rasped.

Oh no. "Oil wells?" she whispered.

Miss Meyer lunged at her like she was the enemy. Grabbing her by the dress collar, she pulled Julie up out of her seat and hauled her to the front of the room. Nervous giggles erupted from students near the back, the ones with a clear escape route.

The ramrod-straight teacher panted. "Class, I want you all to see what happens to stupid kids. Sandford here will write her name in my Stupid Student Answer Book." Miss Meyer turned her face until it was inches from Julie's. "And when you're finished, you will drop and give me ten." The class became pin-drop quiet.

"Ten what?" squeaked Julie.

"Man, you're even dumber than I thought. After you sign my book, you better spend some time in my Stupid Student Answer Chair."

I'm glad I didn't eat breakfast today, 'cuz it'd be all over the floor by now. Julie signed her name in the book of shame, sat in the Stupid Chair, ate lunch by herself, then returned to her desk for the rest of the afternoon, occasionally glancing at the other kids snickering and rolling their eyes and making weird faces at her, especially the boys. When she walked into her house that afternoon, she wondered whether she should tell her parents what happened to her. If they took her side and pitched a fit with her teacher, she would be called a tattletale for the rest of the year. If they said, "Your teacher knows what she's doing," then she would feel stupider than ever. The best thing to do was to push the day way down inside of her and forget all about it. She had to figure out a way to keep it from ever happening again.

Miss Meyer did not run out of stupid students,

ones who kept her attention off Julie for the next several weeks. As word circulated about Miss Meyer's classroom teaching methods, a group of parents made an appointment to meet with other teachers appalled by her thinly veiled abuse. The administration, it turned out, was as overpowered by her as her students were. Rather than taking any action to have Miss Meyer removed from the school, they instead assigned her responsibilities on the Textbook Committee and Extra-Curricular Activities Committee, praying that as she worked with the other teachers, some of their kindness and genuine concern for the students would smooth her edges.

I am stupid in Miss Meyer's class. But it would be so cool to get a part in the Christmas pageant. Then I'd be popular, and everyone would forget about what happened to me. I'm going to try out. Wearing her best dress – a slightly worn, red polka dot with a Dutch girl collar – and her hair held back by a red, plastic headband, Julie snuck into the gym after school one day in late November. Her Keds squeaked on the waxed floor as she walked across the gym to the stage, announcing her arrival long before her courage caught up. When she reached the stage, she looked up at the adults sitting in folding chairs behind a long table, papers and cups spread out around them. *What is Miss Meyer doing there?* Julie's throat closed. A girl in her class who did errands for the judges jumped down from the stage, ran up to her, cupped her hand around Julie's ear, and whispered, "Miss Meyer knows you're here. I wonder if she brought her Stupid Chair with her." When the girl pulled back, Julie saw a mean look on her face and turned around, hoping for a quick getaway.

"Sandford! What are you doing here? This play is for *smart* kids." Everyone heard Miss Meyer's words bouncing around the walls. Julie turned and ran back across the gym, which suddenly felt as big as the whole school. She hoped she could get through the double doors before Miss Meyer heard her sobbing. *I will never try out for anything.* The door banged behind her as she collapsed on the hallway floor and buried her head in her arms.

School was over. Julie had a wonderful, long summer ahead of her before she had to start worrying about the fall. *I hope Miss Meyer doesn't move up to fourth grade.* And then came great news: her family was moving again. This was not going to be another cross-country move – just to Wisconsin. Julie was relieved to leave Illinois and Miss Meyer forever.

"Momma, why are we moving?" Sitting on the sofa next to her mom, Julie remembered the rule: Questions were only allowed during commercials.

Arlene ran her hand down the sleeve of her taupe, silk blouse, smoothing out a little wrinkle. "Why, why, why? How do I know?" She kept her eyes focused on the screen while Julie wrapped and unwrapped a yoyo string around her finger until "The Fugitive" was over. Arlene got up, walked over to the TV, turned it off, swiveled and put her hands on her small hips.

"Your dad says he has buddies from Washington who live in Platteville, and they're ready for us to exercise our visitation rights." Arlene laughed, turned, and headed toward the kitchen.

Maybe I should turn the TV back on and watch

25

"The Twilight Zone." That's gotta make more sense than Momma is.

Everything the Sandfords owned fit in the smallest U-Haul, which Danny hooked to the back of their tan, Chevy Nomad wagon on the last day of June. The family was packed and ready to leave Kankakee by late morning.

The car had no air conditioning. Julie overheard her daddy saying they had a hundred seventy miles and four hours of dad-blame driving. Or something like that – the words were swallowed by the hot air blasting into her ears through the window. She felt like one of her stuffed cats with its legs all stuck out and lying face down on the back dash. Her cut-off shorts and yellow tank top were plastered to her skin. She focused on the fields racing backwards as their car sped forward; and for a while, she was too hypnotized to notice the heat. But when the tall things growing in the fields started looking like upside-down, dancing brooms, she stopped looking out the window. She hoped her stomach would make it the rest of the way to Wisconsin.

A man, a woman, and three boys with haircuts like Miss Meyer's were sitting on the porch when Julie's family pulled up in the driveway. By the time she unstuck herself from her seat and got out of the car, the adults were hugging and laughing. "Rich! Lorraine! Arlene! Danny!" Julie, Dan, and the strange boys were glued to their places, staring at each other.

"The Andersons, as I live and breathe!" Arlene laughed.

"Everyone, come in!" Lorraine put one arm around Julie and the other around Danny. *I hope it's not as hot in there as in our car, otherwise I'm coming back out and finding a shade tree.* As soon as they were all settled inside, Lorraine announced: "Go relax in the living room, and I will call you when supper's ready," then disappeared behind a swinging door.

The children followed their dads into a small room with a brown-plaid sofa, stuffed chairs, and a braided rug. One of the windows had the shade pulled down over it; the other one had a big metal contraption stuck into it that pumped out cold air at full blast. Julie dropped down on the rug, arms and legs spread out, eyes closed. All noise vanished until Mrs. Anderson stood over her and whispered, "Dinner time." She got up slowly, uncertain about leaving this wonderfully cool room, even though her stomach gurgled, waiting for its first meal since Julie had left Illinois.

There was a large table in the middle of the kitchen with picnic benches on both sides and covered with a white cloth. On top of it were dishes filled with sliced ham, little potatoes swimming in something creamy-looking, biscuits, strawberry Jell-O, and a big pitcher of iced tea. On the counter next to the stove was a tall cake with coconut icing. The smells all hit Julie's nose at once; she was starving.

Everyone wandered back outside after supper. The adults settled in lounge chairs on the porch. Dan and the three Anderson boys – Jimmy, John, and Joe, ten, eleven, and thirteen – ran around catching fireflies in the cool dusk; the lone girl asked permission from Mrs. Anderson to explore the house.

Julie meandered around looking at things she figured must be treasures. A framed picture of the family hung on a wall in the living room; a deer head

27

with big antlers and wide-open, pretty, sad eyes, adorned another wall. One of the bedrooms had a bookshelf with lots and lots of books, a golden statue of someone holding a bowling ball; and tall, fat coffee mugs with wooden handles. Her favorites were the paintings and drawings that must have been done by the Anderson boys, taped to the refrigerator. *I have never been in a house like this.* The only things Momma ever hung were stained potholder gloves and a wooden key-shaped thingamajig with hooks to hang keys.

I hope we end up living near the Andersons. At least for tonight, we will get to sleep in their guest rooms.

The next morning, Julie awoke to the smell of frying bacon. The stars outside her window still shone brighter than the top curve of the sun peeking over the horizon. She was ready for breakfast and a new day.

A rainbow arched over Platteville with a pot of gold planted in the Anderson's yard. After breakfast, Mr. Anderson announced to Julie's family that he and his wife had decided to let the Sandfords live in a trailer his family wasn't using. It was eight-by-twenty-eight feet – *whatever that means* – only a year old and parked near the edge of their farm. They would not accept any rent for it, and that was that. Julie had never, ever heard anything so wonderful.

Languid, hot, humid summer days brimmed with adventure for Julie, Dan, Jimmy, John, and Joe. They called themselves the Fab Five; and for once, Julie was okay with her shoulder length, straight hair. *If we are going to pretend to be the Beatles, I can do my part and try to look like one of them.*

There was always something to do around the farm. During the day, the Fab Five watched Mr. Anderson butcher geese and chickens. It was gross to see blood spurting everywhere, but also funny to see headless chickens running around before they keeled over and died. The best part was when Mrs. Anderson fried the chicken and invited the Sandfords for supper. The chicken was crispy and hot and tender and delicious.

As long as Julie stayed with the boys, her mom didn't care what they did. The lawn around the Anderson farmhouse was always neatly mown; but beyond that were swamps, meadows, and good climbing trees. Sometimes the Fab Five were Tarzan, Jane, Cheetah, and assorted monkeys. Other times, they went on an African safari. When they became farmers, they drew straws to see who would be first to ride the five-hundred-pound pig named Benny, the family mascot.

Most days, Julie walked into her trailer at suppertime covered in hay and mud, with parts of the farm clinging to her shoes. As soon as she finished showering and eating, she was back out with the boys. At sundown, they caught fireflies, played midnight tag, and stalked skunks. Julie dragged herself back inside for the night in dirty sneakers now wet with dew.

The oldest boy, Joe, told the others one night after a game of Red Light, Green Light, that he often saw all their parents drinking together when the boys headed in for bed. Joe also said he heard a lot of yelling and cussing, but no one ever sounded mad. Julie thought back to Grandma Hagstrom's time with them and figured when grown-ups got together, they drank. If they had a good time and left the kids alone, she was not

29

worried about it. Besides, it helped her forget Miss Meyer, which was the best thing of all.

Julie learned another new word. She was at the threshold of fourth grade at Christ Lutheran Church School. She didn't know or care what Lutheran meant, just so her new teacher didn't look like Miss Meyer.

Christ Lutheran was a stucco, rectangular building, stained-glass windows on every side, with a steeple, and a heavy, oak front door. It sat on a large, neat lot with flower boxes on the east side of the building and maple trees giving plenty of shade to picnic tables behind the church. The congregation was a close group of a hundred-and-fifty people; sometimes, family members spanning three generations shared the same pew on Sunday mornings.

Mrs. Anderson drove her boys and the Sandford children to school and back every day. On the first day of school, Jimmy, Julie and the other twelve fourth graders gathered in the hallway outside their classroom. Some kids shared their what-I-did-last-summer experiences with their friends; others, like Julie, looked around for any other new kids, the ones Mrs. Anderson said had the deer-caught-in-the-headlights look. On the Anderson farm, Julie saw a lot of deer when the sun went down. She and the boys would get a flashlight and shine it in the deer's eyes, so now she knew what that saying meant.

The fourth graders walked quickly into their room when the bell rang. Julie wore a hand-me-down uniform – navy blue jumper and white blouse – with white socks and loafers, hair pulled into a high ponytail. Her freckles gave testimony to a summer spent outdoors. *When Miss Meyer folded her arms, she looked like Mr. Clean, except that she had a little more hair. I wonder what my new teacher will look like.*

The students scattered to find desks that were either new, used, covered with drawings and initials, scratched, dented, squeaky, hinged, rusted, or plain and small. Julie walked around looking critically at each desk until she settled on one that was scratched. She sat in the seat, lifted the top, and saw a big dent on the inside. *It's perfect for me.*

The class held its collective breath as a woman with jet-black, shoulder-length, wavy hair glided into the room. Her light pink, knee-length dress was stiff as a board. *Not the clothes of an ex-Marine.* Julie's stomach felt like someone had tied a knot in it.

"Good morning, students." *Her voice sounds like a bird's.* "I am Angela Ryczek. You may call me Mrs. R, and I will call you Miss or Mister; today I will start by calling all of you Special."

Mrs. Ryczek reminded Julie of Harriet Nelson, from one of her favorite TV shows. By the end of the day, her stomach had unknotted itself.

Christ Lutheran required all students to attend church each Sunday. Mrs. Ryczek put a check in her Special Book every time one of her students went to church. *I can finally get my name and a checkmark in a book for doing something good.* Julie really wanted to please Mrs. R, one of the kindest women she had ever met; but she couldn't tell her that her parents spent every Saturday night drinking with the neighbors, and then fought when they get back to their trailer. Sunday morning, they slept until noon, while she and her brother

31

ate their bowls of Fruit Loops in front of the TV. The Anderson house was always quiet, so Julie figured they were all at church.

It was already December, and Julie still had a church problem. She thought about asking Mrs. Anderson if she and her family ever went to church. On a morning when she felt brave, Julie arrived at school, took off her jacket, mittens, and boots in the cloak room, put on her street shoes, and entered the classroom ahead of some of the kids with longer rides to school. She straightened her jumper, sat at her desk, and opened her reading book. Mrs. Ryczek was at her desk, reading glasses propped on her nose.

"Miss Sandford?" Julie looked up. *Her voice is always soft. And her eyes are the color of Windex.* "Could you please stay in for a few minutes at noon recess? I need to talk to you." Mrs. Ryczek smiled and then returned to whatever-it-is-teachers-do-at-their-desks work.

What have I done? Oh, please, I hope she's not mad at me. The knot from the first day of school came back and lived in Julie's stomach until the lunch bell rang. After everyone finished eating, they quickly put on jackets, scarves, hats, mittens, and boots, and raced outside to see who would be first to climb the six-foot high snowdrifts piled alongside the fence. Julie walked slowly to the wastebasket, tossed her bread crusts and apple core away, and stood obediently next to Mrs. R's desk.

"Sit down, dear." Julie sat in the desk-for-kids-who-need-extra-attention, hoping she wouldn't start crying. "I have noticed you do not have any checkmarks in my Special Book."

Julie cleared her throat and looked down.

Mrs. Ryczek gently put her hand under Julie's chin and lifted her head. "Do you go to church?"

"No," whispered Julie.

"Would you like to?"

"Sorta."

Mrs. Ryczek did not use any more of her twenty questions.

"Listen, Julie, you are a very smart young lady."

Smart? Lady?

"I have seen how easily you memorize facts. I know how we could get your name in my book."

Oh, I'm listening! Julie clasped her hands tightly together.

"If you memorize a bible verse each week and recite it to me during Monday noon recess, I will put a check next to your name. What do you think?"

"Could ... could I take a Bible home?"

"Absolutely."

"Oh, then I will do it!" Julie jumped up and flung her arms around her teacher. "Thank you, thank you!"

Mrs. Ryczek smiled and waited for Julie to finish her hug and step back. "Julie, here are three index cards with a different verse on each one. You can pick whichever one you want to start with. They are John three-sixteen, Genesis one-one, and First John one-nine. I will be ready to hear you recite next week."

Julie would have done anything for Mrs. Ryczek, and now she would get her name in the Special Book. She could not imagine trying to get through the rest of the school day before going home and starting to read and memorize verses. Sitting on her twin bed that night, Julie opened to the first page of the Bible, expecting to find an index that showed how to get to First John. Instead, she read the words, "This Bible is given to," followed by "Julie Sandford." The next line read, "On this date," followed by, "Christmas, 1966." *My very own Bible! Mrs. Ryczek did this for me!* Julie held the book like a treasure, even better than the doll she always wanted.

Julie had memorized over twenty verses by the end of the school year. She also read exciting stories, like David and Goliath, and sad ones, like when Jesus died. The ones she liked best talked about women like Mary Magdalene. Jesus had loved her even when people made fun of her. *I know Jesus loves me and Mrs. Ryczek loves me.*

CHAPTER 3
CHILDHOOD, INTERRUPTED

The Sandfords were moving again. Julie packed her clothes, stuffed animals, and books, carefully placing her treasured Bible at the top of the box, to keep it from getting squished. She was sad about saying goodbye to the Andersons, who had treated her like she belonged to them; and especially about leaving Mrs. Ryczek, who had made her feel smart. This move was so much harder than leaving Washington. *Mrs. R says that Spring Green is only a hop, skip and a jump away from Platteville. I hope I can come back and visit her someday.*

Fifth grade had to be as good as fourth. And she had all summer to make new friends before school started.

Home was another trailer. Julie was used to them by now and did not expect to ever live in a real house again. But this trailer was dirty, old, and not parked next to a big farmhouse. Instead of looking like the Anderson trailer, it smelled like their barn during mucking out time. The linoleum floor had big cracks in it. The door hung crooked. The windows didn't close all the way. The trailer was in a park (not a real park) surrounded by lots of other old-looking trailers, squished together with a little square of brown crabgrass separating them. Most of the trailers looked like houses on the TV news after being hit by tornadoes.

The Sandfords unpacked their boxes on a sticky, muggy night in early July without a family, home-cooked meal and air-conditioned rooms waiting for them. Julie's mom welcomed them to their new trailer with a Spam casserole eaten outside sitting on prickly grass, swatting mosquitoes.

Julie ate Spam almost every day that summer, usually for supper, but sometimes even for lunch. Her mom found lots of different ways to make it, but it never tasted good, not like the ham Mrs. Anderson made. Julie's imagination added the Spam she ate to Julie and got Jammy, her new secret name for herself.

Owning her own bike was still Julie's dream. There were two for sale one block over from their trailer. Arlene gave her kids five dollars each for a bike and warned them "not to wreck 'em, 'cuz I ain't buying you no more." The blue Schwinns were rusty and mud-spattered; the chains fell off as soon as Julie and Dan hit a curb at breakneck speed on their first ride. They fixed the chains, wiped their greasy hands in the grass, and took off again. Stones shot out beneath the fat tires, sometimes hitting innocent bystanders like well-aimed

BBs from Dan's gun. Deep potholes and crooked speed bumps made the rides a challenge. With hair whipping back and pedals pumping furiously, they attacked the roads and sidewalks like they were being chased. The previous day's cloudburst created huge puddles, perfect for spraying a trail of glistening, oily water in a rainbow arcing behind the bikes.

Julie attracted attention. Even though the trailer park teemed with kids, her bike came at people like a heat-seeking missile. Some neighbors laughed, some cursed, and everyone moved out of the path of destruction.

One man stood outside all day, watching the kids ride bikes. Julie seldom slowed down long enough to notice anybody, but every time she rode on the sidewalk in front of his trailer, her eyes were drawn to him because of his Wellington cap, same as her dad's. She also noticed his dirty-looking, gray hair hanging limply below the rim of the cap, not at all like her dad's hair, and his flannel shirt like her dad's, but with holes around the pocket and collar. The shirt hung loosely and for dear life on his skinny body. Dad's shirt always stretched tightly across his chest muscles. Julie thought it was good that this man wore Wellington boots, but his right pants leg seemed glued to the top of the boot, looking strange to her.

One day the man stood right in the middle of the road. Julie threw her feet back on the pedals; when the brakes caught, the back of the bike fishtailed and the tires screeched, leaving a squiggly path of burned rubber. Other kids stopped their bikes and looked terrified at what the strange man might do.

"Hey, I'm Mr. Thomas. What's your name?"

I'm in deep, dark doodoo now. "Julie."

Mr. Thomas glanced down the street at the group of frightened kids and laughed. "Whoever burns the longest and waviest path of rubber," he yelled, "will get a Tootsie-roll pop!" Their fear instantly turned into cheering and hollering as they lined up their bikes while one of the older boys shouted, "Start your engines!"

Fierce competition eventually drew the trailer park kids into a close friendship. Julie never noticed any of the adults talking together outside their trailers, so she figured they were inside, like Mr. and Mrs. Anderson and her parents always were.

The almost-bald tires on the Schwinns signaled the end of the summer. Julie took one last ride and thought about the beginning of school. *Will I fit in? What is Spring Green like? Who will be my fifth-grade teacher? Will she be like Miss Meyer or Mrs. Ryczek?* Her mind and her bike turned simultaneous circles.

"Look out!" Julie heard, barely in time to avoid a chain link fence. Somehow her circle flattened into a line headed straight for disaster.

"Thanks, Mr. Thomas!" yelled Julie.

"That's okay – anytime. Hey, I can give you a Tootsie-roll pop even though you didn't burn any rubber today! Come over and pick one out," Mr. Thomas shouted back.

Julie headed out to the street to make one more circle, then cruised over to Mr. Thomas' trailer. *I wonder if he's married. Where is his wife?*

"I left the Tootsie-roll pops in my trailer. You can come in and pick out whichever one you want." Julie hesitated because she hardly ever saw the grown-ups going into each other's trailers, and the kids usually stayed outside. But Mr. Thomas was a nice man. All the kids liked him. And he watched out for them. She would only be in there long enough to get her candy, then back on her bike for the rest of the day.

Mr. Thomas opened the aluminum door ahead of Julie and leaned against the railing.

"Go ahead in, young lady."

Julie stepped in and turned around. Mr. Thomas swung the door closed and walked towards her. Before she could ask about her Tootsie-roll, he reached out with both hands, grabbed her tank top at the bottom, yanked it up to her neck, cupped both hands around her developing breasts and rubbed them.

"I've been waiting a long time to do this," he breathed heavily. "And I know you want me to do this, or you wouldn't have come into my trailer."

Julie's lungs burned. She couldn't move. *Where's Dan? Where's my mom? Why is he doing this?* Out of instinct, Julie ducked under Mr. Thomas' right elbow and momentarily froze at the door, trying to remember how to open it. Then she jerked it open, pulled her top down, ran down the steps, and caught her foot on the edge of the bottom one. She stumbled forward, regained her balance, and ran to her bike. For the first time ever, Julie forgot how to ride. She pushed the kickstand back with her foot and walked the bike with her brain all fuzzy, hoping she remembered how to get home. *I hope Mr. Thomas isn't following me. What if he tells my parents I stole his candy?* Hurling the bike against the trailer, Julie collapsed on the dry grass, buried her face in her hands, and sobbed.

All the next day, Julie stayed in her bedroom.

The August sun beat on the metal roof of the trailer until the inside felt like the car the day they moved to the Andersons'. But she stayed in, stayed safe, closed her window, pulled down the brittle shade, and sat on the floor in front of a small fan. She tried to play with Mr. Potato Head, even though most of the parts were missing, and she was too old for it. Her puzzles had missing pieces; and it was no fun playing Sorry by herself. She was bored and hot, and wanted to open her window, but she was not taking any chances on having Mr. Thomas peek in, especially when she got dressed. *I would rather burn to death than see him again.*

Julie was glad her mom didn't ask why she was staying inside, otherwise she might have to tell her about the awful shame. She was used to keeping things to herself, like when Grandma Hagstrom lived with them, and when Miss Meyer said things that hurt.

But this was worse. And harder to keep secret. She felt like she was holding a balloon under water; soon, it would pop up somewhere else. Mr. Thomas turned her inside out and stomped on her, and she almost didn't escape from him. One time her brother had stepped on a bunny in the yard; Julie watched it gasp for breath, stretch out its paws, and then it was still. But Julie couldn't stay still or stay in her hotter-than-a-furnace room any longer. It was time to talk to her parents, or maybe just to her dad. *He will know what to do.*

Late that afternoon, when Julie couldn't take the heat any longer, she exploded from the trailer, sat down on the sidewalk, and waited for her dad to come home from work. She knew the best time to talk to him: right after work and before he stumbled and yelled, kicking anything that made him mad.

Danny pulled up to the trailer, got out of his truck, slammed the door, and walked toward her. Taking off his cap, he ran his fingers through his hair. "Man, it's hotter'n blazes! I need a cold one. What are you doing out here?" Julie's chance was slipping away.

"Dad, I need to talk to you." She stood up and tipped her head down.

"What's eating you?"

She stared at a crack in the sidewalk. "Well … you're not going to like this."

"Are you in some kind of trouble?"

"I don't know." Julie kept her head down and stuttered her way through the story. While trying to figure out how to say the embarrassing part, Danny suddenly turned away from her and ran up the steps into the trailer. *What have I done now? Am I going to be sent to my room? Is he going to tell Mom?* Julie sat down, picked up a stick, and poked at ants racing out of the sidewalk crack.

Julie's father strutted out of the trailer wearing ironed jeans and a red t-shirt that showed off his muscles. His hair was wet and neatly combed. Julie was surprised to see him without his cap. *I wonder where he's going.*

Danny Sandford walked down the sidewalk and turned the corner, Julie following close behind. When she realized where Dad was headed, she panicked. *He's going to Mr. Thomas' trailer.* She ran back to retrieve her bike, riding as far in the opposite direction from Mr. Thomas as she could. If she thought she could get away with it, she would ride for miles and miles.

Walking up the steps of Mr. Thomas' trailer and

41

banging on the door, Danny drew out his menacing voice. "Hey, Ed! Get your sorry butt out here!"

Mr. Thomas ambled to the door and peered through the screen. "Yeah?"

"I know about lizards like you. There's a hole for you somewhere, but it ain't here." Danny was loud, sober, and threatening, making sure everyone around heard through closed doors.

"Get off my property now, before I call the cops!" Mr. Thomas hid behind the door.

"I'd love to see you do that. Maybe they would like to hear what you did to my daughter." Neighbors quickly left their trailers and clustered on the sidewalks, pretending to be interested in each other's conversations.

"Everybody knows I love all these kids. Your kid's just mad because she didn't get the Tootsie-roll she wanted." Drops of sweat appeared on Ed's forehead.

Danny was cool. "Watch your back, Thomas." He turned around, ignored the crowd, and walked back home.

The sun had cast long shadows across the park by the time Julie returned. She dropped her bike near the street and went into the trailer, hoping her dad would be there to tell her that everything was okay; that he had cleaned Mr. Thomas' clock. But he was gone, and she didn't know whether her mom had heard the story. Arlene pointed to a bowl of macaroni and cheese on the table without taking her eyes off the TV. Julie choked down the cold, congealed blob of food, said goodnight, and headed for her bedroom. She pulled up her shade and her window and collapsed onto her bed without changing out of her sweaty clothes.

Julie was done with bike riding. The next morning, she walked her prize bike to the back of the park and abandoned it next to the dumpster.

One of Julie's strongest memories from her earliest childhood was brushing her teeth by herself. She was four years old and climbed on a stool to reach the sink. Grabbing the tube of Crest, she unscrewed the top and aimed it at her toothbrush. When a gentle squeeze didn't work, she squeezed harder, and a huge thing like a piece of long Playdoh shot out and landed on the sink. She was terrified of Momma finding out but didn't know how to get the toothpaste back into the tube.

That was how Julie felt now: Like she had been squeezed and something important had squirted out, and there was no way to get it back in again. Mr. Thomas had done it, and she felt ashamed for letting him.

Fifth grade stared back at Julie from the mirror. *I remember when I cared about who my teacher would be. Now all I want to do is hide from Mr. Thomas.*

Julie hadn't thought about the possibility of getting a man for a teacher. Mr. Davis was short, mostly bald, and wore the same white shirt every day, with a different tie. He was nice, spoke softly, and never lost his temper. He told funny knock-knock jokes. Every day, he encouraged one of his students with something special he liked about him or her. His classroom was covered with posters of animals in funny poses; one hung on the wall behind the desk with a picture of a big, furry calico cat. The balloon over its head read, "Never hold grudges ... they shed terribly." The best part of Mr.

Davis' room was all the books lined up on shelves under the windows. He always reminded the kids to borrow his books anytime, so Julie took home at least one a week. Her favorite books were the "Trixie Belden" mysteries and "Tom Sawyer."

Since I like school so much, why does my head hurt when I'm here? And what about my stomach pains? At first, the aches came once or twice a week, then once or twice a day. By Christmas, they lasted all day. Julie was afraid to go to school because her head and stomach started hurting as soon as she got there. But she was just as afraid to stay home. She watched "Name That Tune" on TV, and this was like "Name That Fear." She did not like the game.

Another school year ended. Julie and the other kids hopped off the bus at the trailer park. As soon as it pulled away, a pick-up truck towing a U-Haul lumbered in. The kids broke into a run and followed the truck. Julie was the first to stop when she saw where the truck is headed. *Is he moving? I want to see everything. Maybe I can get closer and still be safe if I stay in the group.* Strange men came out of Mr. Thomas' trailer carrying boxes while the neighborhood boys begged to help – cheap and instant recruits. The girls stayed back, looked at each other, quietly shook their heads, and drifted back to their trailers. Julie wondered, for the first time, if any of those girls had followed Mr. Thomas into his trailer.

Julie got up the next morning, changed out of her nightgown into shorts, a t-shirt and flipflops, ate a bowl of Frosted Flakes, and walked over to Mr. Thomas' trailer. The truck and U-Haul were gone, along with the lawn chairs, push mower and grill that always teetered crookedly on the grass. Julie wanted to throw a party – but all she could do was run to the chain-link fence and throw up her breakfast.

The headaches and stomachaches went away. Julie talked her mom into taking her to the Salvation Army to buy a bike. *I hope she doesn't ask me what happened to my other one.* They came home with a shiny blue Schwinn. It was missing a pedal but had a big bell on the handlebars. The kids in the park rode in a posse, with everyone taking turns being Wyatt Earp. While they spent the summer making the streets safe, the adults gathered on the sidewalks a little more often than the previous year, talking about President Johnson, school bussing, the weather, and Elvis.

Sixth grade meant a change of schools, but only because Julie would be going to a brand-new middle school. All her friends from last year would be there, and she refused to be afraid of any new teacher. The summer was good, Julie was healthy; and after all, this was middle school. She was almost grown-up.

Mr. O'Keefe was Julie's science and math teacher. Soon into the year, her headaches and stomachaches returned for an encore. To keep things from getting boring, Julie added nausea to the mix. She

The ghost of Miss Meyer lived in Mr. O'Keefe, who told his homeroom class the first day that he used to be a Marine. *This can't be happening.* He did not have a Stupid Chair but enjoyed whacking the knuckles of students who did not catch on to their work quickly enough for him.

had grown since third grade, which made her too tall to hope Mr. O'Keefe wouldn't notice her. Invisibility was not an option.

"Mrs. Sandford, please sit down. *Now.*" Arlene gracefully folded her five-foot-four frame into her daughter's desk chair in the middle of the classroom. It was four o'clock, and the last detention student had left. Jim O'Keefe paced in front of Arlene, then stopped, squared his shoulders, and squinted his eyes. "I'm not sure your daughter is going to make it through sixth grade. She can't seem to pay attention." Arlene stared impassively, stoically – unfamiliar territory for her. "And I've heard that her younger brother seems to get into trouble often. Maybe it has to do with your family living in a trailer court—"

"And that makes my family, what – trailer trash?"

Mr. O'Keefe folded his arms while the words went into free-fall.

"I already live with a bully. You're going to have to do better than that if you expect to win this battle." Arlene narrowed her eyes into slits.

"I don't need to win anything."

"My husband is one part snake charmer and two parts bull fighter. You don't want to mess with him."

"Is that a threat?" Mr. O'Keefe's voice rose slightly.

"It is if you come into my barn and start slinging manure."

"We're not getting anywhere here."

"That's good, because I already got a roller coaster at home, and that's enough of a ride for me."

Mr. O'Keefe and Arlene glared at each other, neither conceding any ground. The janitor walked in and began sweeping the floor. Arlene disengaged from the conference by getting up, walking slowly to the door, and closing it behind her. There was a slight opening of a pressure valve, apparently needed to release tension from both Arlene and Mr. O'Keefe – tension that had nothing to do with Julie's welfare, and certainly not with her knuckles, which – thanks to Mr. O'Keefe – stayed raw the rest of the year.

CHAPTER 4
FRIENDS IN LOW PLACES

Christmas was not merry. Jolly Ol' St. Nick cowered behind Dad, who drank until he fell asleep, usually on the floor, sometimes under the kitchen table. Momma would then get mad and cuss up a storm, using her words to beat up on her kids. When the words were gone, Arlene would clamp her lips shut and not speak to anyone. Julie would hope for invisibility until the middle of January, when something mysterious always happened to make things calm for another year.

Julie jumped off the bus the last day of school before Christmas vacation and took her time climbing over all the snowbanks on the way to the trailer. She opened the front door quietly, trying to escape to her room before either parent saw her. *Maybe Dad will be passed out somewhere, Mom will be in the bathroom, and I can sneak by both.* Julie was startled by her mom standing next to a small evergreen tree propped in a metal stand in the living room. A big bowl of popcorn was on the coffee table, and a box of ornaments Julie had never seen were on the floor. A tangled string of big lights draped over the back of the couch.

Dropping her books and construction paper star, Julie said, "What're we doing?"

"What does it look like? It's about time we put up a tree around here We need to do something special for Christmas."

Darkness blanketed their trailer by the time the tree was decorated. Julie's stomach growled from hunger, but she didn't want to stop until the lights were hung on the tree. When her mom plugged in the cord and the tree lit up in red and green and blue, Julie was sure it was the most beautiful tree ever. *I don't know where Dad is – but I hope he leaves the tree alone when he gets here.* There were even a few wrapped packages under the tree, which made everything look like the picture on the Ace Hardware calendar hanging on the kitchen wall.

For the next five days, Julie sat on the couch reading a book, waiting for it to get dark enough to plug in the tree lights. After that, she stared at the tree, barely noticing her mom and brother eating supper in front of the TV, until her mom chased her to bed.

On Christmas Eve, Julie found her Bible from Mrs. Ryczek and lay on her stomach on her bed, flipping through the first part of the New Testament to find the story of Jesus' birth. She read Matthew while the sky darkened enough to light the tree, even though it was only four-fifteen. Julie turned her Bible over and heard a smashing sound coming from the living room. *Oh no!* She jumped up and ran out of her room in time to duck under red and blue glass balls flying around, while Dad cussed, and Mom cried. With ornaments glittering in a sea of shards, Danny grabbed the pot of meatballs from the burner and threw it against the wall, laughing and yelling, "Mortared mush!" Then he trounced over to the tree and kicked the presents with his Wellington boots. Julie walked backwards to her bedroom, threw herself on her bed and soaked the Bible with her tears. *God, why does Dad smash all my dreams?*

The sixty-degree February thaw in Wisconsin

was the top story on the national six o'clock weather. Julie left home the next afternoon and saw young children wearing shorts and riding bikes through rapidly melting snow drifts. *These kids probably have nice parents looking for a babysitter. If they asked me, I could get away from my trailer.*

"Look out!" Julie was nearly knocked over by two grade school-aged boys riding bikes at Mach speed, headed right for her. The memories of her bike riding – and of being hurt by Mr. Thomas – made her head pound. *Stop it, Julie. Not everyone is like him.* She leaped to the edge of the sidewalk, while a voice yelled, "Michael! Brian! You goofballs be careful! You almost ran that girl over!'

"We're sorry, Mom!" came the stereo reply. The boys jammed on their brakes, bikes swerving in every direction. They turned towards Julie in unison. "Hey, girl, we're sorry."

"That's okay. I used to ride my bike the same way."

"Boys, invite that girl over here, so I can give her something to drink, and maybe you can practice acting like gentlemen for a change."

Are there really moms who talk to their sons like that, and who expect them to show respect? Julie tried to slow her heartbeat, not wanting to look over-anxious to have friends. She walked over to the boys' trailer as casually as she could.

"Hi. I'm Mary Nelson. You can call me Mary. And you've already met the knuckleheads."

Michael and Brian stood close to Julie, overcome with shyness. Ducking their heads in tandem, they parked their bikes next to the porch and scampered up into the house.

"So, what's your name and what's your game?" A pleasant smile played around the corners of Mary's mouth.

"My name's Julie ... and I'm not really sure what my game is ..." Julie covered her confusion by looking down. No one had ever asked her anything that didn't have an assumed answer – a math fact, or a "Yes, Ma'am, I'll never do it again."

"Well, what do you like to do? Are you in any sports? Do you read? What are your dreams? What would you like to be when you grow up?" The rapid-fire questions made Julie uncomfortable, but also curious about this woman. She soon began inventing excuses to walk over to the Nelson trailer every day after school – to borrow a cup of sugar, even though Arlene never baked; to ask Mary to sew on a missing button she had pulled off her favorite red blouse earlier that morning; to get homework help, even though she was getting As in every class. After a couple of weeks, Mary asked Julie to stay at the kitchen table after she had closed her math book.

"Would you like something to drink, Julie?"

"Yes, Ma'am."

Mary got up, pulled a bottle of Coke out of the refrigerator, flipped off the top and set it down in front of Julie.

"We need to talk." Mary's pleasant smile never vacated her face.

Uh oh. I've been a pain here. If she tells my mom, I am going to catch it.

"About what?" Julie gulped down her Coke and her fear.

Mary reached out for her hand. "I don't want you to keep making up excuses for coming here. I really enjoy your company. If you'd like, I could teach you to cook and sew – if that's okay with your mom – and take you grocery shopping."

Tears pooled in Julie's eyes. "Mary, no one has done anything like that for me. I don't know what to say."

"Don't say anything. Give me a hug, and we'll see about sending you home with some fresh chocolate-chip cookies in about an hour-and-a-half. Would that be all right?"

Mary was a mom, grandma, aunt, teacher, and friend, all rolled into one of the nicest adults Julie had ever known. And, by the end of March, her headaches and stomachaches were gone.

Mary took Julie grocery shopping the week after their table talk, and every Saturday after that. They each put a hand on the cart as they pushed it through the produce section, snitching grapes, laughing at the strange-looking fruits, and looking forward to the first ripe strawberries of the season. When they got back from the store, Julie helped Mary put away groceries. *There isn't a can of Spam in any of these bags.* The next lesson was showing Julie what pots and pans were used for, how to make pasta al dente and then lasagna. The best thing of all was when Julie was invited to stay for the supper she had helped cook.

By April, Julie had her own place at the table, between Mary and Lee, and across from Michael and Brian. Each person shared something special about the day; everyone listened, analyzed, laughed, and encouraged each other. Julie's mind heard "The

Twilight Zone" theme song playing in the background. *This must be another world. I didn't know people talked and acted like this – and I get to be a part of it.*

Saturday night in early May found Julie as one of the usual suspects at the Nelson table. Mary had taught her how to make baked curry chicken, mashed potatoes with chives, and fresh green beans. While the family raved over her good cooking, Julie had the courage to share her fear of Mr. O'Keefe. When she was done, everyone voiced sympathy – a new thing for her – and it was Michael's and Brian's turn to talk about school. Next, Lee talked about his job; and finally, Mary's words spilled about wanting to start selling Tupperware.

Mary got up from the table and asked Julie to help her clear the dishes. As they stood at the sink working in perfect washing-and-drying harmony, Mary blurted, "So, Julie, what's it like at your house at dinnertime?"

Maybe I could pretend I cut myself drying a sharp knife, and Mary would forget about her question. If I tell her what my family is like she will never want me here again.

"Well, Mary." Julie took a detour. "My mom makes stuff like sausage and sauerkraut, and the trailer stinks so bad I have to run away!"

Mary didn't follow the rabbit trail. "But I mean, what's it like around your table? Does everyone talk at once, like Lee's family, or do people take turns talking, like here? I'm really interested in how different families do things."

You're right about that. My family is about as

different as you could possibly get.

Before Julie could invent an answer, Mary dried her hands and walked over to the phone. "I know! I'll call your mom, tell her what you said about her sausage and sauerkraut – and after we laugh about it, I'll get a chance to ask her some of these questions without sounding too nosy."

The gig's up.

"Hello, Mrs. Sandford? This is Mary Nelson. My family and I live in the trailer court, and Julie's spent a lot of time over here the past few months. I like getting to know her. You have a delightful daughter."

I wonder what my mom is saying – or maybe I already know.

"Well, anyways, I was calling to share a funny story with you ..."

Julie threw down the towel and ran to the bathroom, slamming the door behind her. *When my heart breaks in here, the pieces will be easier to clean up.* Julie sat on the plush rug, trying not to think about what Mrs. Nelson must be hearing from her mom. After ten minutes, she knew it was crazy to sit in the bathroom any longer. There was no help for her. She got up, quietly opened the door, and tiptoed back down the hallway towards the kitchen.

"Julie, please come here." There was an unfamiliar sternness to Mary's voice. "I talked to your mom, and she said she has never, ever made sausage and sauerkraut. Why did you lie to me?"

"I ... I don't know ..." *Please, Mary, don't send me back home.*

Mary walked towards Julie. "Well, everyone deserves a second chance. But don't ever lie to me again," came the gentle rebuke.

Mary seemed to forget about pursuing a conversation with Julie's mom. Julie thought Mrs. Nelson was good at figuring things out. Maybe something in her mom's voice spoke louder than her words; or maybe Mary heard between the lines and knew something wasn't right. Julie was a beggar hoping for stale crumbs, and instead got a whole, fresh, hot loaf of bread from the Nelsons. She was back on Mary's good side and that was that. She could keep shopping with her, eating with her family, and being with people who unknowingly shone a flashlight of kindness into a shadowed heart.

Mr. Nelson announced that he had transferred jobs and would be moving his family to Colorado. Julie ate one last dinner with them, after which Mary hugged her and promised to write. Michael and Brian gallantly volunteered to escort her back to her trailer. Two weeks later, Julie looked out her bedroom window and saw a moving truck drive past, taking her heart with it.

CHAPTER 5
"STICKS AND STONES
MAY BREAK MY BONES"

The trailer was a compact firing range. Julie sought cover in her bedroom, only to discover that paper-thin walls conducted verbal-assault ammunition. "Tell that damn kid – tell her right now!" she heard her dad scream often. *Tell me what? Why is he calling me names?*

"I'll do it when I'm good and ready! I'm hardly ever good, and I sure ain't ready!" Arlene would slam their bedroom door, followed by the sound of the TV turned up to full volume. Her head was ready to split open like the melons she and Mrs. Nelson often cut and arranged on a platter for a fancy dinner. *Oh, Mary, I miss you.*

The parental door would open and then bang shut, followed by the trailer door opening, and a truck gunning its engine. The last thing Julie ever remembered was crying herself to sleep.

After one of these repeated incidents, Julie awoke the next morning with puffy eyes and an aching head, made worse by the noise of the squealing test pattern on the TV. She walked into the living room in time for her stomach to turn cartwheels from the smell of smoldering cigarette butts in overflowing ashtrays on the coffee table. Julie had trained herself to pick up the ashtrays carefully, balancing them with the empty beer cans. On her way to the kitchen to dump everything, she stumbled over crumpled bags of Fritos or Cheetos, which made the clean-up job bigger and stinkier.

The rhythm of the dance never changed. Julie thought of herself by the name her dad called her and grew numb to its sting. She found out that she could turn on her little transistor radio sitting on her bedside table and fall asleep to her favorite songs, or even to people arguing about war and baseball.

The Sandford family had never done anything special for Fourth of July – unlike her friends' families, who always had picnics at a lake or a park, followed by fireworks at sunset. The summer her family lived on the Anderson farm, all of them had had a picnic together, and then the kids found a tall ladder, climbed up to the flat part of the house roof to watch fireworks, and ignored their parents in the kitchen. That was Julie's best memory of the Fourth of July. For all other July Fourths, Danny Sandford had been gone. Arlene sat inside watching the New York City fireworks on TV, hiding behind the excuse that she did not want to become a mosquito feast. Julie and Dan sprayed themselves with Off and looked for a place to see the fireworks; getting close enough to hear them was too much to expect.

It was another Fourth of July – but the test pattern was about to change.

Arlene shut off Julie's transistor and shook her shoulder. "Julie! Get up! Here's your shorts and shirt. You can throw them over your nightie. C'mon, we gotta go find your dad." She left for Dan's room to give the same command. When the three escapees were semi-dressed and semi-awake, they piled into their automobile wannabe, rolled down the windows, and headed out of the trailer park.

The smell and haze of burnt fireworks and firecrackers hung over the city. It was a balmy night, but Julie was chilled and scared. *We are patrolling a beat without a siren. Where are we going to find Dad? And why are we looking for him?*

Danny's truck was parked in front of the U-Com-In bar. Julie wondered why so many people were outside. She did not want to get out and walk around all those loud people, but it was even scarier thinking about staying alone in the car. She knew her mom wouldn't let her do that anyway. They got out of the car, Arlene leading the charge through the crowd, which somehow parted to let them through. Inside the bar, the air was as hazy as outside, but Julie recognized this thick air as cigarette smoke. People laughed and bumped elbows; some were asleep hunched over little round tables scattered around the room. Others sat at a long, skinny counter in front of a waiter wearing a white apron, pouring liquid from tall bottles into tiny glasses.

"Here. Take this and go buy yourselves a Seven-Up." Arlene shoved a dollar bill into Julie's hand, turned her kids around and pushed them towards the bar, weaving her way through yet another crowd.

Julie and Dan found stools, hoisted themselves up on them and bought their sodas. No longer chilled, Julie was now hot, sweaty, and even more frightened. She drank a few sips of her soda, laid her head down on the counter and cried quietly until she fell asleep. She awoke with her mom shaking her shoulder for the second time that night. "It's time to get home." With her mom half-dragging her and Dan to the car, Julie felt as helpless as her Grandma Hagstrom must have felt.

Julie thought her first and last bar trip would be that Fourth of July. One month and many bars later, she stopped paying attention to the smoke and to the people. The one good thing about the nightly trips was that no one was at the trailer to leave filled ashtrays and messy floors. Julie got up in the mornings and walked a clear path to a cleaner-smelling kitchen and ate her cereal. If it was early enough, she watched TV and enjoyed the quiet house before Mom got up and woke Dad to get to his construction job. Julie made sure she was done eating and back in her room before Danny stumbled around the trailer, yelling and cussing.

I know the Anderson family and the Nelson family, and they are both different than ours. Why do Mom and Dad keep doing these same things every day? Why can't they love each other?

CHAPTER 6
THE O.K. FARM

Crickets, spring peepers and owls fought for supremacy in the night choir. Arlene silently swung her legs out of bed and tiptoed down the hall into Julie's walk-in closet size bedroom. She leaned over the bed, lightly tapped Julie on the shoulder, and held a manicured finger across her tightened lips. Julie awoke reluctantly. *Why are we going out again? We already made the nightly bar run.* She looked at her mom, without understanding the demand for quiet. *Wherever we're going, Dan has to come with us. Who cares how much noise we make?* Something in her mom's face demanded unquestioning obedience. Julie swallowed her yawn and stretched. Arlene reached under the bed, grabbed the handle of a suitcase with a broken latch, pulled it out and set it on the end of the bed. Julie achieved wide-awake status and scrambled out of bed. Arlene pointed to her, and then to the dresser. Julie figured out the clue and took hold of one knob of the bottom drawer, while her mother grabbed the other one. They carefully pulled together, praying it wouldn't squeak on the metal slide. Arlene snatched a handful of clothes and tossed them in the suitcase, while Julie picked up the clothes from her floor and did the same. *What about my socks and underwear and stuff in the other drawers?* "This is all we have time for," whispered Arlene as she tried to close the suitcase. The hinge kept popping out, refusing to cooperate. Arlene looked up to the top of the window and saw a bungee cord attached to the curtain rod at one end and a hook in the ceiling at the other.

"Tiptoe to the hall closet and bring the stool here." Julie did so and climbed up on it to remove the end of the cord from the hook.

"But Mom—"

"Do it!" hissed Arlene.

As soon as Julie unhooked the end, the curtain rod crashed down. For an eternity of seconds, mother and daughter inhaled, staring at the open door with horror-filled eyes. The only sound coming from the adjoining bedroom was raucous snoring. Julie could not remember a time when her nerves were calmed by such a horrendous noise.

Arlene hastily wrapped the cord around the bulging suitcase, attaching the curved wire ends together. She grabbed the handle and motioned for Julie to follow her. Dan hovered in the hallway, still in his pajamas and holding another beat-up suitcase wrapped with a piece of twine. Danny's family walked quickly to the front door, threw on jackets and shoes, and sailed through, victims fleeing their captor.

With one hurdle jumped, there was still a large one looming before the escapees. A faded black fifty-four Buick – their most recent purchase – profaned the gravel driveway, an immovable object challenging passersby to a smack down.

"Kids! Even though the engine's blown, we can still drive this heap if we stop to pour oil into it every fifty miles."

I have a dad who can't seem to do anything without a drink. Now we have a car that's the same way.

"Where are we going?" Julie whispered.

"To see your grandparents in Pineville."

"Where's Pineville? *What* grandparents?" Julie's words were lost as Arlene cursed the jammed driver's side door. She hustled around to the passenger door, yanked it open, and motioned for Julie and Dan to follow her.

After piling their suitcases on the back seat, they climbed in, stepping on crumpled papers and petrified food remnants. Arlene pushed the seat back and slid across to the driver's side as all three settled in the front, enfolded by a reckless sense of anticipation. Arlene spotted a large, unopened bag of sunflower seeds on the dashboard and announced, "Look, guys, we've even got food!"

Arlene started the car, turned on the headlights, and shifted into reverse. A shadow appeared in the low beam of light. She slammed on the brakes and cursed while Julie sat paralyzed. *Please don't let that be Dad.*

A man wearing a sleeveless t-shirt and work pants walked up to the driver's side and made a circular movement with his hand for Arlene to roll down her window. Arlene turned the crank a few times until it was half-way down.

"Hi, neighbor. I've seen a whole lot of what's gone on around your house with your kids and husband. It wouldn't have been right for me to interfere – but it looks like maybe you're trying to run away."

"Please don't call the cops on us," pled Arlene.

"Lady, if I was going to call the cops on anyone, it'd be on that no-good excuse for a husband of yours. I came out here to help you."

The man disappeared behind an old shed and reappeared a few minutes later, dragging a decrepit trailer and hitching it to the back of the Buick. Arlene and her kids scrambled back out of the car, scurried into the house, and swept up armfuls of belongings to load into both the trailer and the car. Danny's snoring resonated throughout the house as the car bounced down the muddy ruts and merged onto the main highway.

The radio and speedometer were both broken. The three occupants rolled down the windows and sang, "Row, Row, Row Your Boat," "Camp Town Races," and "You Are My Sunshine" until their singing overpowered the songs of the night creatures. When Julie started to feel like someone had lifted barbells off her shoulders, she knew they had driven enough miles to escape her dad's drunken tantrums.

Julie supposed these new grandparents were like Grandma Hagstrom. The sun heated the car as they drove past a sign that read: PINEVILLE, MICHIGAN, Pop. 318. *Make that three-hundred twenty-one.* The town looked like a postcard, with one-story houses on both sides of Main Street, guarded by the Pineville Fire Department building at one end and First Lutheran Church at the other. The countryside spread out beyond the town, keeping a polite distance, and the farms were neat, although Julie saw a few tractor graveyards. The swamp of cattails divided the town and country, and Julie looked forward to the fall, when the swamps would look like big, frothy heads of root beer.

Three tired, dirty, hungry people – still wearing pajamas – limped into Arlene's parents' driveway before noon. Richard and Rosalynn Cerbé walked out to the car and enfolded their daughter and grandchildren in enormous hugs. Gulping deep breaths of safe, fatherless air, Julie wondered how long this unknown peace would last. *When will Dad find us and drag us back to the trailer?*

Julie was too tired to worry about anything except stretching out on a soft bed. Maybe after sleep, food, and a little more sleep, she'd be able to concentrate on her grandparents. "Here, darling. And call me Grandma Rosie. You can sleep in the room your mom grew up in." Julie was dog-tired, but still noticed that Grandma Rosie looked like an older version of Mom – same height, same petite build, only her hair was grayer, and she wore a straight, pink-checked, below-the-knee dress with a matching belt tied around her waist. Julie walked into the room and collapsed on the bed. The last thing she remembered was a kiss on the cheek.

The moon shone brightly through the window and the air was a little chilly. It took a while for Julie to remember where she was – but a bathroom was a must. Julie got up, walked out into the hallway and down a flight of stairs.

Voices from another room reached Julie's ears. "Arlene you can't stay here. You and them kids need a place of your own. Why don't you see if Orville Koski has anything for you?"

"Ma, I don't want to beg from O.K.!"

"Like I care—"

Grandma Rosie stopped in midsentence as soon as Julie appeared in the kitchen. "Hey, we thought you were going to sleep 'til next week! Are you hungry?"

"Yeah, and I need a bathroom."

"It's around the corner. Go wash up, and I'll fix

you something." Julie walked out, glad to find the bathroom, and hoping for the chance to finish hearing whatever her grandma was saying to her mom. *Are we going to live in another trailer? And who is O.K.?"*

By the end of the week, Arlene, Julie, and Dan had moved into a farmhouse owned by Orville Koski – who, Julie heard, was a childhood friend of Mom's. The farmhouse was surrounded by more land than she had ever seen, even at the Anderson's. At the entrance to the farm was an arched, peeling wooden sign with "The O.K. Farm" painted in barn red.

The farmhouse was old and deserted, not clean and inviting like the Anderson's. Still, it was big and had a climbing tree right outside the window of the room Julie chose for her bedroom. She could climb out her window onto a thick branch, take a book with her, and not be found by anyone. Julie overheard Mom telling Grandma Rosie that the rent was only twenty-five bucks a month. *Maybe there will be enough money for me to get some new clothes before seventh grade. It would be too embarrassing to wear those torn things we brought from Spring Green.*

Pineville School housed kindergarten through twelfth grade in one building. Julie wore Salvation Army castoffs; shortly after Arlene got a job as a school bus driver, she brought home bags with polyester pants, print blouses, and high-heeled shoes for herself. *I guess there's no money left to buy anything for me, otherwise Grandpa Richard and Grandma Rosie would not have to bring ground beef and chicken and fresh vegetables to us every week. Maybe we would have more if Dad were here. But things are peaceful now. I don't know what I would do with new clothes anyway.*

The seventh graders finished reading "A Christmas Carol," when Danny showed up in Pineville early in December.

"Please, Arlene." Julie heard Dad begging Mom in the kitchen. "I've stopped drinking. I promise I won't take another drop. Ever." *He sounds like he's seen the ghost of Christmas future.* Julie watched a new, sober, busy dad fill holes in their walls, fiddle with wires until the outlets worked, paint all the bedrooms, and reattach door hinges.

"And thanks to you," Julie heard Mom say to Dad one morning, "we don't have to pay the twenty-five buck rent anymore." *I'm glad Dad did all this stuff. The house looks nicer. But will it stay as calm as it was before he came? What do Grandpa and Grandma think about having him around?*

The kitchen was comfortable and inviting. A big, black stove – one that Julie heard Grandpa call "older than Patton" – stood guard in the corner, making everything warm and cozy, even when the rest of the house was freezing, and all the windows were fogged over. *And I thought Wisconsin was cold!*

Julie knew the drill: Dad would start drinking and stay drunk until sometime after Christmas; Mom would swear for whatever reason; but her best skill was her search-and-destroy missions on easy-to-reach self-esteems, followed by hiding in her room.

There was no coal for the stove on Christmas morning. The house was drafty from the wind whipping through every crack. Ice built up inside the kitchen windows, diffusing the sunlight shining on the orange and pineapple wallpaper.

Arlene entered the kitchen dressed nicely and wearing make-up. "Julie, you and your brother get your sleeping bags and bring 'em in here." She raised her arms and swept them theatrically across to the gas stove, turned on the burners and lit the oven. "Your Granny Rosie sent homemade cinnamon rolls that just need to be baked. Now get!" Julie ran out of the kitchen and up the stairs, passing her dad coming down with an armload full of wrapped presents.

Presents? He looks happy – and I'm freezing!

"Who's ready for a big bonfire?" Danny jumped up from Julie's spread-out sleeping bag, licked frosting off his fingers, tore out of the kitchen, and came back in wearing his Carhartt overalls. His family scattered to find their coats, hats, gloves, and boots.

"Last one out's a rotten egg!" screeched Julie, running outside and heading for the nearest snowbank.

"Come on, you guys, we gotta find small kindling sticks for the fire. I'll go back to the shed and drag some big logs over to the pit." Danny stepped into his own footprints from earlier that morning to make his way back to the shed.

The family piled kindling on top of Danny's elaborate log design and when it looked right, Dan yelled "Ready! Aim! Fire!" Danny touched his Bic to the tinder, and within a few minutes, the blaze shot perfectly vertical orange arrows into the cloudless sky. Julie never wanted to wake up from this dream, so unlike anything she ever imagined with her family.

Maybe Dad stopped drinking for good and we can do things like this every night.

The fire settled into glowing coals, and Danny vanished behind the shed, reappearing with four large, sharpened sticks pointed into the air like conquering spears. "Ta-da!" Danny walked triumphantly around the bonfire, carefully handing a stick to his wife and children with a kiss on the cheek for each. He pulled a slightly mashed bag of marshmallows from a deep overall pocket, handed it to Arlene and began singing, "Let Me Call You Sweetheart" in his quiet tenor voice. *I have never heard him sing. The night is full of surprises.*

Richard and Rosalynn had a friend who owned a coal delivery business and was willing to take a load to the Sandford farmhouse on Christmas night. Danny scooped snow onto the smoldering ashes, followed his family into the house, and shoveled coal into the stove. The house was soon as toasty as the bonfire had been. Julie could not remember a more perfect day. And there were still presents under the tree.

On a frigid night in early January, Julie was in her room using the colored pencils and sketch pad, one of her Christmas presents from Dad.

"Julie! Come down here! Your dad and I are watching an eight-millimeter. We want you to watch with us! Hurry!"

Julie dropped her orange pencil on her desk, jumped up from her chair and headed downstairs. Entering the darkened living room and waiting for her eyes to adjust, she saw her parents sitting next to each other on the sofa. *What's the movie? No one has ever taken home movies of our family, like the Andersons had. And we have never had a family vacation, so it can't be that, either.*

Danny undraped his arm from around Arlene's shoulder, moved over and patted the cushion. "Come on in, girl. The water's warm." Julie walked over and plopped down between her parents, with the movie projector humming behind them, directing its beam onto a white sheet draped across the curtain hanging from the picture window. The images were grainy, the sound garbled, but Julie picked out three dogs and a man. They were all climbing on top of each other, and the man was pulling his pants down … *stop!* Her hands shot up to her face, tightly covering her eyes.

"Mom, I want to leave," whispered Julie. *Why do they want me to see this?* While her parents cackled, she fled.

Julie threw herself onto her bed and sobbed. *I wish I could wash my brain out. If I'm going to sit next to my dad on the sofa, I want him to tell me that he loves me. That I'm pretty. And smart. I don't ever want to remember that awful stuff!*

It was January and the end of the first semester. Seventh grade was not too hard. The teachers were mostly nice. And Julie had a surprise for her dad. She bounded into the house with her report card tightly clasped in her mittened hand. Without stopping to shed her winter clothes, she ran through the house, tracking snow on the old, dark-gray, braided rugs.

"Dad! Dad! Look what I got!"

Julie's body followed her voice up the stairs,

boots leaving tracks on each step. At the top, she heard her dad humming softly as she burst through the bathroom doorway, panting and giggling. Danny put down his screwdriver, unbuckled his tool belt, and sat down on the curling linoleum floor. After handing him her report card, Julie pulled off her mittens, boots, and wet socks. Danny had an unreadable expression on his wind-burned face – but Julie was sure he would be happy with her.

Danny talked into the folded manilla card.

"Why did you get this B?"

"But Dad." Julie's eyes brimmed with tears. "I got five A's – in English, Spelling, Science, Social Studies—"

"You got a B in Math. That'll never do."

Oh, but that'll do. And this'll do. It's Thistledew all over again. Where is Thistledew when I need her?

Danny handed the report card back to Julie, who turned silently and walked out of the bathroom, leaving her boots and jacket drowning their sorrows in a puddle of melting snow. If she hadn't needed her mom's signature on it for school the next day, she would have torn the report card into a million pieces.

If that's the way Dad's going to be, I'll find a father somewhere else. It was mid-March, and Julie had stopped trying to get Danny's attention. She was glad to have a nice, newly painted, clean smelling house to live in – but she would trade it all to hear dad say, "You're the best daughter ever."

Orville Koski's sparkly eyes and silver hair turned him into Santa Claus. He spent more and more time around the farm, which made sense to Julie, since he owned the house and all the land. One day he announced to Julie, Dan, and the other neighborhood kids, "You can ride my horses for free in exchange for doing chores around here." It was the perfect thing to chase away Julie's depression. By early May, she had learned to mend fences, feed the horses, and clean their stalls. All the kids fought over who would get the prize for doing chores the best, which was any chore that involved the horses.

Spring gained victory over winter by the end of the month. Patches of dirty snow hid in the shadows of oaks and maples; the brighter, longer-lasting sun encouraged the grass into promise of deep summer green. The earth smelled like worms and damp rocks. New life stomped at the starting gate.

It was a bright, warm Saturday morning, and Orville invited the kids – *I have a posse again* – for a long ride. "The horses are all Quarters, and stand fifteen hands high," Mr. Koski explained that morning, "and there are Bays, Chestnuts, Sorrels, Arabians, and Paints."

Julie couldn't decide between a gray, black, spotted, or white one. All six kids scrambled to get to the one they like best. *Mine is Lightning.* Julie climbed up and waited for instructions.

They spent the morning trotting, cantering, and galloping. Mr. Koski led them on a big adventure, riding on acre after acre of his land, stopping when the horses needed a drink from one of the many ponds. When they walked the horses, he pointed out Queen Anne's Lace, Indian Paintbrush, Mullen, Goldenrod, and Burdick. And when the kids tipped their faces up to soak in the warm sun, they learned about Chickadees, Goldfinches,

Brown-Headed Cowbirds, Evening Grosbeaks, and Starlings – also known as Grackles, Mr. Koski taught.

It was early afternoon and time to return. The sweaty kids rode sweaty horses back to the barn, arguing over who would work hardest at taking off bridles and saddles, rubbing down the horses, brushing them, and feeding them.

Julie was the last one in the barn, inhaling mingled scents of horse and hay. Things in the barn were always right. Even the pungent manure was used for fertilizer around the farm. Nothing was wasted. Everything made sense.

Glancing around the barn, Julie noticed Orville sitting on his usual hay bale, watching her with pleasantness playing around the corners of warm eyes. With impetuous glee, she skipped over to Mr. Koski and dropped down on his knee, not in any hurry to return home to a father who had no interest in knowing anything about her life. Mr. Koski reached into his pocket and dropped several sugar cubes into her hand – treasures for her to share with her horse on their next riding adventure. Excited tears glimmered in her eyes as Mr. Koski softly crooned words of love and comfort, hugged Julie and gently rocked her with the tenderness of a father drawing his child into sweet sleep.

With the same gentle motion, a hand slowly worked its way inside Julie's jeans … down … down … while the other hand reached up inside her denim shirt. Caressing hands mocked caressing words, as Julie's world exploded. Powered by the fuel of betrayal, she jumped up from Mr. Koski's lap, tearing her shirt in the process. Orville reached out, twisted her wrist, and jerked her back.

"Do not tell your mother what happened today, or you will not be living on my land anymore," Orville hissed vehemently as he flung Julie away. She threw the sugar cubes on the ground and raced out of the barn, tripping over a tractor rut outside the door and tumbling into the dirt. At least now she had an excuse for her mom for why her shirt was torn.

Beams of silence supported the roof over Julie's house. Stuffing the incident way below her word shelf would keep her family living in the farmhouse for free. *And besides, who would believe what Mr. Koski did to me? All the kids love him. All the parents love him, probably because he keeps us busy for hours at a time.* Julie wondered if any other girl, last in the barn like she was, had had the same thing done to her. She would probably never find out, but she could also make sure she was never alone with Mr. Koski. She helped Dan with the horses, did chores with him, and perfected her hide-and-survive game.

CHAPTER 7
SWIMMING UPSTREAM

"Get up, Julie. Your dad's moving us to Black Bear, Wisconsin. He's got some fool idea he can find work there." Arlene exhaled her words in one breath before Julie opened her eyes. *Thank You, God.*

"Did Dad—"

"Don't ask any of your usual fool questions, because I don't know anything." Arlene turned around and walked out.

Did he find out what Mr. Koski did to me, and decide to move us away? I really don't care, just so we put distance between us.

Danny found work easily when he was sober. A big construction firm in Black Bear hired him within days of their move into a clean, modern, three-bedroom apartment. Julie was proud of her bedroom with the pale lavender walls, love beads in her doorway, and posters of David Cassidy, the Monkees and the Beatles hanging everywhere. It was the nicest room she had ever had, giving her extra confidence to start a new school.

Kennedy Middle School was overpowered by the smell of chlorine. *I used to dream about being an Olympic swimmer.* The whole school – and especially her new eighth grade class – buzzed about fall sports. Julie found out where to sign up for tryouts for the swim team. "If I don't do anything else," she muttered into her locker, "I will make the team!"

Julie became the newest member of the swim

team and knew the hard work it would take to catch up with all the other girls who had started training in mid-August. There were grueling practices for an hour-and-a-half after school every day. Her teammates complained about the work; Julie lost herself in it. Every stroke pulled her away from her life at home. In her fourth meet, she set the school record for the one-hundred-meter breaststroke, finishing at 1:11:27.

Julie's world was swimming, sleeping, eating, and swimming. It was awesome to be recognized for something besides being the new kid. She dreamed about attending the University of Wisconsin-Madison, home to an Olympic-sized swimming pool. Teammates Abbey and Suzanne talked about sharing an apartment with Julie during college.

Swim season ended in mid-November. Thanksgiving and Christmas – except for the previous year – were a recipe for disaster in Julie's home: mix one-part alcohol with two-parts anger. *Will it be different this year?* Julie willed her dad to stay sober until next spring, when she would then talk her mom into letting her join the local YMCA swim program. She needed to maintain her stamina and speed until team training started again in August.

"Julie, we're moving back to Michigan to be near Grandpa Richard and Grandma Rose. They will help us out when we need it. At least they'll be good for something, because right now they're good for nothing." Danny finished his speech and grabbed a beer from the fridge, strangling it by the neck as he yanked off the cap. Julie was witnessing the end of his sobriety.

Time of death: six-nineteen pm.

Arlene, strangely mute, listened to her husband mock her parents. *Does she agree with him? Does she want to be close to her parents? Does she get along with them? Shouldn't we have stayed near them before, instead of moving away? What about Mr. Koski? Dear God, I hope someone ratted him out by now – or better yet, maybe he got thrown from one of his horses and is paralyzed. How will I keep from running into him again?*

A new job and another move were not in Julie's plans. No one had told her Dad's job wasn't working out, and Julie did not understand what that meant. *You put your head under water – pull, glide, breathe – and you make it work.* A job was no different, was it? There was no way she was leaving; her family could do what they wanted, but she was staying. Maybe she could live with Suzanne or Abbey. The team needed her next year, and she needed the team.

How could Julie leave the only place that meant anything to her? *I'll talk to Mom when she's in a good mood, whenever that is.*

Saturdays at the Sandford house were peaceful until Danny and Arlene stumbled into the kitchen late in the afternoon. Hell sometimes stayed tightly wound, sometimes broke loose, but always showed up. This Saturday afternoon, Julie was in luck. Dad was nowhere near – a good time for a reasonable conversation with Mom. Julie crept quietly into the kitchen, and found Arlene slouched in a metal chair, using one long thumbnail to dig dirt out of the grooves in the red Formica table. Her other hand cradled a cigarette hanging limply out of her mouth while she squinted her eyes against the smoke curling in front of her.

"Please, Mom." Julie sprinted the last lap. "Can't I live with Suzanne or Abbey during swim season next year? You won't have to feed me or drive me home from practice—"

"Absolutely not. What will the neighbors think if I don't take care of my own kid?"

Julie heard footsteps behind her. *Oh no. And here comes Dad. I thought he was still sleeping.*

"Arlene, don't you think it's a good time to tell her the truth, for crap's sake?"

What truth? This is the second time I've heard this. What are they talking about?

"No, it's not, and you shut up about it! I'll tell her if and when I'm good and ready!" Arlene's venom spewed into the air, dangling over the three of them.

"Suit yourself. You always do. All I need is some good, mud-black coffee, and I'm gone."

Julie learned an important lesson that day: her welfare was not as important as what the neighbors thought. Mom must maintain a reputation at all costs. *How can a family that has never been a real family care about staying together?*

An angry blizzard held the town hostage. Swirling, blinding snow, fueled by forty-mile-an-hour wind gusts, turned the snowstorm into a sandstorm. Barely identifiable humans, eyes the only things unprotected against the hostile snow, were in a battle of brute strength with the regal drifts, some already six-feet high. Snow blowers shot plumes of spray in an arc of white blindness, plumes which formed white flags of surrender. The club of determined conquerors conceded defeat, storing their snow blowers back inside garages. Busses, taxis, tow trucks and snowplows were pulled off the streets and highways, waiting for this powerful force to have the last word.

"Maybe winters in Michigan will be easier," Julie heard her dad mumble, laughing like he'd told a clever joke. Two weeks after the storm, snowdrifts were still piled high enough to obliterate street signs. Without waiting for spring and dry roads, Danny ordered his family to put everything they wanted into the back of the Ford pick-up. Julie helped her mom stuff clothes into orange crates and heap them into the truck bed, along with their old bikes, a black-and-white TV that only got reception on one channel, an old Hi-Fi that played seventy-eights, a hot pot, and cardboard boxes of mismatched dishes and pans. *The Salvation Army would reject the stuff we're taking.*

Julie was not sure how four of them would squeeze into the cab; nor was she sure whether the truck would make it as far as Michigan. Some questions were better left unasked. Besides, what did it matter? She was leaving her friends, the swim team, and the nicest house her family had ever had.

Starting a new school in the middle of the year was something Julie should have been used to by now – but it was never easy being the new kid even in a familiar, one-size-fits-all school with twenty-five students in each grade. The school did not have a pool. Since her family had moved with the seasons – so it seemed – and this was only February, she was hopeful she could start high school with a swim team somewhere else. She would train extra hard and regain the strength needed for the backstroke. For now, she focused on getting good grades, so a coach would want her on the team.

Students in new schools always asked where Julie came from. Her standard response was, "My parents moved around a lot when I was young, and I always managed to find them!" She dodged the question and let the kids believe her dad was in the military. *That is partly true. Our house is in a war zone. And the battles never seem to end.*

Mr. Eriksson taught first period math class. Julie arrived at school on the first day early enough to slip into class before anyone else. As Mr. Eriksson marched in and dropped the tools of his trade on his desk, Julie swallowed a scream. *My God, he looks like Mr. Thomas! Does that awful man have a twin brother?* She could not explain the chilling coincidence.

In one week, Julie's paranoia morphed into terror. She began having serious nosebleeds daily in math class. Her mom accused her of making up stories to gain sympathy; Dad thought she was trying to hurt his chances of finding work. She didn't know any of the other girls – or even her old friends – well enough to unload her secret. The school nurse was increasingly concerned and studied all the possibilities of illnesses or allergies to find the source of the problem. When she finally called Mrs. Sandford, Arlene's response was, "Take care of it and don't bother me again."

Mr. Eriksson, initially solicitous toward Julie when the nosebleeds started, gave her opportunity to turn in late work without penalty. In short order, his patience turned into harassments, the harassments became ultimatums, and the ultimatums became humiliation. As he trolled the room, he stopped behind Julie, leaned over, put a hand on her shoulder in his best dramatic fashion and used a perfected stage-whisper. "You want to go to college? You need to get this right. The *dummy* class is down the hall." Other times, he brought the wastebasket for her bloodied tissues, then looked in and announced, "I hope there's no brain matter in there." Julie's only defense was a cocky attitude.

CHAPTER 8
ARLENE'S CAFÉ

Dreams can be put out of their misery. Julie killed hers by scrunching up her swimsuit and throwing it into the back of her closet. She was starting freshman year in Pineville.

"Hi, Julie. It's good to have you back," said Jamie Anders.

"I guess."

"Are you in band or choir this year?"

"Nope. Neither."

"Would you like to be?"

Julie chose to be more thoughtful and less snarky. Jamie was the first person who had tried to make her feel welcome in her new-old school. "What's band like?"

"I love it!"

"What do you play?"

"Flute."

"Didn't you start playing back in sixth grade?"

"Uh-huh. But we're always looking for new people. Why don't you stop in and meet our band teacher? You'll really like him."

"I always thought it would be cool to play baritone."

"Perfect! Our bari is moving to Chicago before Christmas."

"Thanks for telling me, Jamie. I'll see you in band."

"Watch out for Joey Green. You will sit in front

of him, and he's so … well … sort of strange and stuck-up."

"Will do."

The town still looked like a postcard, but with stained and worn edges. One building at the outskirt straddled two worlds – too poor to associate with the houses and too small to be useful to the farms. It had the haphazard, remodeled look of someone oblivious to the original design.

Arlene bought the building and announced her plans to own and run a café. *Her definition of the four major food groups is frozen, boxed, canned, and instant.* Julie watched in mute amazement as Arlene purchased the most run-down, one-foot-out-of-the-grave building in town and nailed an "Arlene's Café" sign to the front wall above the porch. Rough-sawn cedar siding clung to the building in waves of nausea. The garish front porch, wrapped around three sides of the café, was stained in faded burnt sienna. Wooden support posts, painted dark brown, were trapped between a sagging roof and porch. The three steps leading up to the porch challenged all customers to a contest of wits and agility. A corrugated tin roof left diners with suffocating heat in summer and finger-numbing cold in winter. Latticework, usually used to enclose porches, was nailed to either side of the first-story windows in a crude attempt at decorative shutters. A faded Pepsi thermometer graced a porch beam. A lit Grain Belt beer sign hung from a curved pipe attached to the roof. The whole building looked like a little girl playing dress-up, with the colors and styles colliding in the ultimate clothing faux pas.

My mother dresses up our tacky houses to look

like mansions, but she's not fooling anyone. She adorns her body with flair, while I'm lucky to get hand-me-downs. What gives?

The Sandford family lived in a house right behind Arlene's, bordered by a picket fence overgrown with brambles and chokecherries in the fall. The convenience of living next to the café was a trade-off for the size of the house – a bathroom slightly smaller than an airplane lavatory and three bedrooms rivaling Fotomat. The house had a yard inside the picket fence where a previous owner had abandoned a camper, home to field mice, birds, and squirrels.

Leon Bittner, another of Arlene's childhood friends, owned a depression-era housing project in Pineville. Every morning he walked into the café in pursuit of his usual breakfast: three fried eggs, toast, bacon, pancakes, and coffee. And every morning he told Arlene – loud enough for all the morning crowd to hear – that he could give her a great deal on rent for one of his houses. After being dragged into this annoying conversation for the umpteenth time, Arlene went home that night and informed her family they were moving. It was either that, or she would be forced to dump Leon's breakfast in his lap and close shop for good.

The Jacob Bittner Homes, named after Leon's deceased brother, were plain, boxy, two-story structures spread over a five-block area. After weathering decades of paint, Leon had attempted to protect his investment with the addition of low-grade aluminum siding. Some houses were completely sided. Others were only half finished before Jacob had run out of money and interest. Arlene rented one of the incompletely sided houses that a previous tenant tried to jazz up by painting the top half in equal sections of green, pink, and brown – an uncanny resemblance to a box of Neapolitan ice cream

The Sandford house had a kitchen, living room and bathroom downstairs, and three bedrooms upstairs, with a small bathroom, converted from a shared closet. The walls and ceilings were painted battleship gray.

Mr. Bittner stopped by to check on his new tenants on moving day. When Arlene introduced Julie to him, she bit down to keep from laughing. *He looks camouflaged. His skin is almost the color of the walls. Good thing he's bald, or his hair might look like them, too.*

Rent was due at the end of October. "Julie, take this envelope over to Leon's house, three blocks down, number 205. And make sure you're nice to him! He's letting us live here for cheap."

"I got homework. Can't I go later?" Julie didn't really have homework; but absolutely did not want to go to Mr. Bittner's house. He looked at her in the café like a fish in a tank that swims up to the side and bugs out its eyes.

"Don't sass me." Arlene was hanging curtains on the kitchen window with her back to Julie, who stuck out her tongue, picked up the envelope from the table, said, "Yes, Ma'am," and strolled out the door.

Julie christened the neighborhood Bittnerville. Mr. Bittner wasn't mean like the wheelchair guy in "It's a Wonderful Life," but he owned all the houses, and for all she knew, maybe even half the town. She liked their house okay. *At least it's bigger than our last one, it's not a trailer, and it doesn't smell too bad.*

Julie knocked on the front door. *Why doesn't Mr. Bittner live in a mansion somewhere? He must be rich since he owns all the houses. If it were me, I would.*

Leon Bittner answered the door wearing tan trousers, a V-neck, white t-shirt, and slippers. "Hi, Julie-girl. Welcome." Stepping aside to let her pass, Julie felt a tingling in her stomach. *The last time this happened, I was in Mr. Thomas' trailer.* She walked in, took a deep breath, and turned around.

"Mr. Bittner, where's your wife?"

"She had to go grocery shopping, but she'll be back in a little while. I'm sure she'd like to meet you. You want a snack? We got cookies."

"What kind?"

"Oatmeal raisin and chocolate chip."

"Both. Please."

"Done." Leon hobbled to the kitchen, took cookies out of a cannister, stuck them on a napkin, came back out to the living room and put them on the coffee table. "Come and get 'em!" Julie dug the envelope out of her pocket, handed it to Leon, and sat down on the sofa.

"So. What are you doing in school?"

"Well, Mr. Bittner—"

"Hey, I'm almost like an uncle to you. Call me Leon or Uncle Lee."

For the next fifteen minutes, Julie told Leon about her teachers, her classes, and even some of the places her family lived. While she talked, Leon got up to get her a glass of milk, listened intently, chuckled lightly, and gave her more attention than her dad did. He was interested in everything she said, and even expressed pride in her for getting good grades.

"Leon – Uncle Lee – I'd better get home. My mom might wonder where I've been." Julie got up and took her glass to the kitchen sink ... and then Leon was standing behind her. *Phew! His breath smells like garlic!* Suddenly his arms reached around her, unzipped her jeans, and worked his cold hands down inside her underwear, then back up underneath her shirt, rubbing his palms over her bare breasts.

"Don't worry, I'm tickling you," he whispered. "I do this to the girls I like."

Julie burned in fear. *Oh, God, please help me! I'm trapped!*

A big, white car pulled into the driveway outside the kitchen window. "That's enough fun for today." Leon removed his hands, turned, and walked to the door.

Julie zipped her pants and ran out the front door before Mrs. Bittner saw her.

Another month passed. "You must've made a big impression on Leon, because every time he comes into the café, he talks about how much he liked being with you last month." Arlene held out an envelope for Julie to take.

"Mom, please, can't you go this time?" Julie fought back tears.

"Don't be an idiot! If that jerk Leon likes you, maybe our rent will stay down. Besides, what're you crying about?"

Julie wiped her sleeve across her face. "Will you go with me?"

"Heck no. I'll never get away from him and that sappy wife of his."

"But Mom—"

"Forget it. Go." Arlene dropped the envelope on the sofa and returned to the kitchen.

Mom will never believe me if I tell her what her old friend did to me. But I can't go over there again. What am I going to do? Julie ran up to her room, tucked her blouse into her jeans, put on an old sweatshirt and zipped it up. She went back down, put on her winter jacket, and walked out the door headed for the Bittner's. *Please, God, let Mrs. Bittner be home.* At their house, Julie's hand froze, afraid to knock.

The door opened; Julie was shocked to see Leon wearing a black suit and bright, red tie. "I clean up good, don't I? I just got back from a meeting with a bunch of bigwigs, and I seen you standing outside our house. Come in and relax while we wait for Mrs. Bittner to get back from the store."

Doesn't she ever stay home? Julie walked in and stood in the narrow, dark hallway.

"Come with me to the living room. Mrs. Bittner and I went on a vacation out west, and I want to show you some of our pictures." Leon loosened his tie, took off his coat, hung it on a hanger in the closet, and draped his arm around Julie. Julie's feet sunk into the floor. "Let me take your jacket."

"That's okay."

"No, it's not! My wife keeps it hot in here." Leon unzipped Julie's jacket, eased it off her and hung it carefully in the hall closet.

There were not enough layers to shield Julie from this repulsive man, who smiled almost politely as he unzipped her sweatshirt, pushed her gently against the wall, slowly unzipped her pants and pulled them down, running his hands around the inside of her underwear, and then up her shirt. Julie could not even scream. No car pulled into the driveway. There was nothing and no one to interrupt Leon's tickling.

When Leon removed one of his hands, Julie thought he was done, until he clumsily unzipped his pants and started panting. *I don't know what's happening, but I want this over. I think I'm going to throw up.* Leon sighed, muttered a "thank you," zipped his pants and said, "We're all done for today. Where's the envelope?" Julie pulled her pants up, zipped them, dug the envelope out of her pocket, hurled it onto the floor, picked up her sweatshirt, and flew out the door. *What if Mom asks me what happened to my winter jacket?*

By the end of December, Julie knew one thing for sure: there was no way she was ever going to walk into Leon's house again. *Somehow, I need to tell Mom what happened to me. Dear God, I hope something will change. Mrs. Ryczek used to talk about how You are protector. Can You do anything for me now?* When Julie finally opened the can, worms spilled out everywhere. Arlene accused her of telling lies to get out of doing "the only stinkin' job I ask of you around here, to pay our stinkin' rent." Julie's mom left her no choice. No way out.

Arlene sat at the table with her checkbook at the end of January. Julie wandered into the kitchen for something to eat. "Get my purse, look in my wallet for a stamp, and bring it here." Arlene stared at the phone bill.

That's it! When Arlene handed her the rent

check the next day, Julie snuck into her mom's purse, pulled a stamp out of her wallet, rifled through her desk drawer for an envelope, wrote out the Bittner address, slid the check inside, sealed the envelope, licked the stamp, smacked it on the corner, and walked to the closest mailbox – all in one unbroken action. *I hope she doesn't keep a stamp inventory.* Julie stayed away long enough to make her mom think she went to Leon's house. *I don't care if Mom finds out about what I did, and we are forced to move. I am never, ever going over there again.*

Later that week, Leon strolled into the café for breakfast and caught Arlene's elbow. "Hey, I never see my Julie anymore." Arlene noticed Leon's eyes bugged out even more than usual.

"Whatever." Arlene smiled. Back in the kitchen later that morning flipping pancakes over a hot griddle, she muttered, "That man's cake is only half-baked."

It was the one-year anniversary of the move to Michigan; Julie watched a swim season pass without her on the team. Unbelievably, it looked like they would live in Pineville longer than she thought possible. Her nosebleeds finally stopped when school was done the previous June, and she no longer saw Mr. Eriksson every day. She was hardened by the constant teasing; along with her blood, her emotions had also clotted.

The February day was not one of the glorious winter days that made Julie dream of skiing, making snowmen, and burying her low self-worth in the nearest snowbank. An unforgiving, powerful winter wind blew the snow sideways across the road in front of the school. Window screens were covered with blotches of heavy snow that looked like they had been attacked by an angry snow cone machine. Plows fought and conceded the battle, while Julie's thoughts piled into their own drifts. *The maintenance crew must feel like they're trying to bail the Titanic with a teaspoon. I hope we get out of school early; otherwise, we might get stuck here overnight. Where would I want to be stranded? Washington? Illinois? Wisconsin? Michigan?*

Along with owning and managing the café, Arlene had taken a second job as a school bus driver. A voice crackled over the intercom, paging Julie to the office. Did her mom want to drive her home before the start of early dismissal? Was she in trouble? She trudged down to the school office, wearing defiance like a shield.

Mrs. Evelyn Johnson, the school secretary, was accustomed to students like Julie, the ones who used prickly attitudes to protect empty hearts. "Julie, your mom was taken by ambulance to the ER at St. Michael's thirty minutes ago."

Evelyn paused, waiting for Julie to put on her best I-don't-care face.

"Your mom couldn't back the bus out of the garage until she hoisted up the door herself. It seems that the automatic door opener was broken. Anyways, dear, she slipped on a patch of ice. As she went down, she let go of the garage door, which came crashing down on her."

The facemask cracked and Julie's knees buckled. Mrs. Johnson came around the counter, opened her arms, and waited quietly. Julie momentarily hesitated, then walked into those arms, knowing how much she needed someone to sustain her fragile reality.

After a tight hug, Mrs. Johnson made a phone call to a neighborhood school volunteer, who showed up with a four-wheel drive truck to take Julie to the hospital.

Arlene had broken her back. Julie felt a break in the wall of resentment and hostility building in her since being forced to give up the swim team. While Mom was in the ER, love grew in Julie's heart. She waited anxiously for her mom to come out of her grogginess, so that she could show her sympathy.

"Mom! You're awake! What can I do for you?" Julie stood close to her bed.

"You can get out of here and go back to the café. It isn't going to run itself." Arlene continued to mumble. "And you can forget about being in volleyball anymore. Your dad is not," Arlene fought for breath, "going to pick you up after school every day at five." Arlene closed her eyes. "You kids don't know how much I do for you."

I don't care about the stupid café. I want to hear you say you love me and you're glad I'm here. "Okay, whatever." Julie picked the chip back up and set it securely on her shoulder.

It was Friday night and Julie was on an adrenalin rush after spiking the ball for the winning point. Her dad stunned her – after she had returned home from the discouraging visit with her mom – with the announcement that he'd be glad to pick her up after volleyball practice during the week in exchange for her working more hours at the café on weekends.

Julie opened the door to Arlene's at nine-thirty to help the last of the customers and then do her closing jobs. Since no one was waiting for food, she busied her hands wiping down counters and refilling salt and pepper shakers, ketchup and mustard bottles, napkin dispensers, and the all-important toothpick holders. She heard her dad humming behind the swinging kitchen door and assumed he was cleaning the griddle. *He's been in a good mood lately. I hope he stays that way. But hey! If that changes, he can take out his anger on something greasy.*

At ten-thirty, Julie closed and locked the door just as Danny sauntered into the dining area wearing a food-stained apron tied loosely around his waist, hands hidden behind his back. "Ta-da!" He proudly produced a bottle of Bali Hi and shouted, "Julie-girl, let's you and me go to the back room and play a game of pool. A dollar a game sound good?"

When was the last time he asked me to do something fun? Julie raced ahead of her dad to the poolroom, flicked on the fluorescent light hanging precariously over the old table, grabbed the triangle off the nail on the wall, and arranged the pool balls. She was ready to beat Danny Sandford at something! By the fourth game, Danny was joking, laughing, and enjoying his daughter without the jokes being at her expense. *I don't know what's happened to him, but I like this new and improved version.*

Three games in, Danny's hand-eye coordination went AWOL, closely followed by his reasoning skills. "How about Pinball?"

Julie giggled at her dad's inability to keep his hands from slipping off the wooden handles. "Say Uncle!" she yelled as she pushed him aside and positioned herself to take over.

"C'mon, it's no fun drinkin' alone." Danny

bumped into Julie's elbow with his, and some of the wine sloshed onto the slanted top of the machine.

"Oh, ick." Julie used her sleeve to wipe up the liquid. *I can't stand the smell of that stuff, and now it's on my clothes.* "All right, I'll try it." She continued playing Pinball as Danny disappeared into the kitchen, returned with a small juice glass, and poured as much wine on his arm as he did into the glass.

"Here – bottom's up!"

I guess I should be happy he's treating me like an adult. Julie turned away from the lights and bells, tipped the glass and drank the contents all at once. Her dad laughed as she gagged and barely kept from coughing it back up.

"Thatta girl. Try another glass. It'll keep the first one down." Before Julie could object, Danny refilled her glass and brought it up to her mouth. This time, she drank it a little more slowly and noticed, after the last swallow, that she started feeling warm and tingly. *When did Dad start sounding so funny?*

Danny left the room, Julie heard a bell ringing, and then her dad walked back in with his arm sticking straight out, his hand clenched in a fist. "Lookee what the reg'ster drunk and coughed up." He opened his hand, and a shower of quarters fell to the floor, some landing on their edges and rolling in all directions. Julie crouched down to pick one up and tumbled over. Danny pulled her up and walked them over to the jukebox, where she aimed and dropped her quarter into the slot. The song titles and numbers spun, so she leaned her elbows on the glass, concentrated, and pushed the buttons under E, three and two.

"Ray's the man!" Julie turned, lifted her arms

around her dad's neck, and started singing. "I can't stop loving you, I've made up my mind." Father and daughter danced their way to the pool table, where Danny rescued the bottle of wine perched precariously on the edge and took a big gulp. Julie snatched it out of his hands and chugged the rest, then they dropped to the floor. "So, I'll just live my life in dreams of yesterday." Julie finished the song with a sideways grin.

Julie awoke completely naked, covered only in vomit and shame. She focused on a Schlitz wall clock. *Five thirty? Is it day or night?* She gingerly sat up, checked both arms and legs for movement, and realized that, although never having lived through a hangover before, this was The One. Someone had apparently removed her head, beaten it to within an inch of its life and then cruelly set it back on her neck. Her back screamed in pain, shoulders feeling ripped from their sockets.

A dirty, white apron was all Julie had to clean the mess from her body. *I wonder who wore this last?* She collected her twisted clothes and tried to put herself back together again. It was easier to slip her blouse on backwards. She crawled over to the pay phone and used the hanging metal cord to pull herself up, waves of dizziness rolling over her. The quarter sitting on the ledge next to the phone brought a fuzzy memory of something from last night. *Or was it the night before?* With one arm wrapped around the cord for support, Julie reached out with the other arm, picked up the quarter between shaky fingers, carefully aimed it at the coin slot, and dropped it in. She picked up the receiver, brought it slowly to her ear, and almost collapsed at the deafening sound of the dial tone. Uncoiling her arm from the cord and using her elbow for balance, she set the receiver on the ledge and carefully pushed each button of Grandma Rosie's number. She picked up the receiver again and prayed that someone would answer.

Grandma Rosie hardly ever hears from me. When she does, I'm usually angry about something. I wonder if she'll even want to talk to me.

After four rings, someone answered.

"Grandma? It's Julie. Please come ... and get me ... here."

Julie dropped the receiver. "Has your father done something to you? Why did Arlene marry that no-'count drunk? I would love to get my hands on him for sure and for good." Rosie's voice sounded like a clanging cymbal.

Sinking to the floor, Julie remembered she had never told her grandma where she was. She never figured out how her grandma knew where to find her, but by the time she crawled to the front door, both Grandma and Grandpa were using their key to unlock it. Once inside, Grandma Rosie flipped around the Open sign to Closed. *I forgot to do that last night.*

Richard Cerbé picked his granddaughter up while Rosalynn found her jacket and wrapped it around her. As the three walked outside, Rosie sputtered and fumed like the getaway car Arlene had driven when she and her kids escaped to Michigan. Back at their house, Rosie helped Julie out of her jacket and twisted clothes. Julie stepped into the shower while Grandma adjusted the water temperature. Julie never imagined her grandma seeing her like this; but embarrassment is a companion to dignity, and Julie's had been robbed.

When Grandma Rosie closed the shower door, Julie sank to the tiled floor, tipped her face back into the steamy spray, and wondered if there was enough water in the ocean to wash away the dirt from her soul. *Was Dad protecting me from Mr. Thomas so that he could save the merchandise for himself? What kind of father does that to his daughter? He was so drunk. Does he know what he did to me? Am I sure I know what he did?* When the water got cold, Julie stood slowly, turned off both faucets, opened the door and found a terrycloth robe hanging on a wall hook. She put on the robe, wrapped her hair in a towel hanging on another hook, walked into her mom's old room, lowered herself into the four-poster bed and cried salty tears that stung her cheeks.

After a fitful sleep, Julie awoke to shadows falling across the room. *The darkness is a one-size-fits-all for my life, a life where everyone's dreams become my nightmares.*

CHAPTER 9
SPAM-EATIN', WHITE-DOG TRAILER TRASH

Arlene was released from the hospital after one month and returned to driving bus part time. She also spent a few hours each day at the café, although demanding that Danny and her kids cover all the shifts. Julie avoided her dad when she could. When that wasn't possible, she made sure customers were always nearby. She refused to help him clean up and close at night. Her mom seemed oblivious to Julie's morosely defiant attitude, one that dared her dad to challenge her. *Maybe he feels sorry for what he did. Why doesn't he say something to me? And if he isn't sorry, why is he backing down from my stubbornness?*

Arlene's Café was not Julie's dream. She knew they needed the money for food and rent; but that expectation crashed into the reality that extra food never appeared in the cupboards or refrigerator. The only evidence of more money showed up on Arlene: new clothes and shoes and jewelry. If the restaurant was supposed to be a dream recycler, then Julie desperately wanted the building dynamited. *And then we could toast marshmallows over the ashes.*

It was April Fool's Day. *My fifteenth birthday.* Julie walked into the house listening for the familiar sounds of the radio in the kitchen and the TV in the living room, both of which were usually left on all day.

Arlene claimed the noise "scares off the idiots." Julie walked into a spookily quiet house and talked to the dark TV screen. "I think I'll raid the fridge for that Mounds bar I hid in the veggie drawer last night." Plopping her books on the horsehair sofa, she went into the kitchen and yanked on the handle of the GE refrigerator painted gray to match the walls. Julie could not comprehend the idea that anyone would assault an appliance with such a hideous color. "They used ugly wall paint and left thick globs hanging on the sides for dear life! Sheesh!" Jerking open the door, she did not realize at first what was wrong. *Okay. There's no light in here. That explains why everything is so quiet.*

Julie retraced her steps to the living room, and lounged in the unreclinable recliner, lanky legs hanging over the arm, reading a book and enjoying calm in the house. Arlene suddenly and noisily entered and slammed the kitchen door behind her, rattling the pots on the wall hooks.

"So, what, you couldn't start dinner?" shouted Arlene from the kitchen. Peering around the corner into the living room, she modulated her voice. "Why are you reading without a lamp on?" Julie twisted her body, swung her legs to the floor, closed her book, got up and headed towards her room, sending a signal to her mom that she was dog-tired of the constant arguments. "Did those idiots at the electric company shut off our power again?"

Julie turned towards her mom's voice. *How about paying the bill?* "I don't know, Mom. Why would they do that?"

Arlene tossed her purse on the table and everything in it spilled out, running for cover. She retrieved her checkbook and gathered up four pens, trying each one and throwing all but one into the trash. She hastily wrote a check, tore it out of the book and held it up. "Here, run this down to the power company." Julie stared at her mom without moving. "Those good-for-nothings can wait for the rest of their money until we get more." Julie's dad worked construction at least six months at a time, which she thought should have been more than enough to support them year-round if they saved for the down times.

"What does that make me? The elected officer of deceit?" The darkness emboldened Julie in a way she would never have considered otherwise.

"Watch your mouth."

"Okay, I'm sorry." *Why do we have to spend half the year living on food stamps and Spam?* Julie took the outstretched check from her mom and headed for the door, convinced that her life was an in-house arrest. When she finally escaped, it would be to a state of humiliation.

People with dim pilot lights slouched in a long line at the power company, avoiding eye contact and shuffling forward like they had pebbles in their shoes. Julie felt uncomfortable at the possibility of not leaving anytime soon.

It took thirty minutes to reach the Delinquent Accounts counter where Julie overheard a clerk mutter, "Spam-eatin', white-dog, trailer-trash." *We don't live in a trailer. Is she talking about me?* Julie felt as naked as the night in the café with her dad, only this disgrace came from a sober person. She fired the check across the counter, turned, and snaked through the line of semicomatose people and out the door.

Julie startled awake at one-thirty in the morning to arguing, cussing, and the sound of the phone cord being ripped out of its wall socket. She ran downstairs, peeked into the living room, and wondered if there would be a stay-of-execution for the furniture.

"Daughter!" Arlene screamed. "Go to the neighbor's house and call the cops!" *Which neighbors? They all play by the rules of non-engagement. We've lived here for over a year, and no one's done anything about the screaming they have certainly heard. Where am I supposed to go?* Julie threw a sweatshirt over her pajamas and ran out the back door.

The house on the corner, four doors down from the Sandfords, still had a front porch light on. *If the cops come after me, the least I can do is lead them back to my house.* Julie lifted her hand to knock, when the door opened to a woman about her mom's age, wearing a blue terrycloth robe loosely tied around her trim waist. She had short hair, mashed on one side of her head. The lingering aroma of gingerbread made Julie's stomach growl.

"Come in, dear." The woman smiled. "There's hot chocolate on the stove, and you can sleep on our couch if you want to." Julie shivered from cold and fear, too tired to be suspicious. Everything she wanted was here: hot chocolate, a couch, and hopefully a warm blanket, all offered by a woman who radiated an abundance of sympathy, even this late at night, or early in the morning, whichever it was.

"Thank you, ma'am," Julie whispered as she sailed through the door before the woman could change her mind, collapsed on the couch, and cried. The woman disappeared into the kitchen and reappeared with a steaming mug. Julie sat up, wiped her face, and drank as quickly as she dared, since she was expected to dial nine-one-one and get back home.

Officer Seaver banged on the front door. "Come out, Mr. Sandford." Julie was on her third emergency run that week, dealing with guilt over how good it was to leave the arguing house and find shelter with the kind Mrs. Moore. *I wish I could stay there all night.*
"Danny, open the door."
No response.
A little louder, "What's the problem this time? Go back to bed and sleep this off. We got more important things to worry about – bigger fish to fry." The monologue was always delivered to a closed door. With the momentary lull in the hurling of words and objects, Officer Seaver and his partner had no choice but to turn around and walk back to their cruiser, hoping this song-and-dance would end. The officer always mumbled, "God helps those who help themselves," while his partner responded, "That's unbiblical hogwash. Danny has to admit that he's powerless to help himself and turn his heart to the One whose help will change his life." The men opened their doors in tandem to the radio squawking a report of a crime, often a home burglary nearby. The robbing of material objects was less important than the robbing of souls; the officers agreed on that. It was just easier to prosecute.

In the few hours of respite sandwiched between police calls and the arrival of dawn, Danny would pass out on the couch, lying on top of a bent table lamp or torn cushion. Arlene and her children would collapse into troubled sleep, a kind of rough idling until the sunlight overpowered the darkness and shifted the parents into overdrive again. The trophy for midnight fighting went to Danny, while the morning prize went to Arlene, whose job was to harass and manipulate her husband into another day of work – the only way she knew to avoid the stigma of poverty.

CHAPTER 10
MAMA T AND TEDDY-BOY

Norwegians spilled out of their homes at the beginning of May after a winter swimming in Elmer's glue, whiter than the glint of snow in the sunlight and unprepared for shedding layers of clothes to expose alabaster skin.

Julie came home from school, dropped her books on the kitchen table, and headed back outside. Roller-skating sounded fun, but most of the neighborhood sidewalks were a maze of broken chunks of concrete. She decided to walk in the opposite direction from her usual route, and certainly not anywhere close to the Bittner house.

Red, yellow, and purple tulips and bright daffodils bloomed in miniature gardens in almost every yard. *Mrs. Ryczek always had a vase of fresh flowers on her desk in the spring. Maybe if I walk backwards, I can find her again ... or find Mrs. Anderson or Mary.* The black-and-white world of Julie's home was inadequate for her Technicolor dreams. She was lonely for a grandma kind of friend.

Julie walked several blocks until she spied a little, brown, gingerbread house, with gabled windows and blue trim. A sixtyish-looking woman sat on the front porch in an enormous wicker rocker, knitting and singing. She wore a red-checked dress with a matching scarf tied around her head. When she looked up and smiled, her bright lipstick and arched eyebrows complimented a full, perfectly symmetrical face. *If she had dark skin, she would be a dead ringer for Aunt Jemima!* The woman put her knitting needles in her lap, waved, and shouted, "Come up here und talk to me," motioning for Julie to sit in the other rocker. Julie slowly walked up the front steps. "I'm Mrs. Tannenbaum, but everyone calls me Mama T. Und who bist du?"

Julie was the only guest on Mama T's daytime talk show. During the next hour, she shared everything in her life. She wondered why she did not do this with Mrs. Moore, but then realized the Moore house was only for physical safety. For everyone's protection, it was better for her not to be open about her home life.

But with Mama T, it was already so different. She listened and listened to Julie, her attention feeding Julie's starved heart. When she reluctantly got up to leave, Mama T exclaimed, "I vill pray for you! I haf calluses on my knees from praying for so many years, but I down can't get no more, so now I pray sitting on my backside. Der Gott hears from me every day!"

During summer vacation, Julie headed to Mama T's as often as she could. The hot weather chased Mama T inside, so Julie quickly learned to ignore the formality of knocking on the door. She burst into the house and found Mama, who had a no-big-deal way of turning everything into a party for two.

"Come, my Liebchen, is time to haf a cuppa." The coffee pot was always on; it was time to learn to like the nasty stuff. "Ven you come tomorrow, ve make dark rye brodt." Mama T turned on the window fan in the kitchen, poured mugs of coffee, and motioned for Julie to sit down across from her.

"So, I hear you go to school vit my boy."

Julie choked on her first sip of the bitter liquid.

"Ted? Teddy Tannenbaum? I thought he was your *grandson*!"

Mama laughed, as smile lines connected with other lines crossing her face. "Ach, an easy mistake. I was forty-two ven I Teddy had."

"Wow!"

"Ja, he vas a big surprise to his fater und me. I alvays say I had da caboose to give birt to da caboose der Gott gave me!"

Julie rode the wave from shock to laughter. "Mama T!"

"Ah, Gott has humor. He gifs us all tings to enjoy!"

Julie had no answer. She never knew anyone close enough to God to share a joke with Him. Mama got up from the table and brought back an apple pie. "Next, you vill learn to make fruit pies. Ve haf lots to do."

While other teenagers headed to beaches, pools, and movie theatres, Julie was refreshed by Mama T. When it was too hot to bake, grandma and adopted granddaughter went shopping. Mama showed Julie how to find nice clothes at second-hand stores and alter them or freshen them up with special buttons or rickrack, until they ended up looking new. Mama said, "Oh, ja, ve can take da collar off here und move in da side seam dere." Julie's mending eventually became sewing clothes with raw material. *I hope my mom doesn't care that I'm wearing clothes someone else helped me make.*

Teddy never surfaced during all of Julie visits

with Mama T. She assumed bagging groceries at the IGA or pumping gas at Bob's Standard kept him away at dinner time. Mama T's husband had died not long after Teddy was born, and Julie didn't know where the rest of the children were. They were probably married and living far away, but Julie couldn't imagine anyone staying away from a wonderful mom like this unless they had no choice. So, it was just the two of them; Julie did not need to share her new grandma friend with anyone.

The dog days of August barked at the door. Julie and Mama T sat in the living room in front of a window fan, alternating between drinking their iced tea and holding the cold glasses to their sweaty foreheads.

"Mama, you once referred to Teddy as your caboose, so you must have other children."

Mama set her glass down and picked up her knitting needles and a ball of soft, blue yarn. Julie knew she was making a baby blanket for a neighbor's new grandson and marveled that anyone's heart could be as big as hers.

"Ja, I haf Barb, who ist probably about tventy years older dan you. She's married to Bob Fechner, und dey live in Omaha."

"That's funny – my mom has a cousin named Bob Fechner, and I'm pretty sure he lives in Omaha." Julie and Mama T look at each other and burst out laughing. "So, I'm kind of a part of your family after all! Wait 'til I tell my mom! She always says it's a small world, and when things get strange, it gets even smaller." *I don't know about the size of the world, but I feel like I'm the only moon in Mama T's orbit.*

Julie met Teddy Tannenbaum at the beginning

of their sophomore year. *I was wrong about his summer job; he must have been doing heavy lifting outside.* Teddy was lean, muscular, and deeply tanned. His long, blonde hair was sun-bleached, almost white. For the rest of the day, Julie barely concentrated on the meet the new teachers while they're still nice orientation. Teddy was in one of her electives, fifth period art class, where some of the most talented students had work from previous years displayed around the room. Teddy had an acrylic of a fire-eating dragon coming out of the top of a Cyclops' head; a charcoal of a robot tying a noose around its neck; and a colored-pencil drawing of an eagle in flight carrying a snake in its talons. The only thing Julie knew about art was still life, and there was nothing tranquil about those drawings.

"Hey, Sandford! I hear you've been hanging around my ma." Julie carried her hot lunch tray, turned around and almost dropped it as she looked up at this guy, obviously in the dark about how cute he was.

"I have been. She's been good to me." *Okay, that sounds dumb.*

"Yeah." A girl standing next to Teddy put her oar in the water. "He does anything he wants, and his mom thinks he's got it all together. He parties and does drugs and tells her whatever she wants to hear." The girl reached for Teddy's hand.

Julie squirmed. *Maybe I'm more of an artist than I realize. I am already painting a picture of Teddy-boy. I need to stay away from this guy.* Julie took her tray to an empty table and ate her fish sticks. She was so lost in thought that she even ate her dull-yellow wax beans.

Teddy was an edgy guy in a charming package.

107

A few weeks and several stolen glances after that first encounter, Julie hoped for the chance to hitch a ride on his star. She did not have long to wait.

Julie walked down the middle of the hallway at the end of school one Monday in October, when suddenly, Teddy stood in front of her. "Hey, Jules, you're looking mighty hot today." Teddy flashed his butter-melting smile, and she blushed as much from the other kids forming a circle around them as from Teddy's comment. "So, you got a date for homecoming?"

If he's going to humiliate me, he's got the perfect audience. "No, not yet." *Not ever.*

"How would you like to go with me?" Loud applause echoed off the walls, saving Julie from finding her fickle voice.

Mama T was easily persuaded into sewing a new, ankle-length, blue dress with long, sheer sleeves. She was not told that the dress was for a date with her son. Julie did not know why it was important to keep this part of her life separate from Mama T. Maybe she had seen enough of the underbelly of life to know what people might do if they had leverage against her. She loved everything about Mama and had opened deep places in her heart, yet still held back part of it.

Teddy officially became Julie's first boyfriend. She wore his I.D. bracelet, and they were a recognized couple at school. Julie went from having a few friends to suddenly being in the popular crowd, one of the many perks of being with a guy who both chose the play and starred in the leading role.

Most of the sophomore class – and even the older students – waited for a chance to go out with Teddy and Julie. Teddy's black Firebird convertible led the pack to Friday night movies, or to McDonald's, or just to drag race down the main street in town. Everyone assumed Teddy would pick the time and place for the hangouts, and that made Julie feel special. Her boyfriend was good-looking, strong, and decisive.

The tide of Danny's drinking was in the ebb stage, which meant fewer nine-one-one calls at the Moore house. Julie was glad her dad drank less but found him almost scarier when he was menacingly sober, trying to control even the obvious and inevitable parts of his family's lives. *Okay, so what's the diff between him and Teddy? Teddy's strength is starting to look more like stubbornness, and his decisiveness is very controlling. Maybe he's a younger version of my father.*

But Teddy is so cute and fun! And since I've learned to put up with Dad's drinking, this is not a big deal. Besides, I know Teddy loves me, and he would never hurt me.

"I'll come by after I get off work and take you for a spin on the Honda. We have to get in a few more rides before it gets too cold. Wear the leather jacket I got you, and your red bandanna. I'll wear mine too. Okay, babe?"

"I can't wait!" Julie hung up the phone and sighed deeply. No guy had ever treated her like this, and it put a knot in her stomach – *for the right reason this time.*

The Honda wailed into the McDonald's parking lot just as Julie and Teddy saw guys from their class throwing punches in front of a Mustang with a dented back fender. One of the guys was Teddy's best friend. A crowd of guys and girls cheered. Teddy stopped the bike and barely waited for Julie to swing her leg over the seat and jump off before he pushed down the kickstand and sailed into the middle of the fight. *I've seen him do this before. Most of the guys will probably cut a wide path around his temper.* Julie ran inside the restaurant without waiting for the outcome. *Who am I kidding? I can't do this anymore. Teddy has so many girls lined up to date him. I'm sure it won't bother him to lose me, especially if I make it seem like he's dumping me.*

All evidence of a fight had disappeared by the time Julie walked back outside. Teddy was alone in the parking lot, leaning up against his bike and smoking a cigarette. "What do you say we get out and do something fun, babe?" Teddy flicked the cigarette into the weeds and motioned for Julie to hop on.

"Great! Yeah!" Julie secured her feet on the pedals and waited for Teddy to climb on, then wrapped her arms tightly around his waist. *I should probably do this now before I chicken out.*

The Honda cruised down the interstate going seventy. "Teddy!" Julie shouted into the wind. "Let's turn off at the next exit!" Teddy gave the thumbs-up and flipped his right turn signal. Julie hoped for a slower, quieter ride, but as soon as he could, Teddy found a dirt road and pushed the speedometer back to sixty.

Julie loosened her arms. "Teddy, I don't think we should go out anymore," she yelled. Teddy spun the bike in a three-sixty. Rocks flew out from under the tires, and Julie never knew what kept them from laying the bike down. "Stop!" Julie screamed. "Let me off and

I'll walk home!"

The bike came to a stop. Julie quickly climbed off and caught the bottom of her jeans on the tailpipe, yelping as a small hole burned through the jeans to her ankle.

"Maybe you should go back to my mommy and see if she can fix your leg." Teddy was frighteningly sarcastic.

"That's okay," gasped Julie, who sat in the middle of the road holding her ankle. *I won't let him see me cry. That will make him angrier.* "Take me home and I'll be fine. I'm sorry I said anything; of course, you're the guy for me." Julie defaulted to her familiar survival mode.

Back at school the next day, Teddy acted like nothing had happened between them. He sat next to her at lunch and told his audience that they were going to a movie that night and that this date was "for the two of us. The rest of you losers can make your own entertainment."

"Oooooh! Aaaaaaah!" Everyone laughed and pointed at Julie, who blushed without really knowing why.

The cramped back seat of a Firebird had never been Julie's dream of the place to lose her virginity. She had had the image of strolling across a bridge spanning a clear, peaceful river ... but the wind always picked up and the water churned angry images of Mr. Thomas, Mr. Koski, and Mr. Bittner. By the time the roaring water swallowed the bridge, Julie knew there would never be any return to innocence. *Besides, losing my virginity is a silly and wrong phrase. It can be stolen or given, but never lost.* Hers was partially stolen by evil men, and she had given the remainder away freely. The only way she could live with that was to find something in it for her. She was now assured of holding on to Teddy, as well as the far greater privilege of staying in Mama T's life. *Everyone needs a safety net. I've found mine.*

It didn't take long for the net to tear, and Julie's safety fell through the hole. Her dates with Teddy usually ended in verbal attacks, the result of too much drinking and too little care. The gap between life with her dad and life with Teddy was narrowing, and Julie desperately needed some control over at least a small part of her world. *It's time to get out of this. Teddy is great looking and talented, and he can have any girl he wants, especially the unsuspecting ones.* Teddy was coming to pick her up for a date at the movies. Tonight was the night.

"Teddy," began Julie on the way to the theatre.

"Yeah?" He popped open a can of Schlitz and drank most of it in one gulp. "What is it, babe?"

Please don't call me that anymore. I know it should make me feel loved, but it makes me feel controlled.

"I don't think we should be together anymore." Julie ran out of steam.

Teddy hit the gas. Julie glanced over and saw the needle at seventy. *Not this again!* Without warning, Teddy reached across her lap, gripped the door handle, yanked it up, and hurled his weight against Julie's shoulder. The door jammed.

"Please, Teddy, stop and let me out!"

Teddy hit the brakes, and Julie's right shoulder

smashed against her door. She did not want Teddy to see her crying – being a weak chick, he called it – but she couldn't help it. She was tired of this hula-hoop.

"Get out. I've had enough of you anyway. You're about used up. It's time for me to find a new chick who'll appreciate me." Teddy dropped his head back on the seat, closed his eyes, and shut Julie out. She got out of the car and headed back to the main highway, hoping to hitch a ride home.

Devastated at the prospect of losing Mama T and relieved at the expectation of losing Teddy, Julie continued spending time with Mama, but it never felt the same after the break-up with her spoiled son. Julie had nothing to feel guilty about, and was sure that if Mama knew everything, she would not defend her son. But who knew? Maybe it was time to move on. *I hope Mama T keeps praying for me. I need anything that will tip the scale in my favor.*

CHAPTER 11
THE WRONG ROOM

Julie longed for a girlfriend. A close girlfriend. Not the bottom feeders who sucked the life out of her when she was with Teddy. As soon as the breakup was advertised, she became roadkill anyway. *I guess I deserved it.*

Stormy January weather trapped everyone indoors. Julie had not walked down to Mama T's since early December. Even her own mom would have been a shield against the loneliness, but Arlene was in the hospital recovering from another back injury. Danny suddenly had fewer reasons to perfect his rant-and-rave routine. Julie had not been to the Moore house in almost a month.

The unfamiliar sun broke through the clouds in – *what did the weather guy say? Three weeks? No wonder I feel icky!* Julie bundled up and went outside. Freezing to death was better than dying of loneliness.

A house one block over had three gallon-cans of bright, yellow indoor paint sitting on a metal folding table next to the garage with a "free" sign taped to one of the cans. Julie faced a long Saturday ahead of her. *What could it hurt to take the paint?* She made two roundtrips to her house and lined up the cans in a corner of her bedroom. Paint brushes and drop cloths were in the bathroom closet. She was armed and dangerous, ready to attack her bedroom walls. *Attack is the right word. The battleship gray walls look like they've been at war for years.*

How am I going to move my dresser away from the wall to paint? It's as heavy as a boat anchor! None of the kids at school would risk loyalty to Teddy by venturing into enemy territory. Julie's mind scanned the rows of desks in her homeroom class until she stopped at Chris Anderson. She grabbed the phonebook off her desk and started looking for Chris' number. After finding six pages of Andersons in an area of the state top-heavy in Swedes, she was astonished to find the number.

Julie dialed and felt foolish for thinking that moving furniture and painting would be the ticket for a fun afternoon. But Chris also sounded bored, reassured her that she thought Teddy was a creep, and said she'd be over in an hour. By the end of the day, the girls had painted, laughed, and sung slightly off-key to albums. They discovered shared likes and dislikes of jokes and teachers and music. *This is like being with Suzanne and Abbey again. We could use a fourth for our apartment!*

Chris and Julie remained acquaintances at school. They decided to enjoy their friendship away from the shallowness of the other girls. As soon as they each got home from school, they'd talk on the phone for at least an hour. Before long, Chris invited Julie to spend the weekend with her family at their house in nearby Oak Creek.

Chris Anderson's family was like the other Anderson family in Platteville, one in which Julie was both seen and heard. She began to think of Chris as her biological sister. Someone at school started a rumor that they were cousins, and that they must have had some reason for trying to hide it. Both girls were a slender five-eight and shared fair-skinned, German-Norwegian facial features as well as shoulder-length auburn hair. As the rumor took on its own life, it remained uncorrected by girls who each found a friend and decided not to be secretive about it any longer.

Arlene's release from the hospital gave Danny the green light to resume his midnight terrors. At the appointed hour, Julie threw on her jacket and ran down to the Moores. Officer Seaver showed up at the familiar house and delivered his monologue to the same closed door. Julie walked back home and made her own speech in the frosty air. "I'm tired of doing this. It's getting embarrassing. Let Mom start doing it – I'm done. Nothing ever changes anyway."

The human heart is defined anatomically as a muscle; but philosophically, it is a ligament – tough, sinewy, and able to stretch and connect. Julie's heart connected with Chris' and made a bypass around her dad. She was no longer emotionally involved in his tossing-and-throwing of innocent furniture if he left her alone.

"Saturday night's all right for fighting; get a little action in ..." Julie cranked up the volume on her stereo and laughed at Chris, who pulled an enormous pair of sunglasses out of her duffle bag, slapped them on her face and started playing air piano.

"Elton John, you ain't!"

"Thank God," yelled Chris.

Julie had spent every weekend with Chris' family since they met, and really wanted Chris to be at her house for a change. Danny seemed to be in a long stretch of catching his breath before the next round of toss-and-fling, so Julie took advantage of the break in the action to have Chris over. *A friend is finally at my house.*

It was midnight before the girls finished looking through yearbooks, snacking, and listening to stacks of albums. Both fell asleep in mid-conversation on Julie's double-bed while the stereo needle was stuck in a groove on "Send in the Clowns." Julie awoke, grabbed the needle arm and carefully lifted it so that it wouldn't scratch her Judy Collins album. She pushed the arm down into its cradle and drifted back to sleep.

With a bright moon shining through the window, Julie fought to pull herself out of a troubling dream. *Why is my hand wet and why is it moving? What's the matter? I need to wake up!* Julie forced her eyes open and brought them into focus on her dad, standing above her naked, one hand holding a Styrofoam cup, the other gripping Julie's hand to pleasure himself.

Julie withdrew her hand in horror. "Get out of here!" she shrieked.

Danny dropped his cup on the album cover lying on the floor as the smell of whiskey filled the room. Julie sat up and saw the liquid forming on Judy Collins' face. *Now both of us will be stained, probably permanently.*

Danny staggered out of the room, tripping over Chris' shoes as he headed for the door. He caught himself on the door jamb with his shoulder, let out a curse, and disappeared through the door.

Julie's heart ached. *God, aren't there any do-overs?* When word of this horror spun through school gossip, her life would be over, and Chris would never speak to her again. She ran to the bathroom, yanked off her sweatpants and sweatshirt, and climbed into the shower. Turning on the water, she stood sobbing and shaking until her tears and the hot water were used up. She'd been gone at least a half-hour, but when she got back to her room, Chris was sitting up in bed.

"Look, Julie." Chris pulled up her knees and wrapped her arms around her shins. "I will never tell anyone about this." Chris let out a long sigh. "You know what else we share? My grandpa is like your dad. He turns me into hazardous waste."

"Chris, you know you can't sleep here again. I don't know what my dad would do to you." Chris' head nodded slightly as she quietly got up and dressed, organized her suitcase, and waited for Julie to take her home.

Julie was coming unglued. She drove Chris home while her mind drifted over a mental wasteland. *Don't think ... don't think. Drive.* She had no idea where she was. Not even the railroad tracks in the distance looked familiar.

I'd better be careful when I cross those tracks. Every time the gas pedal in this stupid car is jammed to the floor, it sticks and then the car dies, and it takes a crap-load full of cranks to get it started again. I don't want to get stuck on the tracks ... stuck on the tracks ... stuck on the tracks ... I wonder if I'd die instantly ... if I'd feel any pain ... Julie looked around and didn't see any other cars at this rural crossing. She eased halfway across the tracks, stomped on the pedal, listened to the engine sputter and die, and sat back to wait. *The stars are beautiful tonight. There's the Big Dipper. It's getting cold in here. I'm waiting ... anticipating ... I wonder if Carly Simon will get over her stage fright and do a concert anytime soon? I could have been on stage if Miss Meyer hadn't called me a loser. I'll probably lose weight if I keep skipping meals. I didn't even eat supper. But Chris and I had popcorn and M&Ms tonight. That was a long time ago.* Julie's thoughts bounced around the inside of the car for another thirty minutes until the sound of a train whistle jolted her back into the horrifying present tense.

Oh, God, this isn't what I want after all! Julie started the car, stomped on the gas pedal, and finished crossing the tracks as the train – whistle shrieking – barreled down on the space she had vacated. Panting in rhythm with the train engine, Julie lowered her head on the steering wheel and sobbed. *What happened, God? Are You trying to tell me something? Is Mama T still praying for me?*

When the sun spread oranges and pinks across the eastern sky, Julie woke up, lifted her head, and winced at the crick in her neck. Even though there was so much wrong with her life, she wanted to hang on, at least for a little longer. For now, she was in a hurry to get to a bathroom. She turned the key, threw the shifter into drive, stomped on the gas pedal, and the car died.

Julie snuck through her front door and ran up to the bathroom, grateful that everyone was doing their usual sleeping in on a Sunday morning. *These steps are so creaky. How come they betrayed me when they should have warned me last night?* Returning to her room, she tore all the sheets off her bed, threw them in her hamper, and dug out an old sleeping bag from the closet. The floor, though not as comfortable as her bed, seemed somehow safer.

Early in the afternoon, Julie slogged into the kitchen in a bleary-eyed daze, grabbed a mug from the drain board and a coffeepot sitting on the burner, and poured a mud-like substance into her cup. She then poured the contents of both down the drain and plopped onto a chair at the table across from her mom. *How can she drink that poison?* Arlene stared at the newspaper folded crookedly on the table, with her cigarette perched on the edge of an ashtray next to the paper. *I think I made that ashtray in third grade. Was my life any simpler then? Well, there was Miss Meyer. I hope she quit teaching. The Marines can have her back.*

Julie drew her brain back and heard loud snoring coming from the living room.

"Mom." Julie swallowed, wishing she had kept her mug of bitterness. "I need to tell you something."

Arlene looked up, pointed her pencil, and glared at her daughter, who had violated the don't-interrupt-Mom-while-she's-doing-something rule. "Can't this wait? I'm trying to think of a four-letter word for hodgepodge."

You mean like my life? How about crap?"

"Please stay with me." Julie wasn't used to begging.

"Oh, all right." Arlene pushed aside the paper and tossed her pencil over to the counter. "Spill."

Julie was an embarrassed and humiliated victim, unable to look at her mom – so she stared at a glob of grape jam on the floor. *That's about how I feel right now.*

"Last night Dad came into my room—"

"So?"

Julie rubbed her eyes and looked up. "And he was naked and drunk and grabbed my hand while I was sleeping and did stuff to himself and then I woke up." Julie started crying and hoped she would find a point of entry into her mom's heart, or at least a crack in the thick wall around it. She was not prepared for a twisted loophole.

"Oh." Arlene pointed a thumb towards the living room. "Your dad was just in the wrong room." Arlene picked up the newspaper and got up to retrieve her pencil.

Julie wiped her nose with a balled-up napkin sitting on the table. Her face did a slow burn as she looked at her mom's back. "Doesn't he know the difference between *your* room and mine?" Her voice was hoarse from anger.

Shut up!" Arlene turned around. "You've caused enough trouble already!" She glided to the table, took one more drag from her cigarette, ground it into the bottom of the ashtray, and walked out of the room.

Danny took the same detour several more nights on the way to his room. Julie fought to stay awake and avoid him, but emotional fatigue won the battle and left her with the casualties of war – disgust, horror, helplessness. *I still have one way of escape: my mind. I will relive my time on the swim team. I wonder how long I could hold my breath under water. Are Suzanne and Abbey still on the team? With one more girl, we could have had an awesome relay.* Sometimes her dad wasn't satisfied until he thrust himself inside of her, which took longer. *I'm pretty sure I'm drowning. Is there anyone out there who can rescue me?*

Dried leaves crunched under Julie's Converse All Stars as she ran around her neighborhood. When she awoke early enough – and she never slept much after her dad's visits – she went on a run before school. *Even though I'm already a junior, maybe it's not too late to go out for track next spring. If I can't swim, I can tear the cover off the track.*

Julie always got back home with enough time to grab breakfast and a shower before school. She poured milk over a bowl of Cheerios, stared out the window and sighed. *If I keep stubbing my toes over the same sidewalk cracks, I'd be an idiot not to start running a different way. I've stubbed myself over his abuse long enough. There must be a different way to run.* Julie knew her mom wouldn't go to the mat for her, and she was tired of feeling out of control. She looked down and saw that she'd forgotten to get a spoon.

Julie pulled open the silverware drawer, stared at the knives, and saw her different way. Grabbing two handfuls of knives, she ran up and into her bedroom, dropped the knives and slammed the door shut. She picked up one knife at a time and jammed it into the gap around the door until the knives looked like stuck-out quills of an angry porcupine. *The next time he opens the door, the knives will crash to the floor, and I know I won't sleep through that! Danny-the-Drunk will meet his match in Julie-the-Determined.*

That night in her room, Julie listened to albums, snacked, and did her homework. She put her new security measure in place, lay down between fresh sheets, pulled her bedspread over her and fell asleep.

Long after midnight, Danny climbed the stairs. Whiskey sloshed out of his regulation Styrofoam cup and ran down his arm. Julie awoke to the sound of her door handle jiggling, with the knives trembling in protest but holding firm in their resolve. While Julie held her breath, Danny gargled vulgarities around in his mouth, rattled the doorknob a little while longer and then stumbled back downstairs. Julie's racing heart kept her awake the rest of the night.

The next night, Danny repeated his attempt at breaking and entering, and for several more nights after that. Julie's security system held, while Arlene ranted endlessly about their "god-awful garbage disposal," but never found her knives.

CHAPTER 12
"THERE'S NO PLACE LIKE HOME"

The utensil locking system transformed her room into a daytime refuge for Julie and Chris, kindred spirits who pretended to be normal teenagers by teasing each other about zits and fat, even though both had clear complexions, weighed one hundred eighteen pounds, and were the envy of half the girls at school. Julie saw Chris shrug off jealous, petty comments by those girls – but Julie became more and more convinced that she was fat. *I'm already running every day. Maybe I should also start exercising at home.* She had once seen a picture of her mom as a slim, twenty-something girl and knew she had inherited a skinny gene. She also watched her mom fatten and determined never to let that happen to her. She looked in the huge, oval mirror hanging on the wall above her dresser and announced to Chris on the phone one afternoon, "I am going to get skinny again!"

"But Julie, you're already a bean pole!"

"Uh-uh. I can still pinch a little around my stomach."

"Girl, you're nuts!"

Julie started her new exercise routine of ten push-ups, twenty sit-ups and twenty-five crunches. Three Dog Night was the workout album of choice. "Jeremiah was a bullfrog ..." She hummed along as she rose, fell, rose, fell, in perfect sit-up cadence. When the song ended, she got up and stretched before the next set of exercises. Glancing in the mirror to check her progress, she squinted her eyes to get a better look. *Is there light coming through the mirror?* Oblivious to the next song blaring from her speakers, Julie approached the mirror like a detective on a crime scene investigation. She carefully unhooked it from the wall and turned it around. Every cuss word she ever learned flew of out her mouth. Someone had drilled a small peephole through the wall and the mirror. Since her parents' room was right next door, it was easy to figure out who had done it. *He's horrible! He finds new and different ways to violate me. What did I ever do to deserve this?* She put her mouth right up to the hole. "How can you do this to me? What have I ever done to you?" She had learned to live with the loss of her childhood, her innocence, her dignity, and her virginity … and now she had lost her sanctuary. She put the mirror on her bed, opened the door, and slammed it behind her. The needle skipped on the album as her feet pulverized the stairs. *With any luck, they'll break.*

Arlene lounged on the burnt orange couch in front of the TV, surrounded by a stack of old newspapers, a half-eaten cheeseburger, and a Coke can balancing on the newspapers. Julie burst into the room, eyes flaming.

"This time Dad was *not* looking for the wrong room. He was in your room, and he drilled a peephole through your wall into the back of my mirror. He's probably watched me exercise and undress …" There were no adequate words to finish the sentence.

Arlene's eyes focused on "The Tonight Show." "Well, cover it up as best you can. You're nothing if not resourceful. I never worry about you."

WHAT? Is that it? She's not going to protect me from my alcoholic, perverted father? Is she really that pathetic? Or does she stay with him because he gives her money to buy what she wants? In the meantime, he gets her and me for his pleasure, and I get nothing but pain.

Julie dragged herself back upstairs. Where was the hole she was looking to drop into when the world was too much?

Duct tape, it turned out, had many uses. Julie drove to Ace Hardware early the next morning and bought a jumbo roll of gray. Back in her bedroom, she pulled and ripped, pulled and ripped, until she had an inch-thick layer of duct tape strips covering the hole behind the mirror. And just to be safe – *what a sadly ironic word* – Julie slapped a coat of black paint on top of the duct tape. The nightly exercise routine now had an added step: Check the painted duct tape and proceed with caution.

The junior girls were in the locker changing out of their gym suits back into street clothes. Julie felt a tap on her shoulder.

"Hey Julie."

"Hey yourself."

"I heard you're trying to lose weight."

"Who told you that?"

"Who cares? I think it's great. When you're skinny, you're in control of everything."

I'd settle for control of just one *thing.* "Yeah?"

"Yeah. Follow me into the bathroom after lunch, and I'll show you what to do."

"Whatever." *Colleen always gives me the creeps, and she looks way too skinny. Wonder what she's doing?*

The girls' bathroom closest to the lunchroom was crowded and smoky right after lunch. Julie and Colleen hung around until they were the last ones in there, with less than five minutes before they had to get to class. Julie watched in horror while Colleen leaned over the toilet, shoved her finger down her throat and made herself lose her lunch. Then she calmly flushed, walked to the sink, rinsed her mouth out with a little bottle of Listerine she pulled out of her purse, and wiped her mouth on a paper towel. "See? Do this every day and you'll never gain any weight!" Colleen looked in the mirror, fixed her hair, and left the bathroom.

Julie thought she had nothing to lose – *except pounds* – by trying this, whatever it was. At first, it was hard and gross; but after a week, she got used to it. Colleen encouraged her every day, and it felt good to have another friend besides Chris, even if the common bond was strange.

Another week passed. Julie heard Chris' voice in the bathroom as she was in a stall engaging in her lunch-tossing. "Colleen, is Julie in here?"

"Yeah, she's almost done." Colleen slipped something into her purse, walked around Chris and out the door. Chris heard a sickening noise.

"Julie! Are you okay? Should I get the nurse?"

Julie wiped her mouth. "No. I'll be out." Julie opened the stall door, and walked out, headed for the sink, and looking green.

"You don't look well. Are you sure you're not sick?"

127

"NO! I'm—"

"Pregnant? Because I will report your father—"

"No, I'm not. It's—"

"What?" Chris put her hand on Julie's arm, and suddenly there was no shut-off valve for Julie's tears.

"Jules, what's wrong?"

"Oh, Chris, I wanted to get skinnier … and Colleen said I'd have control—"

"You're doing this on purpose?"

"—but my throat hurts, and I'm getting these really, really bad headaches every day like I used to get years ago—"

"Why did you listen to that idiot Colleen?"

Julie walked to the sink, leaned over, turned on the cold water and tried to wash her face. "I can't do this anymore."

"For sure not. It's got to be dangerous. And unhealthy."

Julie dried her face with the bottom of her sweatshirt. "I'm pretty sure I can exercise harder."

"You're my best friend, but you're a knucklehead." Chris put her arm around Julie's shoulder and walked her out the door. "Please promise me that after my family and I move to New York, you won't keep hanging around her."

"I'll do better than that. I'll quit before you move."

"Excellent." Chris exhaled deeply.

Up, down, up, down. *I can't believe I'm finishing my junior year in high school.* Up, down, up, down. *I'm glad Chris is still my friend. I can't imagine my life without her.* Up, down, up, down. *Up. Catch a breath. Wait for the song to end. Stand and stretch. Get ready for the next set of exercises.* Julie always checked herself in the mirror between sets. And there it was: a steady beam of light shining through her mirror. *Can this be happening again?* Julie yanked the mirror off the wall: the duct tape had been torn off and the hole re-drilled. Rage gave Julie the strength to shove her heavy dresser across the room and up against the outside wall. *I'll rehang the mirror tomorrow. I'm not putting anything against that wall again.* The leftover roll of duct tape hung on a nail in Julie's closet, waiting to be pressed into duty. Julie pulled and ripped strips of tape until the covering over the hole looked like a cancerous growth – *not unlike what's in Dad's brain.* Julie jumped on her bed, took down the framed picture of her and Chris at a football game, and hung it where the mirror had been.

Her room was another place of betrayal in Julie's life. She vowed never to exercise or change clothes in there again.

Arlene walked upstairs and into Julie's room, handing her a laundry basket full of clean, wrinkled clothes. "Something's different in here. Did you move your furniture?"

"Mom, you haven't listened to anything I've told you. Dad molested me when Chris spent the night last year. He drilled a hole through your bedroom wall and made a peephole into my room. I covered up the hole months ago, and I found out he did it again!"

Arlene dropped the basket, put her hands over her eyes, and made a pitiful, sobbing noise. "How can you do this to me?"

Julie picked up the basket and clenched her teeth. "How can I do *what* to you? I've been telling you this over and over. I showed you the peephole in the wall. I will not put up with this anymore. Get rid of him."

A snake curled up on a rock was preferable to finding it in a boot, if the person knew where the rock was. The night after Julie's shoot-out with her mom, Danny did not come home. He did not show up the next morning. *Did Mom finally kick him out? Did Dad get sick of Mom and decide to leave? How far away is he?*

A quivering peace rested cautiously on the house, until Danny showed up a week later, sober, mean, and threatening to kill Arlene. Julie saw her dad as way more dangerous sober than drunk when he had the advantage of hand-eye coordination and the motive of revenge. After wreaking his special brand of destruction, he vanished, only to reappear the next week and threaten to "kill all you worthless scum and burn the house down." He settled for beating the furniture senseless, grabbing plates of spaghetti and meatballs from the table, and hurling them against the wall. *I wish I could remember what kind of pasta Oscar threw against the wall. Boy, was Felix mad at him!*

Arlene finally drew a line in the sand and got a restraining order against Danny. When he showed up a third time, Julie grabbed her running shoes and looked forward to seeing Mrs. Moore again. She was aghast when her mom tipped the scale, calmly picked up the phone and dialed nine-one-one. *What kept Dad from yanking the phone off the wall?* Officer Seaver, part of the family by now, appeared almost immediately. Julie thought he did a poor job of covering his own shock at entering the house. After Danny was handcuffed and hauled away, Arlene mumbled, "Good riddance to a bad egg," and disappeared into her room.

Danny stewed in jail for five days.

Mom, you cannot stay on this merry-go-round. I don't think you know how to love me because you've been so beaten down. If you leave your husband in jail for a while, you and Dan and I could start over somewhere. Since you lost the café, this would be a chance for you to get a job that would be good for you. That time before Dad found us was good. You seemed relaxed and almost nice. Sometimes.

Arlene bailed Danny out. He thanked her by violating the Order of Protection so often that Julie considered asking someone to commission the county jail with a special cell in his honor.

CHAPTER 13
STAND OFF

"**W**e're blowing this joint. Time to haul." Arlene issued a take-no-prisoners edict.

"But Mom, I'm ready to start my senior year! We can't move now."

"Yes, we can, and I don't want any more of your lip. You don't know how tough my life's been, and you haven't helped. Besides, we're only moving to Coldspring. You can still see your friends."

What kind of bug-infested place will we live in next? I wish I could live on my own. Before Julie and her mom and brother packed their stuff into Grandpa and Grandma's station wagon, Julie applied for a job at Lakehaven Nursing Home. A buck-fifty an hour would be the beginning of her mutiny against poverty. She would work evenings and every other weekend in the kitchen with bonus pay deposited in her self-esteem bank. When Julie's mom announced, during their first of many macaroni and cheese dinners in their new apartment, "I got a part-time job as a caregiver for some old people in a nursing home," Julie almost choked. *I wonder what it would take for my mom to be a caregiver for me. At least the café is history.*

Rent and groceries were at either end of an income rope that never tied in the middle of Arlene's salary. Julie did the only resourceful thing: called out the grandparent cavalry. Richard and Rosalynn made the thirty-mile round trip from Pineville to Coldspring every week in a big station wagon loaded with baskets of garden tomatoes, corn and green beans, quarts of freshly picked cherries and raspberries, butcher-paper wrapped packages of venison from the previous season's deer hunt, a hot casserole in a covered Pyrex dish, and a pan of lemon bars or brownies. Julie feared more visits to the power company in the future unless Mom got another part-time job or Julie dropped out of school – two scenarios high up on the list of least likely.

The August night was as steamy as a sauna. Julie awoke only mildly surprised that her mom was shaking her shoulder, saying, "We're outta here. A guy at work told me there's cheap, furnished apartments in Fairview." The birds warmed up their singing voices at three forty-five as Julie packed stuff into their car. *I'm always glad when we can move during warm weather and don't have to go far.*

A tenant unencumbered with cleanliness and good taste had vacated the apartment just hours ahead of the arrival of Arlene and her kids. The gold- and green- and orange-striped kitchen wallpaper was splattered with grease and tomato sauce. The avocado stove and refrigerator were obvious losers in a food fight. The rectangular, red, Formica-topped metal table cowered under stacks of yellowed newspapers and overflowing ashtrays. The black linoleum floor was a sticky labyrinth of hardened food and crushed bugs. The rest of the scale-model-size apartment had given its all in hand-to-hand combat.

The late-morning sun raised the internal temperature of the apartment to life-threatening status. Arlene sought relief lying on a flowered sofa in front of a squealing window fan. Julie attacked the kitchen with buckets of Spic-n-Span and ammonia, in preparation for the making of the inaugural Spam casserole.

The Saturday evening shift at Lakehaven had been tiring but satisfying. Julie parked her mom's car in front of their apartment, unlocked the front door, slipped quietly into the kitchen, and almost walked into the back of her mom's chair. She hung her purse on a wall hook and stood behind her mom.

"What do you have there?" All the usual tools – coffee, cigarette, and newspaper – were missing. Arlene picked up the single sheet of paper from the table and handed it to Julie. "What's this?"

"Divorce paper." Arlene sighed. "Am I doing the right thing?"

Julie dropped the paper and covered her epic surprise by opening the cupboard and twirling the handles of several mugs, making a show of trying to choose the right one, finally settling on an enormous dark navy one with "I don't suffer from insanity – I enjoy every minute of it" stamped around it. She pulled the pot out of the Mr. Coffee and poured a thick substance into her mug. *One of these days I am going to show her how to make drinkable coffee.*

"How will we make it without your dad?"

Julie took a sip, grimaced, and sat down. "Mom, I've waited for years for you to do this. You're smart and you know how to get along. One thing you learned from living with Dad was how to survive. You've got lots of time to figure out what you want to do with your life without having a price on your head."

Arlene put her hand over Julie's and awkwardly patted it. Pushing her chair back, she said, "Well, I'll think about it. Those are some good words." Arlene's slippers slapped against the linoleum as she left the room.

The room spun. Her mom had stopped just short of thanking her for her encouragement. *I have no idea what my mom did before she met Dad. Maybe I'll ask her about it someday.* Julie stared at a cobweb near the ceiling and got up to find the broken broom.

Staff meetings at Lakehaven were an Olympic event. Words lobbed back and forth across the room between aides, nurses, and support people. *I spent years training for this sport in my family, and no one's going to intimidate me.* But the outcome was different than anything Julie expected. People were agreeable in their disagreements, encouraging of each other, respectful of opinions, and energized about their responsibilities. *I have some things to learn. This is fun, and everyone is leaving with intact egos.*

A short, plump girl with straight, dark-blonde hair approached Julie after the next staff meeting.

"Hi. Julie, isn't it? I'm Gloria Gustafson."

She is not the most popular girl at school. "Hey, Gloria. I think we might be in first hour together. You have Mr. Johnson, right?"

"Yeah, I do. I like him, but math will never be cool!" Gloria giggled.

"Too true. I just want to graduate."

The girls reached for the instant hot chocolate packets. "Hey, Julie, how would you like to go to a YFC meeting with me next Friday night, if you're not doing anything?" Gloria was so confident, so pleasant, and so unlike any assumptions Julie had made about her.

"What's YFC?" Julie searched around for the pot of hot water, trying not to embarrass herself by pouring coffee over her powered hot chocolate mix.

"It's Youth For Christ, a club for teens. We meet in the town hall to sing, pray, and listen to a speaker talk about stuff we're all curious about – like dating, drugs, things like that – and what the Bible says. It's really fun, and a big encouragement for us."

"Does anyone else from our school go?" Julie was being reeled in.

"There's a guy from our math class, and a bunch of others from our school, plus some from other schools. I could swing by your house on Friday; we could drive together, and some of us go out afterwards."

"I'm in."

Julie and Gloria walked into the town hall at ten to seven.

"Hey, Glo! We saved seats for you. Who's your friend?"

"Julie."

"Hi, Julie, I'm Justine. Everyone calls me Just. Like just too cute, just too perky … I've heard them all. But I don't mind." Justine's almost-black eyes looked like marbles. "Come and sit with me; we're going to start soon." Julie and Glo joined Just on an orange-striped, upholstered sofa. The many-colored armchairs and love seats and beanbags scattered around the room in a clashing of shapes and styles were as offensive as anything Julie had experienced in her accumulated houses and trailers and apartments; yet they looked inviting and comfortable.

Another girl came up to them and interrupted Julie's thoughts. "Hey, Just-fine." She looked at Julie. "I'm Jamie Anders. Aren't you in World Lit with me?"

"Guilty as charged. I'm Julie."

Just popped up out of her seat, said "Bye!" and ran off.

"There goes Just-in-time!"

Julie laughed.

"Didn't you date Teddy Tannenbaum?"

"Guiltier than ever."

"I was afraid to talk to you back then."

"Why?"

"You seemed so together—"

"I was messed up." Julie sighed.

"What happened?"

Julie was thoughtful. "I think he was kicking the tires to check out the car, and then decided against it – against *me*."

Jamie was quiet.

"I'm sure you didn't come here to listen to this."

"But I'm glad you shared. Have you been keeping this inside?"

"Pretty much. No one wants to attend my pity party. My best friend Chris moved to New York last year, and I haven't found anyone to talk to since then."

"I'm not going anywhere. I know I'm not Chris, but I'd be glad to listen to you anytime." Jamie smiled and touched Julie's shoulder.

"Thanks. Thanks a lot. I'll catch you at school."

The room quieted down when a few guys near the front started strumming guitars. Song after song washed over everyone in ripples of melody and harmony. Julie heard a song about a spark and getting a

137

fire going and was back with her dad building a bonfire on Christmas day. *I don't want to remember anything good about him.* When the last chord hung in the air, whispered notes faded into intense silence.

A twenty-something looking guy carrying a duct-taped book strolled to the front of the room and hopped up on a wooden bar stool. He wore Nike running shoes, patched jeans, and a Grateful Dead t-shirt. When he turned his head to shout something to a guy on the far side of the room, Julie noticed a wavy ponytail hanging under his John Deere cap.

"Hi. There's still couch space and plenty of floor space for those of you who are looking for a spot. I'm Bret."

Whistles and greetings filled the room.

"Great singing. And let's thank the guitar players."

Everyone clapped, some kids whistled again, and Bret waited patiently for the room to regain its equilibrium.

"Here we are again. I usually talk about dating and sex and peer pressure. Is there anything else?"

Julie joined the easy laughter.

"Tonight, we're going to talk about God as our heavenly Father. I know that some of you come from divorced homes and your dads live far away. You hardly ever see them, and you really miss them. Or maybe you're okay with them being gone because they drink too much, too often, and it makes you uncomfortable … or sad … or mad … or all three.

"I know some of you have good and kind fathers. I met some of them when they helped carry in this cast-off furniture. They're the dads who order your homes – and sometimes you resent that, but mostly you feel safe. Your friends give you a hard time because your dads are too strict, and then they look for your dads when things start falling apart in their homes. They want someone to care about them, so they borrow your dads for a while."

Bret looked around the room and made eye contact with some, those unafraid to look back. "Before the night is over, you will be asked to enter into the dad world of someone else whose experience might be very different than yours – maybe much better, maybe far worse."

The students had a quiet space to sift through his words. Some whispered to their friends; others crossed their arms and wore looks of challenge or disdain.

"The toughest thing for me to talk about – and the hardest for some of you to hear – is aimed at those of you whose parents are still married, but whose dads beat you or your mom or your brothers or sisters … or do stuff to your siblings that you wouldn't dare bring into the light of day."

Julie's face flushed. *Did Glo tell this guy I'd be here tonight? Or is this a coincidence?*

Some of the students squirmed, stared down at their shoes, reached for a friend's hand, or clasped their own tightly together. The only sound in the room was the rhythmic humming of the Coke machine at the back.

Bret continued. "How many of you are waiting for the Jaws of Life to snatch you out of your homes?"

Hands shot up and burst the tension bubble.

"Your Father with a capital F knows who you are."

Hands lowered. Bret's voice was authoritative

and soothing. "The Bible uses many words for God: Protector. Provider. Creator. Lover. Grace-Giver. Satisfier. Healer. Nourisher. Restorer. Jesus even called him Abba, which means Daddy."

When Bret flipped open his duct-taped book, Julie saw that it was a Bible. "Psalm sixty-eight, verse five, says God will be a father to the fatherless. Whether you have a loving father or an abusive father – or anyone in-between – you can leave here tonight knowing that your Heavenly Father, your daddy, loves you with a forever-love. It is a love that doesn't depend on your grades, your looks, or your accomplishments. He loved you enough to send His son to die for you, and He loves you enough to be your enough every day."

John three sixteen: "For God so loved the world, that He gave his only begotten Son, that whosoever believeth in Him should not perish, but have eternal life." I got my first check for memorizing that verse.

A tapping foot echoed loudly, while a girl's voice rose timidly from the back of the room. "Bret? Isn't one of the Ten Commandments to honor your father and mother? How do I honor a father who's a ... creep?" A slow burn crept into her face.

Bret eased slowly off the stool. *He looks like he's stepping into a minefield.* He put his Bible down on the stool, took off his cap, and twirled it around his fingertip before tossing it on the floor. Everyone watched and listened intently.

"I could easily concede defeat right now. I attended YFC meetings in high school, and then moved on to Concordia Bible College and Trinity Seminary. I've studied the Bible and spent a lot of time wrestling with God over things that make no sense to me. Up 'til now, I thought the hardest battles were behind me."

Bret pointed to his cap. "Let me try to explain what I think God has shown me. We all want connections to our dads, and that cap shows it. Bret Johnson senior is a regional distributor of John Deere equipment. When I wear his only high school graduation gift to me, I am reminded that God expects me to honor him. Someday, I hope he'll see what I do as important and valuable.

"When I take off my cap at the end of the day, I remember that God is the Father who matters most. Even if my dad never says he loves me or is proud of me, I know that God loves me more than I deserve."

Bret noticed some of the guys removing their baseball caps and tossing them on the floor.

"The question was about the commandment to honor your parents. I believe that when you do that, you're obeying God and giving honor to Him. Honoring your parents doesn't have anything to do with whether they've earned it. It's showing what I call UR – Undeserved Respect. You should give it to your dads and moms, your teachers, and even your bosses.

"And yeah, you might feel like that makes you a doormat. UR makes it easy for people to stomp on you and wipe stuff on you. But, as Christian young people, you can choose a different image. You can be a bridge – still walked on, but more importantly, walked *across* by people who need to find God on the other side.

"I've done this with my father many times. He calls me every Sunday afternoon and asks me when I'm going to get a *real* job. 'When I was your age,' he says, 'I was already married, had three kids, and worked two jobs. I had a lot of responsibility – something you seem to know nothing about.' If I try to explain myself to him, it becomes a game of Battleship. Hit and a miss. Hit and a miss. Ultimately, hit and sunk. Even if I make a convincing argument – like how I think I'm making a difference in some of your lives – he disengages and moves on to some other game. I don't want to win an argument or a game. I want his encouragement. I want him to believe in me.

"After he hangs up, I stomp around my apartment, yelling my anger and hurt out to God. And then I ask Him to help me exchange the picture in my mind from being a doormat to a bridge – a bridge that will take my dad to God. He needs God's love and forgiveness like we all do every day."

Bret paused, picked up his cap and started twirling it.

"Lately, I've learned that there's a hidden blessing in my relationship with my dad. God loves me, believes in me, and is always in my corner. If I had the kind of father I've always wanted, maybe I would never have found a Heavenly Father."

Bret put his cap on. One of the guitar players cleared his throat.

"Bret, what about someone who never knew their dad? My mom and dad were both sixteen when my mom found out she was pregnant, and her boyfriend left her without a forwarding address. How do I honor him?"

"I'm sorry that happened to you. But you can still show UR – Undeserved Respect – to your father by honoring him in your mind and in the words you use to tell your story to someone else. He may have fled the scene of the crime because he was scared. Maybe he didn't think much about it. But wherever he is today, he needs the bridge of Jesus to lead him to our heavenly Father. Remember: Even if our earthly fathers abandon us, God never does. Never will.

"We're going to try something for about fifteen minutes. I want you to find a partner – guys, find a good buddy; gals, find another girl. When you've found your partner, get together in a quiet place. No pressure here – if you're comfortable, share with each other about your experience with your dad. It doesn't need to be much, just enough for you to pray for each other. I'd like you to promise to pray for your partner every day this coming week. Let's hold everything spoken here in confidence. I will let you know when the time is almost up. If you are one of those people blessed with an amazing dad, freely and happily share that. This time will be different for each of you. God knows who your partner needs to be, and so we'll trust Him to put the right people together."

Oh God! What would my life have been like with a different father? I can't ever forgive him, and You can't ask me to. He probably doesn't think he did anything wrong. If You are my real father, why didn't You protect me from my dad? Does that make You any better of a father than he is? I want to believe Bret when he says You care about me.

Julie leaned forward with blurred eyes. Glo and Jamie sat down on either side of her, each putting a gentle hand on her back. Julie wept as Jamie whispered, "I'm sorry he abandoned you," in her ear. *Is she talking about Teddy? All I can think about is my dad. I wish I could tell him what he did to me.* The new friends cried with Julie, and then she thought maybe God was also sad about her father. Maybe He really did love her like Bret said He would.

Bret's shrill whistle quieted the room. "You are welcome to stay after we're finished. I want everyone to hold the hand of the person closest to you, and let's form a big circle, or ellipse, or oval, or some sort of geometric shape." Everyone laughed and grabbed a hand while someone near Bret started singing acapella. It was the most beautiful three-part harmony; Julie caught on to the melody and words quickly. She closed her eyes and joined the rest: "Father, I adore You; lay my life before You; how I love You."

When the singing stopped, Bret spoke quietly. "Abba, Daddy, some of us can't think about our dads without feeling blame or shame. I used to blame You for the father I thought You had cursed me with … but I'm trying to see the blessing in him, because that's how I found You – the best Father – the One who has never, ever left me. Please be the father every one of these teens needs. In Jesus' Name, Amen."

It was ten to eleven before Julie, Glo, Just, and Jamie piled into Glo's car. Julie felt refreshed and unburdened as they headed to Pizza Hut. *God, I know I didn't deserve any of this tonight, but thank You for it.* Julie got home at one-thirty and pulled out a box from her closet. On the bottom was her Bible from Mrs. Ryczek. *Did she suspect something wasn't right in my family? Thank You for putting her in my life. Bless her!* Julie got comfortable on her bed and paged through her Bible, looking at all the verses underlined in red pencil. Sunlight dimmed the light from the stars before she fell asleep.

The ink was still wet on the divorce papers when Danny showed up at the new apartment. He was sober and ready to defend his title. Boots trampled the defenseless ground as he exploded through the front door. Had there been a fasten seat belt sign, it would have lit up and given fair warning of expected turbulence.

Julie was in her room listening to "Jesus Christ Superstar." As she turned up the volume, it occurred to her that the soundtrack of her dad's life was really one song he played forever – a predictable, methodical melody about an angry man toying with lunacy.

Julie's violence radar detected specific forms of destruction even from her bedroom. Lamps were overturned. Furniture was tipped. Breaking glass was the exclamation point for every cuss word bouncing around the living room. The contents of the kitchen cupboards were the next targets. When Julie's curiosity drew her out of her room, she found a totaled apartment. A pile of plastic plates formed a fraternity of the safe-for-now in a corner of the kitchen. Every other flat surface was buried under the shattered remains of broken dreams.

Arlene sat on the brown-carpeted floor in a corner of the living room. *If you're hoping for invisibility, forget it. It never worked for me.* Julie's brother ran to the hall closet, snatched his denim jacket, went to the front door, and grabbed the brass doorknob so hard it came off in his hand. He turned around and hurled it at his dad, catching him in the abdomen. Dan swore, stuck his fingers into the doorknob hole and managed to yank the door open. He was out the door while Danny was still doubled over in pain. Julie slipped into auto pilot mode, raced to the kitchen, and pulled a serrated bread knife out of the kitchen drawer. She ran five steps back into the living room in time to see her father stagger over to her mother and cock his arm back. Julie reached out, caught his arm, and planted herself between her parents. Trapped in a strange moment of time, she faced her dad. *I am about to become either a murderer or a victim.*

"If you touch her, I will kill you." Her blood was ice cold.

Danny's eyes had the wild look of a trapped animal. His clenched fist, still in Julie's grip, burned from the drip of her salty sweat. "I could break your neck," he choked.

"Take your best shot." Julie barely breathed.

Father and daughter looked at each other. Julie heard her mom whimpering as though she were underwater, all senses focused only on her dad. Danny looked down at his wife, shoved Julie aside and walked to the front door. Turning around, he leaned against the door frame and pointed to Arlene. "You might want to tell her someday soon." He dropped his arm, turned around and walked out, leaving the door open behind him.

Julie slumped to the floor, overcome with relief but still angry. *I didn't honor my father, but I also could not harm him. I cannot stop hoping that someday he will love me as his daughter. And for crying out loud, what is my mom supposed to tell me?*

CHAPTER 14
REVELATION

Balancing home and school was like a lumberjack on a log roll. Julie's fear of losing her footing competed with her urge to plunge head-first into water that would swallow her, pain and all. It was a wobbly dance of survival and despair.

After Miss Meyer, Mr. O'Keefe, the nosebleeds, and headaches, school settled into an uncomplicated routine. Julie's teachers were practical people interested in her academic progress. A few were heavy-handed and self-absorbed, but they were lightweights, and no match for some of the tyrants who had buried Julie's innocence long before her childhood ended.

Mr. Schroeder, the band teacher, was Julie's north star. Called Sir by students and teachers alike during his twenty-plus years of teaching – although no one knew where the nickname came from – he was a bright light in everyone's sky. Sir joked with his band students with a sideways brand of humor, but also demanded hard work and expected great music. There had only been a few honorable and respectful men in Julie's life, and none as genuine as Sir. The best part was having band seventh period; it usually put her in a good and confident mood for the evening.

The only downside of band was Joey Green. Julie hoped he and his family would move; or at least, that he would stop using his drumsticks to beat on the back of her head. When he gave a play-by-play account of his previous night's female conquests, Julie ignored him, and was greatly consoled by the evident and unusual disdain Sir seemed to have for him.

On a glorious Friday afternoon, the band flexed its muscles, practicing for the halftime show at the home football game later that night. The windows in the room were open. Brasses and reeds blasted their notes to an audience of squirrels, passing cars, and early-dismissal seniors heading out to jobs.

Sir gave last-minute instructions about the order of songs – the perfect time, in Joey's twisted thinking, to lean over his snare and tap Julie's ear with a stick.

"Hey Sandford. I got a scoop."

Julie turned and glared. "You idiot, I don't want to hear about your stupid date last night. Any girl who would go out with you must have Loser tattooed on her forehead."

Joey did a rim shot. "If you're the last one to hear about this, there will be no joy in Mudville."

Julie figured there was no way to shut Joey up until she relented. "Okay but make it quick. I really want to hear what Sir is saying."

"Are you sure you're ready for this?"

"Joey!" Julie turned back around and looked straight ahead.

"I'll tell you about it after the bell rings."

Oh great – now someone I don't even care about is dismissing me. Is there no end to these guys in my life?

The bell signaled the end of Sir's pep talk, the end of the school day, the end of the week, and hopefully the end of Joey's attempts to get Julie's attention.

Julie leaned over and opened her baritone case as Joey flipped his chair around, straddled the seat, rested his sticks on a slightly bent music stand and tickled her back with his fingers.

Straightening, Julie turned and glared. "This isn't a social call. State your business and leave." She secretly wished she wouldn't take every opportunity to carp at Joey, but theirs was an oil-and-water relationship, and she still didn't have tools for dealing with guys specializing in humiliation. "I mean, okay, what did you want to tell me?" *I could at least give this guy a chance to act human.*

Joey pressed his advantage. "Sandford, maybe I should wait 'til Monday to tell you."

"Suit yourself." Julie bent back down to finish packing her bari.

Joey gently touched Julie's shoulders and pulled her upright. The hard, cynical lines around his mouth softened. His eyes pierced a deep place in Julie. She felt strangely drawn to him. "Julie, I was in our kitchen last night, really late. I'm sure my parents thought I had gone to bed much earlier. I was up in my room studying for our AP English test, and I went down to get some ice cream. It was Rocky Road, unbelievable stuff! Anyway, I overheard my parents talking in the living room. I figured they were talking like mushy parents, until I heard Mom say, 'I wonder if he knows that Julie Sandford is related to him? Her mother, Arlene, married my cousin Eugene. That makes Joey and Julie some sort of first cousins once removed, or something like that. I never quite understand how the family tree grows.' Dad answered, 'We should probably tell him tomorrow.' Well, that's today, and Dad left for work before I got up, so I guess they'll tell me tonight."

Joey picked up the drumsticks and did another

rim shot on the music stand.

"I really thought you were trying to be a nice guy, but I guess everything's a big joke to you. Why do I bother listening to you?" Julie jumped up, knocking over her music stand, and completely ignoring her open instrument case at her feet. She had a sudden urge to flee from this ridiculous, far-fetched, but strangely disturbing conversation.

Joey flipped his drumsticks, raised the stand, and laid them on the edge. "Julie, we've done lots of fighting. It doesn't take much for me to set you off. I could do that without making up something like this. I don't like it any more than you do, so why would I tell you if it wasn't true?" Joey was talking to Julie's retreating back.

"See you then." Joey picked up his sticks, set them back near his drum, and walked quietly out of the band room.

Julie could not concentrate on her normal after-school routine. Her backpack was forgotten in her locker. She didn't know how she got home, only that she was walking towards her back door. *God, if You are out there, please help me.*

Julie paced around the parking lot in front of her apartment building waiting for Mom to come home from work. She had no idea what she would say to her mom. *Hey, Mom, I heard something crazy in school today. Is there something you want to tell me? And who the heck is Eugene?*

The late afternoon breeze cooled Julie's forehead and played a soothing melody through the trees. Julie was finally ready to go inside.

Grabbing a Coke from the refrigerator, Julie wandered into the living room and turned on the TV. Phil Donahue was interviewing some guy who had had a sex change operation. Julie flipped the channel to an after-school special, something about a mom learning to love her son who was gay. *Isn't there anything normal on TV? But why should there be – there's not much normal in my life.*

Arlene came through the door, muttering about her tired feet, her lousy job, and her empty checkbook, and found Julie lightly dozing on the couch.

"So, are we having T-bone steaks for supper? With all the fixin's?" This was Arlene's standard after-work greeting.

Julie roused and rubbed her stiff neck. When her brain defogged and she remembered her talk in the band room, she suddenly felt chilled.

"Mom, can I tell you something I heard today?" Julie sounded far more tentative than she felt.

"Don't tell me coloreds are moving next door to us!" Arlene looked dismayed.

Julie sighed. "Mom, can we please not beat that dead horse? They're called blacks, and no, there aren't any moving next to us that I know about."

"Thank God!" Arlene dropped onto the couch and propped her feet up on the coffee table.

Julie made her approach on a different runway. "Do you remember when Dad used to beg you to tell me something?"

Arlene rubbed her eyes. "Your dad used to say lots of fool things. I never listened to most of it, and you shouldn't either."

"Right before Dad left us for the last time – *I*

hope – he looked at you and said, 'Don't you think you should tell her soon?' What was he talking about?"

Arlene got up slowly, rolled down her nylons, pulled them off, tossed them behind the couch, and crossed a leg under her as she sat back down. "I need a cigarette."

Julie jumped up, rifled through her mom's purse, handed her a flip-top box of unfiltered Lucky Strikes and an orange disposable lighter, and sat cross-legged on the floor.

Arlene lit her cigarette, took a deep drag, tilted her head back, and released a trail of pungent smoke. "Well," Arlene said. "Well."

I am not letting her off the hook. I'll sit here all night if that's what it takes, until she tells me whatever it is I should have heard a long time ago.

"I guess you're old enough to hear this. Mind, I'm not ashamed of any of it. I've done my best by you and your brother. You have no idea what I've been through."

"Okay." Julie waited.

"You know I went to high school in Coldspring. A guy named Eugene and I were high school sweethearts. We started dating our freshman year all the way through high school and kept dating for four more years after graduation. We were the Eugene-and-Arlene duo. It sounded so ridiculous and hokey, and everyone figured we would get married and go on 'The Dating Game' on TV together!" Arlene stared at the gathering shadows on the far wall. "I just wanted to live with him for a while after graduation, but that would have been very unacceptable, especially for this hick town. I loved him, but I felt trapped."

152

Arlene locked and reloaded. "Anyway, we set our wedding date. The only thing I remember clearly from that day was standing next to your Grandpa Richard in the lobby right before we walked in the sanctuary. The 'Wedding March' was playing. I took my father's arm, leaned over, and whispered, 'I don't know, Dad. This doesn't feel right.' 'Don't do it,' my father said. 'We can stop this right now.' But we walked down the aisle – kinda felt like I was walking the plank."

"And?"

"And I figured since I did the right thing and married Eugene, instead of just living with him, that somehow God would reward us with the perfect life together. Eugene promised me a big house, a white picket fence, the whole enchilada. The only catch was we would have to move to Washington state to chase that dream.

"For the fifties, I was a very independent woman. I owned my own car right out of high school. I had a full-time job. I knew what I wanted out of life. If Eugene wanted to move us out to Washington, fine by me, if he could make good on his promises. Besides, I wasn't about to be embarrassed by returning all our gifts and admit that maybe I had made a mistake. Our marriage was going to work."

Arlene ground out her cigarette in a metal, beanbag ashtray. "I guess I wasn't completely honest with Eugene, but he wasn't honest with me, either. When we got out to Bremerton, I found out that there wasn't a house, no job for Eugene ... I have no idea why he even wanted to move out there. Maybe it was for adventure. We had both felt trapped in Coldspring. I was too angry and disappointed to ever ask him why.

"Anyways, when you were born, there was finally some good that came out of living there. I hadn't really thought about being a mother, but that was another one of those expected things for the fifties."

Gee, Mom, you really know how to turn a daughter's head.

Arlene made a lane change without signaling. "Eugene left me and you when you were three months old and took up with a fourteen-year-old chick named Barbie. A while later, I heard they got married. I guess he got what he wanted, and so did I. I'm going to change into some comfortable clothes. Start some supper, will you?" Arlene retrieved her nylons and left for her room, trailing them behind her.

Julie stayed on the floor, eyes blurred, thoughts whirling in a blender. *Why didn't I hear this a long time ago? I have a dad somewhere out there named Eugene. Danny Sandford isn't my real dad! At least the man who did that horrible stuff to me doesn't belong to me. I'm never going to forgive him for what he did. Maybe someday I will find my real dad, and tell him what my life was like, and he can track down Danny, and ... and ...*

Julie's mind wandered too far to return that night. She still had to go to the football field and play in the pep band, pretending that her Friday night was as normal as everyone else's; but she had so much to think about. Julie remembered the YFC meeting, and Bret's teaching about earthly fathers and the Heavenly Father. *Thank You, God, that Danny isn't my earthly father.*

CHAPTER 15
ERIK

Erik Martin's high school yearbook inscription under his picture read: "There was never a saint with red hair." Green eyed, freckled, cocky Erik played varsity football and attacked life with the same full-tilt, reckless abandon. He was six foot two, muscular and handsome. As though that weren't enough to seal his popularity, he swore, smoked, drank, and flirted with all the girls and with most of the boundaries of legal behavior.

Erik had graduated from Coldspring four years ahead of his sister Lori. He lived in Detroit, worked construction, and came home in the fall for high school football games.

"Hey, Erik!" Lori – slightly overweight and pleasantly quirky – motioned Erik to her seat on the top row of the home team bleachers. "I want you to meet someone."

Erik walked through a gauntlet of high-fives and arm pumps, his legendary football prowess making him a Friday night attraction.

"Hey yourself, little sis. Who's your pal?"

"This is Julie, my friend, and hopefully, partner in crime."

Julie didn't miss the once-over glance from Erik or the hunger in his eyes. She was already in way over her head.

"Hi, Erik." It would have been foolish to pretend she didn't know who Erik was, or *what* he was. Her sixth sense from years of living with her parents told her that Erik lived on the wild side. *He's a guy who picks his kicks and doesn't care about the kickbacks.*

"Maybe I should join you. It looks like you're coming apart." Erik had a keen grasp on old jokes, oddly endearing to Julie. Squeezing between his sister and her friend, Erik wore his letter jacket like the mantle of a conquering hero. For the rest of the game, Julie barely paid attention to touchdowns and extra points, aware instead of Erik's shoulder brushing up against hers, tingling sensations doing a tap-dance up and down her arm. When Erik leaned in close to explain the finer points of football to Julie, his breath smelling of beer and Fritos, Julie knew she was in trouble. *This guy is a definite bad boy. If I were smart, I would run while I still can.* But here was a guy – strong, older, probably a hard worker – paying attention to her, acting like it mattered to him that Julie understood a game that represented all that was good for him. She was being invited into a guy's life for all the right reasons. When the game ended, Erik gave Julie a chivalrous kiss on the cheek, planted another tender kiss on top of Lori's head, and wove through the bleachers, cradling an imaginary football, pretending to duck his opponents, and doing the touchdown dance as he hopped down the final step to the track. Erik waved a benediction over the crowd. "Smoke 'em if you got 'em!" he yelled.

"Come back and visit us! Don't be a stranger – you're already strange enough as it is!" This was Lori's signature send-off to Erik. "And tell George to get off work next Friday night, so he can come back up with you!" Erik turned around and started running backwards as he waved and shouted, "Later, Laurence!" Julie knew she was already swimming in deep water. *Hopefully it's not shark-infested.*

Erik, Lori's boyfriend George, and two other guys shared an apartment in Detroit. Erik, the oldest of the four, decided it was past time to christen their new apartment with the party-to-end-all-parties. The three guys' girlfriends lived in Coldspring. Erik hoped Julie was willing to drive down with them and get to know him better. As soon as Erik returned from his trip to Coldspring, he told George about Lori's friend Julie. He was unusually open about his feelings, not trying to hide being smitten with her.

"Georgie-Boy, Julie Sandford is so different than any chick I've met here! The ones my age are too into their careers to get involved with a lowly construction worker. The younger ones are airheads, even though it's nice to be the object of their adoration for a while." Erik slouched back on the sofa, rearranging the cushions to cover the broken hide-a-bed mattress springs. "Julie is sweet, and a girl who's a good thinker. She has deep brown eyes ... I could lose myself in those eyes. Her hair is thick. She's got these bright, red lips ... it was all I could do to keep from kissing her and running my fingers through her amazing hair."

Erik and George raised their legs and plopped them onto the water-stained coffee table in perfect harmony, while the wobbly table protested in disharmony. "Then it's settled." George's best trait was using an economy of words. "When's the party?"

"How about next weekend? You're off work, and maybe we can get the girls' parents to let them all drive down together. Do you think you could call Lori?"

"Done deal."

"Do I look stupid to you?" *Mom is famous for her unanswerable questions.* "Why in the world would I let you drive down to Detroit to see a guy you just met? What do you know about him? What's his family like? Are you going to spend the whole weekend in his apartment? Does he have an extra bedroom for you and the other girls?" Arlene's rapid-fire questions were thinly veiled accusations of Julie's inability to figure anything out on her own. *I may not have thought of everything – but you aren't exactly a poster child for wise advice.*

Was it only three weeks ago when Bret talked about honoring our parents? Julie pushed aside the thought. *God, I promise to think about it again later if You will just let me do this one thing now.*

Julie had already seen some of Erik's rough edges. He drank. His reputation as a wild driver in high school was still talked about in driver's ed classes. But he was tall! And muscular! And he had a good construction job. If he already has a steady income, and plans to provide for her ... maybe someday ... well, who was she to pick nits? *Look at my father. If there's one thing he's done for me, it's lowering the bar on my standard for men. It's not hard for any guy to jump over it. And Erik leaps over it.*

"Mom, I really, really want to do this with my friends. I promise I'll find out all the details before we go. I'll get you a phone number, and I'll make sure the four of us sleep in our own room together. I'm a senior; you hafta start learning to trust me."

Julie knew that her mom had very little energy to drag herself to her part time job, and then home to veg out on the sofa for the evening. With no excess to do battle with her daughter, and nothing to gain from it, Julie thought Mom would eventually cave. For the next three days, Julie wrote little notes pleading her case, which she taped on Arlene's bedroom mirror, on the bathroom mirror, and on the refrigerator. Suddenly the notes disappeared without an explanation.

Arlene walked into Julie's room, stood in the doorway until Julie looked up from her English homework, and crossed her arms. "I really don't care if you go, but make sure you bring the car back with a full tank of gas. And if you have a baby nine months from Saturday, don't come cryin' to me, because I am not raising a bratty grandkid!" Arlene stalked out of the room while Julie raised her fist, pumped her arm, and shouted, "Yes, yes, yes!"

Julie Sandford had had few adventures aside from almost yearly moves, and none with three girlfriends. It was impossible for her to concentrate in class for the remaining days until her trip. She could not believe her mom had given in to her; maybe she realized that her daughter was graduating from high school in eight months and would be out on her own anyway. Julie also couldn't believe she had the whole weekend off work – it just meant taking an extra shift for Gloria when she got back.

Tuesday night at Lakeview, Glo listened to Julie talk about Erik, about his roommates, about the construction job, and about how strong and capable he was.

"Have you prayed about Erik and this trip?" Glo's sincere eyes held Julie to her seat in the cafeteria.

"No. But I know Erik's a good guy, and I can

help him with the things that aren't so good. Once he falls for me, he's going to want to change those things." Julie spoke with more confidence than she felt. *Glo, if you only knew what kind of life I've lived with my family, you would also know how different Erik is from all of them. He cares about me, which is more than I can say about my father.*

Glo got up from the table, pushed her chair in, said, "Julie, friend, I will pray for you this weekend," and went back to work. Julie stared at her pop can, hoping she was making the right choice.

Michiganders have a standing joke with outsiders about their four seasons: Winter's Coming, Winter's here, Fourth of July, and Road Construction. Julie awoke Friday morning to a spectacular fall day, the kind that is a carefully guarded secret to keep out all the undesirables, she supposed. The humidity masqueraded as Phoenix. Late-summer tulips and phlox flaunted vibrant colors. The air was laced with the pungency of wood smoke. The sky was an indescribable blue, spread like a vast ocean undulating in gentle waves. Pencil thin clouds knifed through the sky, mingling with a jet trail arching over the horizon.

Julie was a racehorse at the starting block, ready to burst through the gate and explode down the track. She didn't know how she would tolerate seven periods of classes before the beginning of The Great Adventure.

At three-thirty, Julie, Lori, Melissa, and Jacqueline slung their backpacks into their lockers, slammed the clangy metal doors, and sped out to the parking lot. Cars and trucks were a mix of gleaming chariots – some, gifts from upper-middle class parents;

others, rusted knights, held together with baling wire and prayer. Arlene's blue Chevy Nova was on loan, pressed into reluctant service by semi-grateful teens. The Nova's front and back bumpers were plastered with faded stickers which read, "Kiss Me – I'm Desperate," "A Closed Mouth Gathers No Feet," and "Mr. Potato Head for President." Julie and Lori scampered into the front seat while Mel and Jaq stood outside the back doors, waving to friends, fixing their hair, and tipping their faces to the sun, reveling in the magnificence of the day.

Julie rolled down her window. "Hey, you guys, let's boogie. This car's heading south!" She started the engine and looked at Lori, whispering, "One, two, three." On her cue, she and Lori sang, in perfect unison, "Get your motor runnin'—"

"Head out on the highway." Mel and Jaq joined in as they opened their doors, slid in, slammed the doors, and rolled down their windows. "Lookin' for adventure, in whatever comes or way. Born to be wild!"

The Nova hit cruising speed on Interstate Seventy-Five heading to Detroit. The fall colors changed to summer green as they drove farther south. With the gradual decrease in daylight and the increase in traffic, Julie concentrated on navigating, while the speedometer crept up from sixty-five to almost seventy-five. *I hope we have enough money between the four of us to pay for a speeding ticket.* Mel and Jaq giggled in the back seat and sang with songs on the radio, while Julie and Lori, more subdued, monitored the traffic, watched for cops, and talked about the gas gauge.

At seven-fifteen, three happy travelers and one relieved driver eased into a parking spot at their boyfriends' apartment complex on the south side of the city. They unfolded themselves from the car and Julie went around the back to open the trunk. The girls pulled out duffle bags and heard "Incoming!" from across the parking lot. Erik, George, J.J. and Zeke ran toward them. George reached the quartet first, pitched aside Lori's duffle bag, wrapped her in a bear hug and swung he around until she screamed, "Enough already – I'm gonna hurl!" J.J. and Zeke did the same with Mel and Jaq. Julie and Erik faced each other, surprisingly comfortable rather than awkward. Erik put out his hand, Julie gingerly took it, and all eight walked slowly back to the apartment. It was natural and easy for Julie. *Where has this guy been all my life?*

The L shaped sectional living room sofa supported eight pairs of arms and legs wrapped around each other like tendrils. Erik disentangled himself and shot up, almost knocking Julie to the floor. Everyone laughed – including Julie – as Erik said, "Let's get this party started!" While he disappeared through the swinging door into the kitchen, more people appeared at the front door. By nine o'clock, the party of eight had tripled.

Julie tried to stay in the background, feeling slightly out of place among Erik's roommates and friends. She and her friends were the only high schoolers there. Everyone else looked much older; the guys sported bushy mustaches and beards; the girls had that been-there, done-that look. Adding to Julie's nervousness was an empty stomach. The last thing she'd eaten was a bagel for breakfast. The living room began to fill with the sweet and sour smell of marijuana and the yeasty smell of beer. It was suddenly too much for her.

God – I think I made a big mistake. I should not be here. I'm not sure why Erik invited me. I would rather wait to see him again after he comes back up for a visit.

The Big Adventure slowly became more frightening than daring. Julie had spent enough years living in the wake of the raging torrent of alcohol to know what kind of destruction it left. She had determined never to drink or do drugs, especially after the bar room episode with Danny. Now she found herself back in the roiling water.

J.J. sauntered into the living room, unbuttoned denim shirt hanging over khaki shorts. "Presto!" He held up a pan of brownies like the spoils of victory. "Who's hungry?" he slurred. Julie caught the pan as J.J. tipped it forward.

"You're a lifesaver!" Julie had found the Holy Grail. She parted a group of guys standing in front of the kitchen door, went in, set the pan carefully on the red tiled counter, yanked open a drawer and found sharp knives and spatulas. She cut the brownies and took two before the others dove into the pan.

The broken springs on the sofa ambushed Julie's backside as she plopped down on the only vacant spot on the sofa. Hunger overcame good manners as she consumed both brownies in four bites each. *I know there's an abundance of beer here – not good to chase brownies down. I need cold milk.* Julie headed back to the kitchen, once again parting the sea of guys blocking her way. Foraging through the cupboards, she found a plastic McDonald's cup. A lone carton of milk stood sentry over the bare fridge. Julie emptied the carton into her cup, tossed it in the sink, took her cup to the table and sat down on a duct-taped, vinyl chair. She gulped the milk, dropped the cup on the floor, folded her arms on the table, lowered her head and closed her eyes.

Bells clanged in Julie's head. *That milk must have been bad. My head feels like it wants to vacate my body; and my stomach doesn't feel too good, either.*

J.J. walked into the kitchen and used the knife to dig out a brownie. "Julie, what do you think of the brownies?"

Julie muttered something incoherent, face still buried in her arms.

"Have you ever had hash brownies before? They're the best trip I know!"

Julie slowly, painfully, raised her head. "*What?*"

"Yeah, girl, you're going to be stoned good for the rest of the night!" J.J. was proud of his newest convert.

The bathroom was far away from the kitchen, but fortunately, unoccupied. After Julie emptied her stomach, she opened the door and wandered down the hall to a room that looked like a bedroom. Piles of clothes, shoes, tennis racquets, record albums, and fast-food containers littered every inch of the floor. Julie didn't care what she stepped on, just so she made it to the bed. Pushing aside a football and a cap, she fell backwards onto the pile of sweatshirts. A cool wind blew through a wide-open window. *Can someone? — anyone? — come in and cover me with a blanket?* Julie passed out.

Erik missed his girlfriend. "Hey Tin Man, where's my woman?" J.J. sat at the kitchen table, using his finger to dig the remainder of the brownies out of the corner of the pan.

"I dunno, man. She was here, she wasn't lookin' too good, and then she vanished. Poof!" Erik wandered down the hall, looked in his roommates' bedrooms, and then checked his own, where he found Julie lying spread eagle on his bed, head turned to one side, a thin line of drool hanging out of her mouth. Erik crept inside, quietly closed the door behind him and turned the lock.

Julie stirred. Her hand instinctively reached up and gingerly pressed down on her forehead. With eyes in slits, she made out a blurry outline. It looked like Erik, but who knew what tricks her drugged brain might be playing on her? Was this guy – Erik? – straddling her? She felt hands groping for her buttons, while a rush of cold air hit her exposed chest. Julie tried to push her numbed brain out of its fog.

"Don't ... do ... this ..." Julie's voice was hoarse. "Please ... wait ... no ..."

Erik finished, got up, pulled his shorts back on and left the room. *Have I been dreaming? Was Erik here?* Julie fell asleep again.

The next time she awoke, her eyes were in better focus. She sat up, swung her legs over the side of the bed, buttoned her blouse, retrieved the rest of her clothes, and put herself back together. *I wonder how much time has passed since I stumbled, mostly dead, into this room? Maybe an hour ago. Maybe three. I'm freezing. I need to get out of here. Where are my flip-flops?* Julie wanted to gather her posse and leave. Even her mom's I-told-you-so would be better than staying here any longer.

Julie grabbed the doorknob just as the door pushed towards her. Erik's surprised look turned to delight. "Hi, hon." He stepped inside, turned, closed, and locked the door, grabbed Julie's elbow, and pulled her back toward the bed. Too weak to resist, Julie sat down.

"I thought we could, you know, fool around a little bit. I locked the door so we wouldn't be interrupted." Erik put his arm around Julie.

"Are you kidding me? Didn't you get enough last time?" Julie shoved Erik back and rose slowly to her feet. "Get over there and unlock that door before I scream!" Julie shook from fear, anger, and cold.

Erik erupted in an eerie laugh. "Who do you think you're kidding? No one'll hear you from in here." As if on cue, someone amped up the volume to the max in the living room.

Julie turned and glared. "There's nothing you can do to me that my own father hasn't already done. But you're no match for him. I had a showdown with him, and I'm not afraid to have the same with you."

Erik rose, clapped his hands in mock applause, and strutted over to the door. He turned the lock, opened the door, bowed, and swept his arm across the air. "M'lady," he said in a British accent. Julie ran past him, resolve melting into despair. *Why do I always end up in these sink holes?* She hurried around the apartment despite the feeling that someone had attached a ball and chain to her ankles. Passed out bodies were scattered on the floors in every room like the aftermath of a train wreck. Lori, Mel, and Jaq were the lone survivors, huddled in a corner of the living room watching reruns of "I Love Lucy." When Julie spied them, she

166

practically launched herself at them.

"Julie! What's the matter with you?" Genuine concern etched Mel's face.

"Can we leave? I don't know what time it is, and I can't talk about it right now, but I want to go home. I need to go home. If we take turns driving, we should be okay." Julie melted into tears.

"Sure, girl, we're about through with this stupid party anyway." Mel unfolded her legs and got up from the floor, rubbing out her stiff muscles.

"Did my brother do something to you?" Lori's voice was equally concerned.

"I'll be fine." Julie couldn't believe how stupid that sounded. The girls quickly gathered their purses and duffle bags, left the apartment, and walked to the car, staying close for safety, huddling together for warmth. After wiping the condensation off the windows, Julie handed Mel the keys and shuffled into the back seat.

No one talked or sang. Mel flipped through radio stations until she found one with a man's blaring voice lamenting the poor treatment of returning Vietnam vets. *At least the war's over for them. Battles keep finding me.* Julie turned her head from the window and wept silent tears. The common denominator in all the chapters of Julie's life was alcohol: her parents, Grandma Hagstrom, the Andersons, creepy men, Teddy, Erik. Even though someone else bought the booze, she paid the biggest price in innocence and dreams.

Four girls collapsed in their beds by the time the sun rose on another day in Coldspring. Julie awoke to the sun low in the sky, her head not yet clear enough to discern dawn from dusk, or even to know what day it was. *I wonder why Mom didn't come into my bedroom and ask me why I'm home already? I should know better by now: If nothing rocks her boat, she will let me struggle in the water by myself. An occasional lifeline would be nice.*

A shrill ring broke into Julie's thoughts. Moments later, Arlene appeared at her bedroom door as though it was the most natural thing in the world for Julie to be home early and sleeping at … whatever time it was.

"Your friend Erik's on the phone." Arlene twirled the receiver connected to the phone in the living room by a twenty-five-foot cord.

"No! I don't care what you tell him, I am *not* going to talk to him! Ever!" Julie's voice hammered inside her head.

"Suit yourself – I don't care one way or the other." Arlene turned and walked back down the hall, the coiled cord submissively trailing her.

Julie didn't expect Erik to take rejection casually, but that was her plan – to reject him. He was coming up for one more football game, and she would find an excuse to be somewhere else. *My avoidance infrastructure is secure. I wonder where my heart fits in.*

The next day, Sunday, Erik called repeatedly. Arlene quit answering the phone after the third call. Julie's nerves were on the ragged edge. Answering the phone would be better than the unrelenting ringing.

"Julie? Hi. It's Erik. I'm really sorry about the misunderstanding when you were down here."

"I understood perfectly." Julie gave no ground.

"Babe let's start over again. The hash in those

brownies, the beer … everything made me looney. I'd never hurt you. We won't have sex again until you're ready. I really want to see you again, and this time, we'll go out to a movie or something. And hey, what did you mean by, 'I had a showdown with my father?' Did something happen before you came down?"

"Not really." Julie hated that her heart was thawing.

"Would it help if I talked to your dad?"

If only. "No! I mean no, it wouldn't. My dad's a …pervert …"

"So is mine, especially when he ogles the babes in the swimsuit issue of *Sports Illustrated.*"

"No! He really is! He's done stuff to me. What you did to me last night was him all over again."

"I'm sorry."

"I wanted you to know why I was so mad."

"Could we start over?"

"Really?"

"Really."

Erik called Julie every night at eleven-thirty to make sure he'd catch her at home after her shift at Lakehaven. They talked about work and movies and books and high school and football, each reluctant to hang up on the other. Julie didn't think it was possible to have a guy for a best friend until Erik came along.

A rare surge of common sense held Erik back from inviting Julie to his apartment again. When he traveled home to Coldspring over Thanksgiving, he asked her to share dinner with his family.

Winter arrived early and carried a grudge after a long and balmy fall. Arctic wind roared down from

Canada, plunging northern Michigan into temperatures flirting with zero, well below normal for November. After a filling Thanksgiving dinner and a delightful time with Erik's parents, Lori, and his two younger sisters, Erik pulled Julie into the vacant den.

"Babe, lets you and me go for a drive. My Firebird has a good heater, and we'll have a toasty ride up the shore. How about it?" Erik touched Julie's face. For a fleeting moment, her mind raced back to times in the car with Teddy-Boy. *I haven't driven with Erik before. Do I have any reason not to trust him? Okay, Julie, get a grip.*

"Sure, that sounds great." Julie and Erik hugged his family, bundled up and ran shivering and laughing out to Erik's car. Julie sat on her gloved hands, waiting for them to warm up.

"Honey, let's sit here for a few minutes. There's something I've been waiting to give you all night." Erik took off his polar fleece glove, reached into his parka and removed a small, black, velvet box. "This is for you."

Julie sucked in her breath, pulled her hands out from under her, stripped both gloves off, and reached for the box. She opened it to a simple ring, with a diamond chip in the center. Expelling her breath in a puff of cold air, Julie said, "Erik, does this mean what I think it means?"

Erik smiled. "What do you want it to mean?"

"It ... it looks like a promise ring."

"That's exactly what it is. I want us to get married someday." Erik took the ring and slipped it onto Julie's left hand. "When I make more money and move us into a nice apartment, I'll get down on one knee and do it the right way."

"Oh, Erik, do we have to take a drive? I want to run back in the house and share this with your family!"

Erik shut off the engine. He held both of Julie's hands in his, one still hidden in a warm glove, and said, "Julie, you've made me a very happy guy. I'll do anything for you!"

For the rest of the evening, the family – *I am now part of a real, together family* – played Monopoly, Risk, and Rook. By ten o'clock, happy and hungry people rummaged in the refrigerator for leftover turkey, stuffing, and pumpkin pie. It was the perfect end to a storybook day. Julie's life had been miserably devoid of happy families and the love of a good guy like Erik, her husband. *Someday.*

Julie's days were filled with school, her job at Lakehaven, girlfriends, and Erik – everything she always wanted. She spent a big chunk of her paycheck on long-distance phone bills, counting the days until Erik came home. The one sadness in her life was avoiding Gloria, who was pleasant, always solicitous, and continually inviting Julie to YFC meetings. *If I go back to those meetings, I'll have to face the possibility that Erik shouldn't be in my life, and I can't do that.*

With the approach of Christmas, Julie's white knight fell off his horse more and more frequently. Erik's visits began with a pleasant evening with his family. Board games were set up; the popcorn popper was brought out of retirement; and a game of silly story one-upmanship was played into sudden-death overtime. The increasingly predictable ending was Erik and Julie having a free-for-all argument either in the den or out in the driveway in his car. Julie begged Erik to stop drinking; Erik promised that this would be his last time. Each incident was another dejá vu. At some point, Erik passed the social drinking mile-marker with his temper headed toward a dangerous curve. Julie longed for his family to step on the brake, but Erik's charm always won the day. He sent money to his parents every time his dad was laid off work. If they weren't completely blind to their son's drinking, they certainly squinted their eyes and saw a good ol' boy having a good ol' time. *What if my life with him becomes a carbon copy of life at home?*

The next time Erik came home, the family gathered in the den for a lively game of Life. At the end of the game Julie had three kids, a mortgage, and the prospect of bankruptcy. *My life is full of irony.*

"Erik, can we go for a drive?" As soon as they got into Erik's car parked in front of the house, Julie determined to speak her mind before getting trapped in a speeding bullet with an angry Superman. "I need to tell you something." Julie reached for Erik's hand and willed her teeth to stop chattering. "These past months have been so wonderful. I know you care about me, and I care about you." Erik stared straight ahead. "You also know what life with my dad was like. Maybe another girl wouldn't have a problem dealing with you when you drink, but for me, it pushes rewind buttons that play bad memories. I can keep your ring. You know part of me will always love you. But I'm sorry. I can't marry you."

Julie waited for some sign of rage but was instead shocked when Erik dropped his head on the steering wheel and began sobbing uncontrollably. Julie had never seen a man cry, and it almost undid her resolve. She opened the car door, ran back into the house, and found Lori coming out of the bathroom.

"Lori, please take me home and don't ask any questions. I'll tell you what happened when we get back to school Monday. Say goodbye to your family for me." Julie ran through the kitchen to the attached garage and waited in the Martin car for Lori.

Lori was mute during the ride home. Julie used the blunt weapon of her emotion to chip at the impenetrable wall of silence that surrounds alcoholic families, but it was nevertheless seen as a threat, and she was locked out. By the time they were back at school Monday, Julie was no longer in the orbit of Lori's friendship.

CHAPTER 16
THE REVOLVING DOOR

It was too soon to assess the damage done by Hurricanes Teddy and Erik. The deadliest impact of both storms was Julie's self-worth, tossed and blown and strewn around the shallow cove of her heart. She planned to bury the leftover bits and pieces without any rebuilding, not even a temporary relationship shelter.

Christmas snuck in and out without Danny. Arlene's new apartment was pitiable and bleak, but intact. Julie decided to focus on graduation five months away – a chance to choose a path not bordered by emotional and financial poverty. *If I ever get married, it's going to be to a guy who will work hard, drink easy and love me totally. In the meantime, I have work and school to keep me busy.*

A school-weary teacher in a threadbare sweater seemed clueless about whether his students understood the world financial markets during fourth period economics. Everyone in class stared out the window at the enormous snowflakes swirling around the flagpole while Oblivious Mr. Silvius sat in front of an overhead projector, using a pointer to illustrate a sequence of vastly tedious economic ideologies.

Julie pulled her attention back to the room and noticed a guy looking her way. *I shouldn't be thinking about anyone else! I'm not even over Erik yet!*

"Tom – Tom Dietrich. Have a minute?" Mr.

Silvius usually did something to wake up his class about midway through the period. His most creative effort was reminding his students of their names, first and last.

Julie gathered her books and headed out the door toward the cafeteria. Tom was leaning against the vending machine near the lunch lady, watching Julie walk toward him.

"Hi. I'm Tom. I noticed you in November and I've wanted to meet you. Word on the street is that you were dating Gin Martini." Tom's easy smile reached his eyes partially hidden behind glasses. He stood a few inches taller than Julie, and had a crease around his forehead from the rim of a cap. His black t-shirt stretched tightly across his chest and upper arms, barely containing well-defined muscles. The beginnings of a wiry mustache gave Tom a rugged look. Julie liked the whole package.

"Would you like to go out sometime? Maybe tomorrow after I get off work at six."

"Yeah – I'd like that." Julie's face flushed.

"Let's meet at McDonald's out on the highway. I'll be there around six-thirty."

"Where do you work?" Julie wanted Tom to stay a little longer.

"Knutson Sod. I load and carry big rolls. I'm really into grass!"

That's obviously a well-rehearsed line. What a goof! Julie smiled, said, "Bye, then," and got in the hot lunch line. *I'm trolling through unknown water, and I don't know how deep it is. Maybe I should go slowly.*

The first date set the relationship-wheels in motion. Tom was a good listener, interested in Julie's opinions. They had fun together going to movies, hanging out with Tom's friends, and driving around Pleasant Lake.

On a frigid Friday night in mid-February, Julie, Tom, and four of their friends rode in Tom's car, laughing and singing to the eight-tracks, checking out the movie theater, bowling alley, and pool hall looking for cheap entertainment. They did not, however, want to leave the warm cocoon of their car for the icy blast of winter waiting to ambush them. When his gas gauge and energy level hovered on empty, Tom deposited their friends at Jim's house and shouted, "Close that door and move your dupas!" He laughed, cranked up the heater to full throttle, and blew out his breath in puffs of warm, moist air, immediately frosting the windows. He turned to Julie.

"Hey, girl, would this be a good time?"

"A good time for what?" Julie's heart sank.

"You know. We've been dating for a while. Guys at school tease me about not getting to home base with you yet." Tom turned his head and caressed the steering wheel with his left hand.

"What do I care about what your friends think? A bunch of jocks aren't going to decide anything about my life." Julie's anger became a good furnace.

"Look, Julie, I have a right to expect this. I care about you, and I know you care about me. What's the deal?" Tom faced Julie, eyes boring into her courage.

"Tom, I am not ready for this. There's stuff you don't know. I need more time." Julie was in the middle of a maze and could not find her way out.

"I don't need any more time! If you're not ready, then you're probably not the chick for me. I'll take you home." Tom gunned the engine, cranked up the radio, and drove the next ten minutes in stony silence. When they pulled into Julie's apartment complex, she turned to Tom, who seemed intensely interested in the streetlight. She turned away, opened the door, and turned back to say goodbye to a stiff body, eyes unblinking. Julie was dismissed for the umpteenth time in her life. She slammed the door and ran to her house, tears freezing on her cheeks.

Julie walked in on her mom lounging on the sofa in a house dress and fuzzy slippers, working a crossword puzzle. If there were any roads of sympathy leading to this place, they yielded the right-of-way whenever Arlene's welfare was in jeopardy. Julie's full-out, head-on collisions with both Teddy and Erik had not attracted any attention from her mom. Julie shrugged out of her parka, hung it on a hook in the closet, and walked toward the kitchen.

"Julie, is that you?" Arlene did not look up from her crossword puzzle.

Yes, Mom, it's me. I walked right through your intersection. "What do you want? I'm kind of tired." She spoke into the refrigerator, desperately wishing for a comforting friend instead of day-old Spamloaf.

"Come here. I need to tell you something."

Julie pulled out the meat drawer, grabbed a slice of wrapped American cheese, slowly closed the drawer and then the fridge, and wandered back out to the living room. Unwrapping the cheese, she watched the clear wrapper flutter to the coffee table. "Yeah?" She folded the cheese into quarters and popped it into her mouth.

"We need to move. This place gives me the

creeps. There's a guy down the hall who's always watching me when I get the paper in the morning, no matter what time it is. I heard of a good apartment not far from here. You can take me to work and then drive you and Dan to school. I know you want to finish out your senior year here." Arlene's attempt at sympathy sharpened Julie's suspicion radar.

"Are we being evicted again?"

"What're you talking about?" Arlene sounded only mildly offended.

"It's taken years to connect the dots, but I finally get that we didn't move all those times because of a creepy neighbor, or a better job opportunity for Dad – for *Danny* – or to be closer to Grandma and Grandpa, or to anyone else. We moved because we couldn't pay our rent." Julie walked back into the kitchen in search of something to drink.

"That's not a very respectful way to talk to your mother!" Arlene crumpled up the newspaper and threw it at a defenseless aluminum plant, half dead, hanging in a plastic pot from a hook in the ceiling. A carpet of dried, brown leaves was spread on the floor underneath it.

Julie popped the cap from a bottle of Coke, pitched the cap on the counter, and took a big gulp of the fizzy, throat-burning liquid as she walked back to the living room.

"I didn't mean to be disrespectful. I'm very tired. And I'm trying to figure out my life."

"It isn't rocket science. Some people say God works in mysterious ways, but it's no mystery. When you're down He squashes you, so you gotta make sure you stay out from under His thumb." Arlene shifted gears. "You think Teddy-Boy could bring over his truck and help us move?"

Mom, try to keep up! For cryin' out loud, he was three boyfriends ago! "Why can't Dan help us?" Julie had perfected the art of deflection.

"When he got fired, his truck was repoed. His fool boss didn't believe him when he said he got to work late last week because he had trouble with his truck."

Dan must be Danny's biological son. Blame and excuses are both in their DNA, and there's obviously no lifeguard in that gene pool.

Julie had an inexplicable surge of sympathy for her mom; and after the earlier events of this long night, she had no desire to fight her. "Okay, I'll call Mama T and see if she knows where Teddy is." The last Julie had heard, Teddy had dropped out of high school – *probably with Mama T's blessing* – to try to get into an over the road trucking school.

Climbing into bed, Julie ached for a friend like Glo, whom she was still avoiding. Erik's family filled the gap for a while, but that ship had sailed. All Tom's friends would jump the fence when they found out he dumped her. Julie pounded and folded her pillow. *I wonder where Eugene is, and if he ever thinks about the infant girl he left behind.*

Julie dialed Mama T's number. A voice answered after the third ring. "Ja? Wo ist dis?"

"Hi, Mama. It's me."

"Julie! Es ist so *gut* to hear from you!" Before she could ask about Teddy, Julie was invited over for dinner that weekend.

Teddy had changed. He did not show any

179

awkwardness about helping Julie's family move the week after her phone call. Julie decided not to tell Teddy that their new apartment was up a long flight of stairs, and Teddy surprised Julie by counting the steps and good-naturedly laughing about it.

"Twenty-three steps! Good thing you packed everything in small boxes. And thank God for furnished apartments!" Teddy laughed and headed back down the stairs.

"Thanks for helping!" Julie shouted, thinking he was finished and heading home.

"I'll be back – got three boxes left." Teddy reappeared five minutes later. "Maybe twenty-three is our magic number," he exclaimed after the last box was stacked against a wall of the living room. Putting his arm around her, he whispered, "We could get married on March twenty-third. We could have twenty-three guests at our wedding. I could lay twenty-three rose petals on your pillow on our honeymoon night." For the moment, the surge of romance in Julie's heart was stronger than the warning bells going off in her head.

Mama T sewed a wedding dress for Julie within a month of her rekindled relationship with Teddy, who also insisted on getting to know his future mother-in-law. But his behavior defaulted to the rhythm of anger and apology, rage and remorse. *This is recycled Teddy. Or Erik reversed. I can't even keep the players straight.* Julie was the ante in a high-stakes poker game, tossed into the middle of something she was increasingly desperate to flee.

Teddy ate another Sunday brunch at Julie's and conducted a fact-finding tour of Arlene's personality.

Good luck with that. Teddy kept up a lively monologue; Julie knew it was time for a dialogue between her and Teddy. Alone. As soon as they finished eating, Julie took Teddy's hand and led him to the worn, brown, Naugahyde sofa in the living room. *Whatever happens in this conversation, I am for sure not going to do sixty-five in a car or on a motorcycle.* Even though Julie had not experienced her mom as a protector, she doubted Teddy would explode with Arlene nearby.

Julie did not entrust more than a small corner of her heart to Teddy. She simply told him she wasn't ready for a serious relationship after all. Teddy got up and spewed a torrent of cuss words, then walked to the front door, turned around and erupted in a fountain of tears. Julie stared at him as he opened the door, wiped his eyes on his sleeve, walked out and slammed the door behind him.

"Wait!" Julie leaped to the door, pulled it open and walked out in time to see Teddy pounding down each step, counting backwards from twenty-three as though erasing Julie from his life. As he shouted "thirteen!" he looked up in time to avoid plowing into Erik. Teddy blew past Erik, ran down and threw his weight into the front door, pushing it open so hard he practically fell out. Erik turned as a blast of lingering winter air snuck in before the door banged shut. Turning back around, he looked up at Julie and said, "Who was that?" as he took the remaining steps two at a time.

"Never mind. What are you doing here?"

"Babe, I haven't seen you in over three months." Erik put his hands on Julie's waist. "I'm here for the weekend, and I found out where you and your family were moving to. I had to come over and see you. Let's go in and sit down."

A force from the past pulled Julie into the apartment – a force that left her feeling colder than the wintry air. Erik guided her to the sofa and sat down on the floor in front of her. "Julie, my family confronted me about my drinking the night you left. I promised them I'd quit, and I haven't had a drink since. I sold my car and bought a little Plymouth Duster. I'm going to change, and I want you to marry me."

This can't be happening. If it were a Movie of the Week, people would yell, 'Psych!' and flip the channel.

"Before you say anything," Erik continued, "I bought you a real engagement ring this time." He started to reach into the inside pocket of his camouflage hunting jacket.

"No! Stop!" Julie jumped up. "This is nuts! I can't marry you. I wouldn't marry Teddy, the guy who almost mowed you down on the stairs. Please, please, leave me alone!" Julie sobbed.

Erik slowly rose, wrapped his arms around Julie and pulled her head into his shoulder. Her arms hung loosely at her sides.

"Julie, I know this is what you want." Erik waited.

Measure twice, cut once. Julie pulled her head back, breaking his hold without touching him. "No, Erik, it's over. Please go."

Erik reached into his pocket, took out the velvet ring box, threw it through the still-open front door, and walked out. Julie ran into her bedroom and flung herself onto the bed. *How many girls are lucky enough to have one guy propose to them, much less two, and on the same night? I don't know what I want anymore.*

Sharon Dietrich had heard from a reliable source that Julie Sandford was going to marry Teddy Tannenbaum. Sharon liked Julie, saw how happy her brother had been when he dated her and wanted to at least give her brother a chance to throw his ring in the ring.

Sharon waited for Tom to get home from work. As soon as she told him about Julie, Tom quickly showered and drove over to her new apartment, tires sliding over ice-covered roads.

Tom opened the front door of Julie's apartment and raced up the stairs. His attention was drawn to something hitting the wall and a guy headed towards him.

"Erik Martin?" Tom stopped and grabbed the handrail.

"Yeah?" Erik glared, face and hair the same angry shade of red.

Someone was shaking her shoulder. "Julie, I don't know what's going on outside our apartment, but you better get out there!" Arlene materialized and vanished without leaving any footprints. Julie sat up, rubbed her stiff neck, ran her fingers through her hair, and emerged from her room into the gathering darkness of the living room.

"Get out of my way!" A familiar voice yelled outside the building.

Julie reached the front door and looked out as Tom and Erik squared off on ... *the thirteenth step?* "Stop!" Julie's face was ashen.

Erik dropped his clenched fist, turned, and glared at her. "It's him or me!"

"I'm sorry, Erik. Nothing's changed." Pity, fear, and anger mixed into a sour taste in her mouth.

Erik shoved Tom into the wall, tore down the steps and out the now popular, well-used door.

Tom looked at her. "This isn't exactly what I had planned."

Julie crossed her arms. "Oh? And what exactly *were* your plans?"

Tom climbed the remaining steps and put his hands on her shoulders. "I don't know. I was wrong before. I shouldn't have pressured you, and I was dumb to let you go. I want to marry you. I'll be good to you. I'll work hard. You know I will." Tom knew when to fold his cards. He let go of Julie, turned around, and slowly descended the stairs.

Three blind mice; see how they run.

CHAPTER 17
SMOKE AND MIRRORS

Julie stood in the narthex of Redeemer Lutheran Church adjusting the bobby pins holding her wedding veil in place. Ceiling fans circulated air-conditioned relief from the relentless heat outside the stucco building. Beside her was Grandpa Richard, looking both nervous and glad that she had asked him to share this special day with her.

Danny lurked outside in the shadow of a maple tree, dressed in his regulation blue jeans, Wellington boots, and cap. Julie saw him through the tall, narrow window next to the heavy oak door, and simply turned away from him. This was not a day for her to dwell on what he had taken from her.

The organist launched into the "Wedding March," while Julie crooked her arm in her grandpa's and turned to him. *I love you, but I can't help wondering what it would be like if I were holding the arm of my biological dad right now. Would he be dressed in a white tux, or a plain, black, slightly out-of-date suit, like you? What advice would he give me? If he thought he made a mistake in marrying my mom, would he tell me to stop the madness I may be doing here and now?*

"Grandpa, I'm scared. I don't think this is the right thing to do."

Grandpa squeezed Julie's hand and whispered, "Don't make the same mistake your mother made. You can walk away right now. Or you can run!"

Tears threatened to make rivers of mascara

down Julie's cheeks. "I can't. I just can't." *I think this is a mistake – except that Tom works hard, and he'll give me financial stability. Besides, we have shower gifts, and wedding gifts, and we can't return them. I'm through the turnstile now – time to ride the ride.*

After the simple ceremony, a small group of friends and family gathered around Tom and Julie, balancing cups of punch and plates of cake and trying to stay cool in the basement fellowship hall. As the newlyweds prepared to leave the reception, Arlene found her daughter in the restroom changing from her rented wedding dress into white pants, blue tank top and white blazer.

"Here, Mom. Could you please return my dress for me?" Julie handed her mom the dress on a hanger. *I never did get a new dress, did I?*

"I hope you know what you're doing. We all make mistakes—"

Julie turned and looked at her mom's reflection in the wall-to-wall mirror over the double sinks. "It's a little late for this talk now, isn't it? I made the right decision. Tom will take good care of me." She picked up her white shoes, shoved them into a plastic Payless bag, and turned back to her mom. "Could you take these, too?"

Arlene shrugged, draped the dress over her arm, took the bag, and said, "Well then, enjoy your honeymoon. Could you get the door for me?"

Julie opened the door, patted her mom's shoulder, and watched the door close behind her. Glancing once more at the mirror, she said, "Mirror, mirror, on the wall, I am *not* my mother after all."

Coldspring Hotel was a perfect place for a

romantic honeymoon, the kind Julie had always dreamt about before giving in to Tom's premarital sexual desires. Their wedding night was not memorable for Julie, who emerged from the bathroom in a new negligee to find Tom sound asleep. She did not know why they were given a room with two double beds but decided that since Tom was already snoring in one bed, she would get a good night's sleep in the other. *I am not going to let this bother me. We can start over again tomorrow.* Julie was surprised, both at how tired she was, and how content she felt to have her own bed.

At five-thirty the next morning, Julie pulled aside the heavy curtains and looked out at a spectacular view of Pleasant Lake, marveling at the color of the water changing from light blue near the shore to deeper blue, then blue-green, and finally to a blue too intense to describe. *The lake is an eternity of mystery and promise.* She turned from the window as Tom sat up, ran his fingers through his hair and said, "I'm starving."

Okay, so he's not the most romantic guy on the planet. "Where do you want to eat?" Julie walked towards Tom, hoping he would get excited over her figure showing through her nightie, pull her into bed and start their honeymoon over.

Tom got up and headed for the bathroom. "I figured we'd grab a quick bite at that family restaurant in town. We've got to get home. I've got work to do. We're burning daylight here."

Julie sank onto the bed. *Ohmigosh. What have I done?* Within an hour, the newlyweds were showered, dressed, packed and out the door. *Remember, Julie, this guy is a hard worker, and that's what you wanted. Maybe romance is highly overrated.*

Tom and Julie graduated three days after their wedding. Julie returned to school to pick up her diploma cover, say goodbye to friends, brag about how Tom had wanted her to have his last name on her diploma, and close the door forever on the Sandford years.

I am moving into another trailer. This time Julie was happily surprised – the trailer was clean and nicely furnished. Days before the wedding, Tom had told her about a ten-by-fifty-five-foot trailer for sale for three thousand. The seller was an older man who nursed his wife of forty-five years through a hideous battle with brain cancer; after she died, he did not want any memories of those months. When Julie heard the story, she hoped she and Tom would never live through anything like that.

What will I do if Tom tells me he wants to park our new trailer in a trailer park? Speaking of memories, I sure don't want that one popping up. I am not ready to tell Tom about Mr. Thomas. He was depraved and I was deprived – sounds like a bad country western song.

Bill Kenney, Mayor of Coldspring, was a good, older friend of Tom's. When Tom introduced Bill to Julie at their wedding reception, he said, "Julie, meet my friend Bill, giver of great wedding gifts!" Bill's gift was greater than Julie had ever known in her life: an acre of land outside Coldspring city limits on scenic highway twenty-three.

Julie moved her few belongings into the trailer and rummaged through a small box of keepsakes, looking for something to hang on the bare walls. She found a picture of a doll with masking tape still stuck to her back; a framed picture of her and Chris; a certificate from Mrs. Ryczek for memorizing bible verses; and a poster of zoo animals. *Is this all I have from my childhood?*

Tom walked into the trailer after work, found Julie, took her hand, and led her out and up a short path. As they tried to outrun the mosquitoes, Tom said, "Whenever I tell my grandma that the mosquito is the Michigan state bird, she tells me that it's God's way of reminding us that there really is a hell!"

The path opened into a clearing surrounding a large farmhouse. A stout-looking, sixtyish woman sat in an aluminum lawn chair on a porch that wrapped around two sides of the house. *Reminds me of how I met Mama T!*

"Julie, this is Grandma Emma." Tom smiled at his grandmother.

The woman hoisted herself up and laughed as she disengaged from the chair suspended in the air by her wide hips. Ambling over to Julie, Grandma Emma engulfed her in a suffocating hug. Pulling back, she grabbed both of Julie's hands in a bone-crushing grip.

"You feel dese hands? I haf milked tvelf cows mit dese hands for almost fifty years. My husband, he drank da beer too much, und could nefer do da work he vas s'posed to do. Dese hands raised kinder und grandkinder. I by myself am now, und I don't mind at all!" Grandma Emma released Julie's hands and caught Tom in an adoring hug. "I haf my boy back home! Every ting I haf is yours. Now come in und haf dinner mit me." *She sounds like Mama T! I have stepped into fairy land!*

After a simple, filling meal with Grandma Emma, Tom and Julie walked back to their trailer in the cool dusk of June. "Julie, I know I never told you much, because this is kind of painful. I've tried to forget about it. But maybe you should know." Tom stared at the familiar ruts on the ground.

I thought I was the only one dragging overloaded luggage into this marriage. They came to a fire pit, and Tom motioned for Julie to sit on a stump, while he eased down onto an overturned pallet.

"My dad was killed when I was thirteen." Julie held her breath. *Every time I asked you why your dad couldn't come to our wedding, you shrugged it off and said he was busy. I should have pushed you harder for the truth.* Julie remained quiet. "About six months after Dad died, Mom married a bozo named Archie, a real loser who couldn't stand me or my sister."

We have more in common than you think. This is almost bizarre. Julie got up and started collecting sticks to throw into the pit. When she thought she was out of earshot, she talked to the crickets. "How much should I tell Tom? Am I being fair to him? What should I do?" Julie wandered back, tossed her sticks, and sat on the stump.

Tom got up and arranged the sticks on top of a few large half-burned logs. "Mr. Archenemy robbed me and my sister blind! We never saw one penny of our monthly social security survivor checks. I don't know why my mom didn't stop him. By the time I turned sixteen, I couldn't stand it anymore. I was not going to get the money, and I hated that jerk, so I figured I'd blow. I threw all my stuff into a big army duffle, got in my car, and drove to Grandma Emma's. About six months later, Sharon showed up. That's where we were living when I met you." Tom pulled a lighter out of his pocket, lit the kindling, waited for a good blaze, and walked to the trailer. Julie stayed outside until the fire was reduced to embers.

"Grandma, can I fill these jugs with water?" Julie was on her daily water run. She and Tom had been in their trailer for most of the summer without running water. *Maybe I should be thankful that we have electricity.* Tom ran a very long, heavy-duty extension cord from the trailer to her house. Their light source was a small K-Mart desk lamp, which Julie carried around the trailer, plugging it in wherever she needed it.

Tom had promised to take care of his wife, which meant picking up construction jobs with his buddies when his hours at Knutson Sod dropped below full time. Julie knew a good man was taking care of her, and she felt like she was finally on the right road, driving in the rhythm and flow of traffic. She was sad, though, to give up her job at Lakehaven, since it was twenty miles from their trailer, and they only owned Tom's truck. *I should be thinking about what I'm going to do when I grow up.* Glo had graduated with Julie and been accepted into Michigan State University. College was way too expensive for the Dietrichs for now, but Julie longed to go when she and Tom were settled somewhere, maybe after they moved into a house.

Hot'n Cold General Store became the place for Julie to get a job, meet people, relieve some of her boredom, and contribute her buck-sixty-five an hour to the family treasure chest. Since she would have to depend on coworkers to drive her back and forth to work, she hoped to be welcomed into the community as a full-fledged adult.

"Tom, who needs an alarm clock when we have your grandma?" The six o'clock sun threatened to blister the siding off the trailer. Tom was getting ready for work as Julie rolled out of bed to answer the familiar knock at the door.

Julie brushed past Tom. "You should have married Grandma Emma, so you would have someone to take care of you. I am definitely not her." Julie sneered, as she opened the door and tried to greet Emma with a genuine smile. She puzzled over this relationship between her husband and grandmother-in-law; it was unlike anything she had experienced with any of her grandparents.

"I yust wanted to know if you haf enuf to eat dis morgen." Emma was annoyingly spunky for this time of day.

"Yes, Grandma, we're fine. Tom is leaving for work."

"Okay, den, I come back tomorrow."

Julie's job sometimes kept her past four, when Tom got home from work. By the time Julie returned, Tom was at Emma's eating dinner. *I am Tom's wife. He should be eating my cooking in our trailer.*

The end of July brought unrelenting heat that sizzled Julie's nerves. "What are you doing here, Tom?" Julie had arrived home from work at five-thirty and walked into an empty trailer, oppressive heat clinging to the walls. Without stopping to change out of her work clothes, she angrily marched up to Emma's house and banged through the door without knocking.

Tom swallowed a forkful of meatloaf. "Well,

you weren't home, and Grandma had dinner for me."

Julie seethed. "Your house is over there! *I* am your wife. I cook your meals."

Grandma Emma sheepishly responded. "Vell, Julie, you're velcome to eat mit us here."

"No, Grandma, I am not hungry. Tom's house is not here anymore."

"I am sorry, Julie. I did not mean to offend you. Of course, Tom shoudt be at his house mit you."

"Oh Grandma, it's okay, I guess." Julie sat down at the table, rested her folded arms, and lowered her head. A large window fan blew cool air across her back.

Emma got up, opened the freezer door, took out a frosted mug, dumped a handful of ice into it, then opened the refrigerator, pulled out a pitcher of lemonade, and poured it over the ice. The crackling sound of ice-verses-liquid caught Julie's attention. She lifted her head as Emma placed the glass in her hand "Here, Julie, I haf someting to make you feel better."

Julie took a large gulp and held the glass to her forehead. *Am I nuts? Here is a kind, capable, loving woman who's glad to cook for Tom. If I come home hot and tired, she'll cook for me too. Get a grip, Julie!*

In bed that night, Julie listened to Tom's even snoring as she lay perfectly still, hoping to catch a breeze through their window. If there was one thing Julie had learned that day, it was not to turn away from purposeful acts of kindness, especially when they came from someone as wonderful as the woman in the farmhouse. *Seems like people in farmhouses have been good to me.* Julie turned her head to see stars littering the sky. *Lord, thank You for Grandma.*

Grandma Emma was Julie's rock, strong and

stable and dependable. If Tom picked up extra work on the weekends, Julie wandered over to Emma's, where there was always a surplus of food and drink, wisdom and sympathy.

On an oppressively hot Saturday, Emma's floral housedress clung to her back, as curly tendrils of gray hair lay plastered to her neck. Julie sat at the table while Emma plodded into the dining room from the kitchen, humming and carrying thick slabs of German chocolate cake on chipped china plates with a faded floral pattern. She set a plate down in front of each of them.

"Ven I vas your age, Julie-girl, my husband Herman und I had a baby. A month later, I vas carrying vater in jugs across my shoulders from da vell to da haus. It vas one-quarter mile trip, und I vas balancing our baby boy on my hip vile I valked. It vas very tough life, but I saved all da money I could." Emma thoughtfully chewed and swallowed a bite of cake. "Herman died of da cancer, und I know I shouldn't be mean, but he vas no gut! Venever he could, he vould take da money, go into town, and treat his friends to da drink. He vas a bugger, und dat's da troot!" Emma laughed, finished her last bite of cake, and scraped all the crumbs onto her fork.

I don't own the real estate on broken families. Emma has a claim on her turf of hardship and grief. But she's not a miserable person seeking miserable company. This woman is full of joy, with tough, callused hands but a soft heart. Julie was grateful for the good sense not to push Emma out of her life.

CHAPTER 18
FIRST COMES LOVE,
THEN COMES MARRIAGE ...

Winter made a dry run before Thanksgiving, coating grass, trees, abandoned trucks, and piles of tires with a layer of wet, heavy snow. Julie bundled into her fleece-lined jacket, pulled on her Sorrels, and trudged over to Emma's, dragging her body in slo-mo.

Emma always seemed to know when Julie was coming and greeted her at the door with a steaming mug of hot chocolate. "Come in, come in, und da door close. Es ist nicht vunderbar!"

Julie collapsed on a kitchen chair, pushed back her hood, and wrapped her hands around the mug. "Grandma, I have something to tell you." Her eyes pooled in enormous tears.

"Let me guess: You are wit da child already, ja?"

"How did you know? Tom and I have only been married six months. I'm not ready for this." Julie sighed deeply.

"Honey, du bist never, ever ready to be pregnant, no matter ven it happens. Da gut Lord sees fit to gif you everyting you need to get troo dis. And ven da baby comes, the tree of you vill feel like a real family." Emma smiled warmly.

"But – I'm only nineteen! I don't know what I want to do with my life."

"Vell, it looks like it has been decided for you already, ja? Ven your baby comes, you vill be vay too busy to vorry about your future. Da best ting you can do now is sleep ven you can, eat vell, and stay healty."

195

Julie gazed at this incredible woman and then around the kitchen where things always seemed right. *Emma will be here for me. She's Mom, Grandma, Aunt, and even Best Friend.* "I love you, Grandma."

"I luf you too, Liebchen."

"Sleep when you can, eat well, stay healthy" – simple words spoken in broken English from an unbroken heart. Julie was certain she could do those three things.

On Christmas night, a virulent intestinal bug knocked Julie down for the count. Five days later, she saw vultures circling when she awoke from a fitful sleep with her heart racing, her body sweating buckets, her hands and arms numb. Panic took over when she got up and felt something sticky running down her legs. She hobbled to the bathroom in intense terror. Sinking to the cold linoleum floor, she focused on realigning her gray matter. *If I can crawl to the living room and reach the phone, Emma will know what to do.*

Emma had never driven anything but tractors and the occasional rusty pick-up truck around her land. Tom's sixty-six Ford was in her barn for emergency transportation. Within minutes of Julie's call, Emma had thrown a coat over her robe, pulled on her boots, and climbed into the truck. Amazingly, it started on the first crank. She drove down to Julie's, shifted into park, leaned over, opened the passenger door, and left the engine running. Inside the trailer, Emma lifted Julie, carried her to the truck, tucked old wool blankets around her and ignored the speed limit and winter driving precautions on the way to the Emergency Room. "Dear Gott, spare Julie's life und the life of dis precious baby," she uttered over and over.

Anxiety filled Julie's heart. *Where's Tom? Did he come home after I fell asleep last night and then leave again early this morning? He never works on Saturdays. God, please get me to the hospital on time.*

As soon as Julie was resting comfortably in the maternity ward, Emma found a phone in the family waiting area and began calling all Tom's friends, most of whom had been in his life since childhood. No one knew where he was. A few joked that he had gone AWOL from the marriage army. Emma dismissed the puzzled looks from people staring at her pink robe and men's winter boots. Tucking runaway gray hairs back into her bun, she headed back to Julie's room, whispering prayers for the courage to tell her what she did not want to hear – that no one knew where Tom was.

Julie slept quietly while Emma settled into a leather recliner. The room soon filled with soft humming; Emma had a head-full of hymns and was ready to pass the rest of the day singing peace into the room. Her friend Amy said that the word PEACE stood for Pray Early And Cheat the Enemy. That was Emma's plan. Julie may have been sleep-deprived, but she was not going to be peace-deprived if Emma had anything to say and pray about it.

Late afternoon sun flashed high beams across Julie's bed, flooding the room with optimism. She awoke groggy and thirsty and saw Emma sitting in a chair with her legs up and head tipped sideways, snoring lightly, and smiling even in her sleep. Julie looked at the needle taped to her hand and at the tube attached to the IV bag. *Why did I ever doubt that I wanted this baby?*

A cheerful nurse came in bearing Epiphany treasures: toothbrush, toothpaste, and comb. Emma opened her eyes, looked down at her robe and chuckled. "Maybe I need fixing more dan you!" She got up, rubbed her back, and watched the nurse raise the bed and help Julie comb her hair. When Julie suddenly grabbed her stomach and moaned, the nurse reassured her that she was fine and that these new pains were probably from hunger. Julie's stomach rumbled and Emma laughed as the nurse handed the comb to Julie and left the room to answer a call bell.

"Emma, could you—" Julie's arm stopped in mid-air.

"Vat is vrong?" Emma's eyes signaled alarm.

"Those footsteps ... in the hallway. They sound like Tom's. Oh, I hope they are. But where has he been?" Julie felt like someone had pulled a string in her emotions and she was unraveling. She dropped the comb on her blanket, lowered herself onto the pillow and flung her arm over her eyes.

Heavy footsteps clumped down the hospital corridor, along with the sound of banging metal carts and swearing. Julie froze.

Tom appeared in the doorway, jacket hanging open, work boots untied and a look of disdain on his reddened face. Bleary eyes glanced first at Julie, then at Emma, then at the floor. Julie's feeling of relief was overpowered by anger and sadness. *Where has Tom been? Does he care about my baby and me? Our baby? Is he glad we're okay? Will he ever tell me I'm beautiful?*

Julie wondered if there was any difference between her husband and her adoptive father. And what about Eugene? Was he different than those two? What if he knew he was going to be a grandpa? But he had abandoned her when she was a baby, which left three men in her life who had more important things to do than care for her.

Tom walked unsteadily into the room, stood at the foot of Julie's bed, then walked over and put his hand on her forehead. "Julie, I'm sorry. I'll try—"

"Don't. Say. Anything. Just leave me alone. I'll be fine here with Emma." *Go home.*

Winter sloughed off her heavy coat, revealing a spring wardrobe. Buds burst into leaves that accessorized dignified oak trees and flamboyant forsythia bushes. Emma made the short walk to Julie's every evening, cradling a thermos of hot tea and a Cribbage board, a fairy godmother in galoshes. Julie's isolation and discouragement transformed into belonging and contentment. Often, grandmother and granddaughter sat in companionable silence, drinking tea, and watching Julie's stomach ripple with the movement of unseen body parts. "I don't know if this baby will have good hand-eye coordination, but he will have good elbow-knee coordination!" The laughter helped them observe the code of silence where Tom was concerned. Most of the time he was gone when Emma visited. She never asked where he was and Julie did not volunteer information, usually because she didn't know herself. She knew that Arlene was busy slaying her own dragons, which made Emma the core of all things good and kind in her life.

Her pregnancy was in the home stretch. Julie lugged around an extra thirty pounds while July heat and humidity turned the trailer into a sauna. Her doctor off-handedly mentioned, during her final check-up, that she would probably be scheduled for a C-section, since the baby was positioned feet-first and unlikely to turn itself before labor began. Julie did not understand the lingo but figured if she followed her doctor's orders, she would reach the point where someone else could carry her baby around for a welcome change.

Tom's friends occasionally dropped by to check on Julie. Through them, she found out that when Tom was not at work, he was drinking with Bill and Bernice at one of the Coldspring bars. Julie assumed Bill was Bill Kenney, terminal bachelor. The only time Julie ever saw Emma closed and evasive was when she asked her about who Bernice was. "She vas my sister-in-law. Dat's all." *And apparently as much of a bugger as Emma's husband.*

With less than a month until her due date, rest was an elusive dream. No sooner would she drift off, long after midnight, than Tom would pull up to the trailer, open and slam his truck door and stumble up the steps in a tragic-comical attempt at quiet. Julie would stir awake in time to see Tom standing over her with a silly grin on his face, holding out a can of Mountain Dew and a Snickers bar like the proverbial peace offering. *How does Tom drive home safely every night? How many lives does he have, and which one is he on?*

"Mom, this baby is coming soon. Could I stay with you until I deliver? You live so much closer to the hospital."

"I suppose. If you insist."

On a muggy night when air conditioners lost ground in their battle with the unyielding humidity, Julie was lying on a bed in the Emergency Room at St. Michael's – shivering, crying, desperate to hear the familiar footsteps of her doctor.

The on-call doctor ran in and out of cubicles in a blur of frenzied activity, pulling privacy curtains back and forth like a magician on stage and reassuring Julie that he was monitoring her closely, even though her baby was still several hours away from entering the world. *Does this doctor know I have a breech baby?* Arlene paced around the cubicle muttering about going back out to find a cheaper parking spot on the street so that she wouldn't have to pay the crooks in the parking garage. Every fifteen minutes she escaped to the waiting room for a cigarette, then returned to Julie's space, slightly more stressed after each trip.

I wish I knew what was happening. Where's Tom? I hope they find my regular doctor soon. As her pain intensified, Julie was free-falling through a haze of terror. *Why aren't they prepping me for a section? What's happening? Could I die from pain?* Her baby's first step into the world was with one foot out and the other hung up in the birth canal. Julie was cut horizontally and vertically. She tore. She bled. She screamed. Christina Rose Dietrich was born. Julie's last thought before she drifted off in a drug-induced euphoria was that she finally had a doll to dress.

Tom drove Julie and Christina home from the hospital five days later. As soon as he had them settled, he announced that his responsibilities toward his wife and newborn daughter were to get up in the morning, go to work and bring home a paycheck every other week. It was Friday – Tom kissed his two women and drove off to work, leaving Julie with all the left-over jobs.

None of her life experiences prepared Julie for the punishing triathlon of diapering, breast-feeding and round-the-clock pacing with a colicky baby. A healthy body would have made everything easier, but Julie dealt with excruciating pain for six weeks, without the time or ability to lie down. Her bed was the most neglected piece of furniture in their trailer as Julie hurtled towards a meltdown. The energizing, late-summer sun mocked her weariness.

Julie was confined with a baby whose daily activities were nursing, gulping, burping and projectile vomiting. Grandma Emma was the benevolent guard, making her rounds every morning at seven, delivering homemade cinnamon rolls with a hug, a smile, and the reassurance that, "Dis, too, shall pass, Liebchen." After Emma left, Julie and Christina were alone for the rest of the day. Julie never considered leaving the trailer; even if her body had been strong enough, her pride left her unwilling to take a colicky baby into a world of ideal mothers with perfect babies. There was too great a chance of being wounded by friendly fire.

Thanks to Bill's baby gift – paying to have a well dug for Tom and Julie's trailer – their new Whirlpool washer became Julie's most cherished friend, while the old Plymouth Duster – a recent better-than-soda-and-candy peace offering from Tom – sat forlornly in the weeds.

Mid-October brought renewed energy. "Maybe if I get the wash done this morning," Julie whispered to Christina, "you and I can go for a drive. I'll put you in that cute, yellow, hand-smocked dress with the matching bloomers." The air was crisp and the sky a deep topaz. This was one of Julie's favorite times of year: The temperature was close to sixty; the bright sun was invigorating; wood smoke hung languidly in the air;

and best of all, the mosquitoes were gone. It would be good for her to go out, maybe even show off her new baby to a few of her former coworkers at the store. Those friends would love her in the Midwestern-nice kind of way and fuss over her baby, something she craved. *Maybe I can do this mother thing after all. If I've survived these first months, I can do anything.*

Julie tucked Christina into her infant seat on the floor, poured a cup of powdered laundry detergent into the washer, pulled out and twisted the knob to start the water, and gathered up an armful of clothes. That's when she noticed red spots on the back of the green shirt she had worn the previous night during Christina's last feeding. The spots looked like dried blood and could only have come from Christina's post-nursing vomiting. Julie dropped the clothes on the floor, slammed the palm of her hand into the knob to shut off the washer, picked up Christina's seat, tucked it under her arm, grabbed her purse hanging from the kitchen chair, pushed open the trailer door and raced out to the car. After belting in Christina's seat, Julie shoved the key into the ignition. *Jack be nimble, Jack be quick.* The car started on the first try.

God, forgive me – but maybe they'll ask me to take Christina to St. Michael's for an overnight stay, and I can pass out. I could stay on a cot in Christina's room, be right there if she needs me, and let the nurses take care of her.

Julie shook herself out of her daydream, pulled into the clinic parking lot and headed inside. After checking in, she took her baby to a waiting room filled with big plastic blocks, cardboard books, climbing equipment for toddlers, and four deep, leather armchairs. Julie set Christina's infant seat on the floor, lifted her out of it, and wrapped her arms around her baby as they both sank into one of the chairs.

The nurse entered the waiting room fifteen minutes later and found Julie and Christina zoned out. She gently woke Julie and led them back to an exam room. The pediatrician walked briskly down the hall and entered the door right behind them.

Dr. Johnson listened patiently to Julie's concerns while he thoroughly examined Christina. "Mrs. Dietrich." The older doctor sat in his swivel chair, removed his glasses, and looked kindly at Julie. "Your baby is fine. The blood in her vomit is from irritation in the lining of her throat. You need to settle down, maybe have a glass of beer. It will be easier for Christina to nurse that way, and easier on you." Dr. Johnson made a few notes on his clipboard.

I know I was sleeping, but am I hearing you right? Do you know what damage alcohol has done in my life? "Doctor, I'm relieved that Christina's okay. Hopefully we won't see each other again unless it's at a party!"

"Deal." Dr. Johnson patted Julie's shoulder, rubbed Christina's head, and walked out. Julie was overcome by embarrassment and relief. This was not how she pictured her first mother-daughter outing, but at least she found out that she was up to the challenge. For today, that was enough. She drove home and laid Christina down for a nap. Mother and daughter slept for five hours – the longest stretch of uninterrupted sleep since Christina's birth.

The outing to Hot'n Cold General Store never happened. Over the next several weeks, Julie and Christina visited Dr. Johnson at least once a week. Julie was usually convinced that Christina was dying from a variety of childhood ailments. The green machine navigated itself to the clinic while Julie agonized through all the possible scenarios of Christina's impending death. She never experienced more than a cold, congestion, or an ear infection, while Julie suffered from an acute case of affirmation starvation. In her high-alert level of stress, she had only the minimum daily requirement of energy to make it through twenty-four hours. Emma still showed up at Julie's door every morning armed with cinnamon rolls and ready to start the coffee pot – but Julie turned her away more and more often. She was simply too tired to be loved.

Christina's colic decreased while Julie's sleep increased to six hours a night. On a Monday morning a week before Christmas, Julie – full of remorse for sending Emma away every day – surprised that gentle soul by inviting her to stay for seven o'clock coffee. Emma graciously accepted Julie's invitation, acting as if it were a normal occurrence rather than one that had been interrupted by months of distress in Julie's life.

Tom faded from Emma's dinner table – and from Julie's, as well. She had learned to cook basic casseroles, set the table, wait, watch game show reruns while the food stayed warm in the oven, nurse Christina, put her down for the night, and finally give in to her hunger pangs. She would then wash her plate, leave the other one on the table and go to bed, all the while wondering if, and when, Tom would come home.

Julie determined to stay married. She had no skills, no job, and no way to support herself. She was not going to end up like her mom – who, Julie thought, could leave that horrible excuse for a husband – for a human being – if she worked hard, saved her money, and carved out her own place in the world. For Julie, there were no do-overs. She could not go to Arlene for financial or babysitting help. Her mom lived thirty miles away and made it clear that she raised her kids and was not about to be tied down with grandkids.

The noose was tightening. It was merely a question of who, or what, would finish the knot.

CHAPTER 19
SLEEPLESS IN MICHIGAN

Julie was in a tug-of-war between Christina and her marriage. One side promised joy, the other, helplessness. Looking out her bedroom window as she rocked Christina, Julie's battle was reflected in the changeable early April weather. Some days brought the promise of spring hovering in the air as temperatures neared fifty, beckoning people to page through catalogues advertising Burpee seeds, barbecue grills, and patio furniture. Other days, winter regained its authority by freezing recently melted snow into hazardous patches of ice. Low-hanging clouds waited to dump wet snow on people who had packed away their warm clothes prematurely.

Several weeks had passed since Julie's last visit to the clinic. She was finally convinced that Christina's bouts of cold and flu were the stuff of normal babyhood; and she was learning how to care for her baby. Her body had healed from the breech birth. She fit into pre-baby clothes and did not have to dress for breast feeding.

When nausea hit, Julie relaxed. She was bound to get the occasional flu bugs that hit Christina. Tom never seemed to get sick, but he was never home long enough to catch anything from them.

The nausea continued for over a week. This time, she had no reason to take Christina to see Dr. Johnson but wondered if he might be willing to give *her* a check-up. After all, she reasoned, he should be an adult doctor as well as a pediatrician, and she was comfortable with him.

Julie held tightly to Christina's infant seat as she pulled open the door against the wind-whipped snow. The antiseptic smell inside the clinic intensified her nausea. Although she wanted to be here, she had an increased sense of fear and dread. *What if something terrible is wrong with me? People get cancer and other life-threatening illnesses, even mothers of babies.*

The familiar waiting room felt like home to Julie and was intentionally decorated for the safety and enjoyment of toddlers. Three of the walls were covered with brightly painted murals of animal babies and human babies frolicking together. The fourth wall proudly displayed a magazine rack mounted high enough to be out of reach of tiny hands and boasted magazines like "Parenting." Mothers whose children were well behaved handed out "Highlights" magazines like candy. Some overworked mothers – maybe all of them – were glad for a chance to share moments of uninterrupted adult conversation.

Julie thought for the hundredth time that this room would do far better at meeting their needs if there were a coffee pot and "Newsweek" or "Time" or "Reader's Digest." She peeled off her coat, ski hat and gloves and distractedly unwrapped the layers bundling her precious baby. The room was inviting and pleasant, and if Julie's nausea would settle down, she would gladly sit in this comfortable warmth for as long as it took for her name to be called.

After a routine check-up and a pleasant chat with Dr. Johnson, Julie was left alone in a room with animal murals on the walls. While Christina cooed and babbled and smiled, Julie's head drooped forward onto her chest. Soon she dreamed of a knocking sound. Drowsily pulling her head back into wakefulness, she saw the door open cautiously and a nurse tiptoe into the room.

"Mrs. Dietrich, I have wonderful news for you. You're not sick at all – you're pregnant!" The nurse's face broke into a grin reaching the tops of both ears, clearly enjoying this part of her job.

Julie covered her face and burst into tears. *Ohmigod, what have I done?* The startled nurse reassured her that everything would be all right. *No. Everything will not be all right. I don't even know what all right is. But whatever it is, it is not my life.* Julie scooped up Christina and the diaper bag and walked back into the waiting room, avoiding eye contact with the other mothers. She threw on her jacket and forgot to zip it, quickly dressed Christina, and sprinted out of the clinic. The snow turned to sleet, pelting against her face like sharpened needles, mixing with Julie's tears and freezing her face and spirit into numbness.

Emma Lynn Dietrich was born during a January snowfall when Christina was sixteen months old. Emma was an easy baby, one described as normal in all the child development books. Julie whispered a word of thankfulness to God and crossed her fingers behind her back, covering all the bases in the game of faith and luck.

Casting a wide net to pull in sufficient resources for her baby girls was Julie's daily challenge. Tom gave her fifteen dollars a week to cover groceries, diapers, clothes, and all other needs. *I hope he enjoys the planet he's living on, because fifteen bucks on earth buys a cup of coffee, a tube of toothpaste, a package of diapers, and Spam.* Mayor Kenney, owner of the Hot'n Cold, helped by extending credit to the Dietrichs during the winter months when Tom had fewer hours at work. If the grocery credit was paid up by the end of the month, Tom and Julie went out to the bar for a beer and a soda.

With the coming of spring, Emma taught Julie how to plant a garden and promised to teach her how to can vegetables when they came in. Julie also learned how to bake bread and sew her own clothes – things she had started to learn from Mama T. With some creativity and determination Julie knew she could provide for her family on a shoestring. But she wanted to own the whole shoe.

Fairview State Hospital, built in 1937, was a well-ordered, sprawling compound of red brick cottages and buildings with two, three, and four stories, all connected by walkways and tunnels. The largest and most imposing of the structures was the central building, the only one that boasted concrete steps leading up to a wide portico flanked by four enormous granite columns. The hospital complex was set back a distance from the highway; even from afar, those columns drew admiring eyes up the gradually narrowing edifice to the copper-topped cupola towering over the grounds in a proclamation of good will.

Driving across Coldspring River, Julie often stared at the beautiful, majestic hospital and meticulously manicured grounds, wondering what went on in those buildings. When she finally decided to test the waters by asking Tom what he thought about her trying to work there, he told her she was too stupid to pass a job placement test. Anywhere. *Okay, Miss Meyer, someday I'll show you what I can do.*

The January blahs that had hovered over Julie since her teen years were still a part of her emotional DNA. She decided to fight the depression, bundle up her daughters, drop them off at Grandma Emma's and check out job openings at the hospital. An older woman at Hot'n Cold used to tell Julie about her years working in maintenance at that hospital; how the basement was a labyrinth of tunnels opening into storage rooms with antique furniture, outdated, fiendish-looking medical equipment, and coffins in the abandoned morgue. It all sounded far more intriguing to Julie than her view of the cans of Campbell's soup on the back shelves of the store.

New snow covered the shrubs around the hospital in a layer of whipped cream, chasing away the apprehension that threatened Julie's resolve. By the time she walked across the wide parking lot, she determined to make a change in her life.

The central building looked like the best place to start. Julie walked up the steps and through the door, craning her neck back to admire the twenty-foot ceiling and the massive white pillars spaced throughout the sun-drenched lobby. Feeling like she was somehow defacing the marble floor with her snowy boots, Julie stopped at the information desk and stomped her feet on a rubber rug, then asked all the necessary questions to obtain an application. *There's no reason to tell Miss Meyer what I did today. I probably won't be called back for an interview anyway.* Julie finished the application, gave it to a pleasant woman at the desk, and drove back home feeling like she'd left some of her blahs at the hospital.

A week and a half later, Julie received a phone call from someone in Personnel at the hospital, asking to set up an interview for Human Services Technician. Julie also heard about a woman named Miriam Evans who ran a daycare a mile from her trailer, and who was willing to charge just a dollar twenty-five an hour for

211

both daughters! Things were heading in a hopeful direction.

CHAPTER 20
THE HOUSE THAT TOM BUILT

Human Services Tech was a forty-hour-a-week position. Motherhood added sixty. Cooking, cleaning, tending a vegetable garden and splitting wood consumed another forty. The sleep balance in the weekly ledger was four hours a night. The lines that separated hours from days, days from weeks, and weeks from months crisscrossed into a web threatening to entangle Julie and swallow her few remaining functional parts. Tom was caught in a tug-of-war between drinking buddies and home.

Grandma Emma unknowingly pulled on Tom's rope. "Tomboy." Emma wrapped her hands around a cup of black coffee, sitting across the table from Tom as Julie sprang up to close the windows of the trailer against the late fall air, chilly and damp, pursued by the wintery wind racing down from the north. Storm windows rattled as Julie wondered how much longer the four of them would survive in this sardine can without becoming airborne.

Julie poured coffee for her and Tom and sat down next to him across from Grandma, who tucked a loose strand of coarse gray hair back under her babushka, as she called her headscarf.

"I haf a gift for you. There has a farm been in my family since mine fater owned it, und his fater before him." Julie never tired of the charm in Emma's convoluted English. "It's a forty-acre farm in Kale, down road from vere you are, and I vould like you to haf it. You can build nice haus on it for your family."

213

Maybe Tom will be home more now. We can be a real family and I can live in a real house that I own. Julie dropped her head on the table and cried, releasing tears of fatigue and relief.

Tom spent the winter cutting trees, clearing an area for the house, and then hauling the trees to the sawmill. During the following spring and summer, while the boards air dried, Tom designed the house, hired a well digger, removed rocks, and poured the concrete foundation. The boards were planed during a warm, dry autumn, and Tom used every spare minute to build before the snow flew.

On a cold, crisp Saturday in early November, Julie drove through Kale – a modest looking town of seventy-one people living on neat farms with flower beds and miniature lighthouses along the road, railroad tracks bordering the back of their land. Pick-up trucks parked in the front yards were stocked with hay bales and gun racks. *I bet they raise Cain here along with the cattle.* Tucked in a knoll at one end of town were two churches whose front doors faced off across a dirt road. St. Andrew's had peeling wood siding, new oak doors painted forest green, and a third-story bell tower. St. Luke's had new white siding, cross inserts in the door windows, and a fieldstone lamppost guarding the front steps. Spruce trees showing no denominational preference grew freely on both sides of the road and in the churchyards.

Julie slowed down as she passed the churches and assumed that one was Lutheran, the other, Catholic. *This is Michigan – it's a good guess.* The towering spruces protected the churches, and Julie wondered if her new house would protect her from—*what?*

214

I can't believe I did the Kale tour seven months ago and that I've been married five years today. I'm still waiting for something special to happen in my life.

Julie shook off her pensive mood and laughed at her daughters playing in the inflatable wading pool like puppies tumbling over each other. The trailer was way too small and hot to stay in any longer than necessary. Being outside in the scorching heat without any shade was not much better, except that the open space kept Julie from wanting to gnaw off her leg. Tom promised they would move into their new house by early July, and Julie convinced herself that having more room would fix the problems in their marriage. *Click my heels together. Say, "there's no place like home," and open my eyes in my dream house.*

Tom and Julie took their girls and celebrated their anniversary with dinner at McDonald's and a drive to their split-level house. Tom stayed outside and played with his daughters on the swing set while Julie wandered through the rooms imagining all the decorating she would do. The kitchen counters would be reddish-orange and the walls would be paneled in dark tongue-and-groove walnut. Scandinavian teapots and plates and trivets would be displayed on shelves and special hangers. The dining room would have cream and tan wallpaper with a fern design. The three bedrooms would be decorated to match the personalities of the occupants. Everything in the house would be the best and classiest in country-living-on-a-budget.

Even the christening meal was planned way ahead of time: fried chicken, home-made biscuits with freezer strawberry jam, real mashed potatoes with sour cream, and iced tea. And not a Spamloaf in sight.

Tom's buddies unloaded the last of the boxes at

the new house, followed by a celebratory trip to the bar and activity that kept them there until closing time. The deliverymen had set up the new bed three days earlier; and with her bedroom door closed against the happy screeches of her daughters and a blanket thrown across the window to keep the room dark, Julie stayed in bed nursing a migraine while Emma drove over to take care of all three of her girls. Julie hoped the violent headaches and migraines, resurfacing early in her marriage, would stay back at the trailer – but they found her at the new house. When Emma suggested that her friends at First Evangelical Free Church could help relieve Julie's stress and "achy head problem," Julie was willing to try anything and agreed to go to church with Grandma.

The EV Free church was five miles outside Kale city limits. Within three months of Julie, Christina and Emma attending, Julie had earned the nickname, "Shake-n-bake." Her chicken casseroles, yeast rolls, cracked wheat bread and cinnamon buns were in demand for every wedding and funeral and potluck. When Tom cycled through his drinking binges, Julie was up late waiting for bread dough to rise instead of feeling her blood boil.

CHAPTER 21
DANCING TOO CLOSE
TO THE FLAME

Stress would certainly evaporate in a new house. But Julie soon discovered that little girls and household chores were messy, unpredictable, and left no margin of error. Whatever else happened, control – for Julie – had to outrun chaos, which meant working five days a week at the hospital, making meals from scratch, planting and weeding and harvesting her garden, canning the produce, splitting wood for heat, baking bread and rolls, and collapsing into delirium-filled sleep for three or four hours before the madness started again.

Patients who bit, spit and hit without warning constantly challenged the control Julie craved at the hospital. Order came from organizing and filing reports, ridding the floor of feces and cleaning windows.

Persistent headaches dangerously thinned the edges of Julie's sanity. Home chores were non-negotiable; but she thought a job change might bring some relief. *If I don't find something else to do soon, I'll be sharing a room with one of the patients.*

Tom's sister Sharon had been accepted into beauty school. *This is what I've been looking for.* She thought back to all those times when her mom sat her on a stool and whacked off her hair in an offense against good taste. With beautician's training, she could style her daughters' hair to look like dolls; they would save money on haircuts; her hair would always look right; and she would work well with the clients. Everyone who

217

came to her shop would want their hair precisely styled a particular way, and she could do it.

"Tom." Julie scurried around the kitchen cleaning up the supper dishes while the girls played in the living room. *Tom is home, sober, and maybe even agreeable.*

"Hmm?" Tom was lost in "The Dukes of Hazard."

"Sharon is going to beauty school." Julie scraped plates of half-eaten spaghetti into plastic storage containers.

"Yeah, so?" Tom got up, walked over to the TV, cranked up the volume and sat back down on the end of the couch.

"I was thinking that I might like to do that too," Julie yelled from the kitchen as she sealed the lids on the containers and popped them into the fridge.

"Yeah."

"The tuition is less than a thousand." Julie stood over a sink of hot, sudsy water, beads of sweat dripping down her face.

Tom got back up, turned off the TV and watched the screen fade to black. He turned to Julie.

Here it comes.

"What have you been drinking? We don't have that kind of money. I need a tractor and other equipment to get this farm up and running." Tom fell back on the couch and picked up a magazine from the local farm and fleet store to emphasize his point.

Julie had him in the crosshairs. "Everything is always about you, isn't it? This house is *your* dream; you never asked me to help you design it. You don't have any idea what I want!" Julie plunged the dishrag into the water and stormed out of the room, shaking her

218

hands over her head as she left.

Her pastor had preached many sermons on the husband being the authority of the home; whatever he did was supposed to be supported by the wife. What Julie heard was, "You need to do anything and everything your husband wants." *Blah, blah, blah. I am not doing it anymore.*

Julie dropped her daughters at Miriam's and drove to the hospital thinking about the heap of manure her life had become. The stench was getting to her, and she wished someone would come along and shovel out the mess. *I have lost my glass slipper. And I'm at the wrong end of the horse.*

At morning break time, June Harrison walked up to Julie wearing a bemused smile and carrying a mug of coffee and a Hershey's bar. She held out both hands to Julie. "You look rattled. Want to pick your poison?"

June had a knack for showing up when Julie needed her. *Why haven't I ever realized how much she reminds me of Glo?* "I'll take both."

June sat across from Julie at a small, white, metal table. "Julie, would you like to come to a prayer group some of us are starting? No pressure. If you would like us to pray for you, we would do that." June fumbled through her purse for a notebook and pen.

"No. I mean yeah; I don't want you to just pray for me. I want to go with you. When and where will it be?"

June set her purse aside and looked intently at Julie. "The first one will be tomorrow at six-thirty right here, and then probably every Friday morning after that."

"I'll be here." Julie crumpled up her candy

wrapper, tossed it into the garbage can, put her coffee mug in the sink, and headed back to work.

"Thank You, Lord," whispered June.

A dozen people had gathered at six-twenty the next morning when Julie walked in.

"Hey, Julie, glad you could make it."

"I'm not sure why I'm here. I've never prayed out loud before—"

"And you don't need to if you don't want to. We are here to help each other, to grow together. We all struggle with jealousy and resentment and anger and gossip. We pray so that we can ask God to take those things from us and make us into the people He wants us to be. Some of us will pray out loud and others will follow those prayers silently."

"That's a relief, June. I'll be one of the silent ones."

"Cool."

Julie got a cup of coffee and sat next to June. "Can I ask you something?"

"Shoot."

"How did you get here?"

"You mean—"

"To wherever you are in your life?"

"I'll give you the Cliff Notes version now, and someday when we've got more time, I'll give you the whole story."

Julie laughed.

"My dad was an alcoholic."

"*Was?*"

"He died ten years ago from cirrhosis of the liver."

"Sorry."

"Don't be. By the end of his life, he had made himself right with God and it was a blessing that he didn't keep living in constant pain."

"Oh."

"When I was twenty-five years old, I realized that I had spent my childhood feeling out of control. When I became an adult, I tried to compensate for it by being obsessed with perfectionism. I drove everyone crazy. I was very unhappy. I didn't feel like I could trust any man, including the one I was married to."

Maybe there are people rowing in my boat after all. "What changed?"

"A deeply caring and brutally honest friend told me that I wasn't a little girl anymore. Regardless of my childhood, I had a will that needed to bend toward God just like everyone else in the world. I hid behind perfectionism and resentment and righteous anger – but God saw me as someone who needed the forgiveness He offers all of us."

One of the older men in the group broke into the conversations and asked them "to come together now that so that we don't fall apart later." A short time of sharing illnesses and financial needs, emotional struggles and praises was followed by a longer time, the most vulnerable praying Julie ever heard. When a younger gal prayed for the strength to love a father who did not deserve it, Julie's mind drifted back to Bret's talk. *Didn't he say God was a perfect Father? I've tried this long enough on my own, God – Abba – it's time for me to find my way to You. I'm sure You can do a better job with my life than what I've done.*

Prayer time ended. The group headed for the time clock to punch in and begin their shifts. Julie felt wrapped in peacefulness, seldom experienced in her

221

life, especially as an adult. She would be at the next prayer meeting.

Church was different for Julie, as she listened to the pastor's sermons with a new attitude. The next time he preached on the women of the congregation honoring their husbands as though they were honoring Christ, Julie determined to try it. She knew that her stony heart needed softening; and if she focused on that, then it was God's business to work on Tom's words and attitude.

Maybe Tom would settle down and become a better husband and father if he had a son. Julie knew Tom's number one dream: to pass down their farm owned by the one person who had ever created good memories for him. *I can do this for Tom. It's totally in Your hands, God. This is all new to me; but I believe – I want to believe – that You know what's best for me, for us.*

Oblivious to the lengthening days and robust smells of the beautiful spring morning in early May, Julie shifted into autopilot as she opened the door to the hospital's employee entrance. *My feet need rest. Did I really want to be pregnant again? How long until lunch? I'm already starving.* At eleven-thirty, she navigated through the accumulation of male patients – many of whom were social misfits from the fourth floor Chemical Dependency Unit – forming a broken line in the second-floor cafeteria. All patients were expected to step aside and make room for employees on their half-hour lunch breaks. Julie had finally gotten used to the catcalls, gestures, and recent additions of poking and rubbing her growing belly. *The presumed mating activities of the species.*

Reaching for a plastic tray, Julie was at the head of the line when she received a sharp crack on her backside. Reeling around, she faced a man slightly taller than she, with greasy looking, graying hair and an unkempt beard.

"Hey, Sandyford, who's the hot chick?" The bystander smirked as the guys around him whistled and yelled.

"This ain't no chick!" The whistles grew louder. "This's my kid!"

Julie stood in paralyzing horror. *That son-of-a ... why is he here?* Evading Danny's outstretched arm, Julie ran out of the cafeteria, eyes burning in tears of anger and shame, and collided with her supervisor. Grabbing her arm and dragging her into a nearby conference room, Julie slammed the door behind them.

"Jennifer, do *not* give out any information about me to Danny Sandford – not where I live, anything about my girls, my life, or my home ... not even about my car ... nothing." She left Jennifer retrieving her jaw from the floor while she found the office for her next filing assignment. Her hunger would wait.

The crudest male patients moved on to other female targets of ridicule, but Julie could not avoid Danny during her daily duties. He often looked at her with an unreadable expression and without attempting conversation. Although patient records were confidential, their bragging let staff in on more than they really wanted to know. Grapevine news traveled quickly about Danny, mainly that he had had three DUIs and faced either jail time or ninety days in detox.

Danny sat alone at a table farthest from the vending machines. Julie approached him, dropped her tray on the table and glared at the broken looking man sitting hunched over his lunch. *God, I do not want to feel sorry for him.*

"What was up with Grandma Hagstrom?" Small talk was unnecessary.

Danny looked up at Julie, his face registering no surprise at her out-of-the-blue question. "Leona was no mom. My family told me all about her." He stabbed a glob of congealed macaroni and cheese with a bent fork.

Julie sat down across from him and opened her carton of milk.

"She slept around, married some guy, shacked up with someone else, kept sleeping around, and her old man died when I was six months old." Danny set his fork down and pushed his tray aside.

"Where did you and Leona go after that?"

"God only knows where she went. I was juggled between an aunt and uncle, a grandma, and friends. They all told me I had cute hair and I was a happy baby – but they were all a bunch of drunks."

Have you looked in a mirror lately? Julie sighed. And waited. "How come Grandma came to live with us?"

"Beats me. Your mom invited her – felt sorry for her or something. We didn't know she was going batty—"

"Which explains why I overheard Mom say she had 'awful hard arteries,' and that she was 'looney.' She must have had hardening of the arteries and could have used some real help."

"I wasn't going to do anything for her."

"But why did you let her babysit Dan and me? Most of the time she was passed out on the couch while we did guerilla warfare. You never knew that we

224

drowned every turtle we had in the toilet."

Danny chuckled.

"It was like 'Cuckoo's Nest' around there." Julie shook her head, got up, left her food untouched on her tray and walked away.

Danny left Fairview cleaned up, sober, and connected to an AA chapter. He earned his sobriety pin, regained his license from the Steamfitters Union, reclaimed his old job, and went looking for Arlene. Julie guessed her mom was in serious financial trouble or emotional trouble – or both – to open her door to him.

"So, your dad—"

"*Danny*—" Julie crooked the phone under her chin as she washed dishes.

"Whatever. He says, 'C'mon, babe, let's put the past behind us. I'm different now, changed, and my life's good. I can give you the stuff you've always wanted.'"

Isn't that what it was always about anyway – your stuff? No good can come of this.

Danny wore down Arlene's defenses and arguments in one month. They rented an apartment together and remarried on a blustery day a week before Christmas.

CHAPTER 22
ENCORE

Christina and Emma had been given unique names. Julie dug in her heels against any second-generation Julie or Tom, Arlene or Danny.

"Oh, baby," Tom pleaded. "If we have a son, please let me name him after me. That's all I've ever wanted." Julie caved, hoping to weave a thread of peace into their marriage. Their son, Tom Allen, was born on a bright January morning a few months before Julie's twenty-fifth birthday. She had access to maternity leave and stayed home with all three kids. *Tom might not approve, but he's got his namesake, so we'll both be happy. And my baby boy will always be Tom-Tom to me.*

The Dietrich home was shrouded in calm for three months after Tom-Tom's birth. Even the clouds cooperated by thoughtfully releasing huge flakes of snow, which Julie loved to watch while rocking her baby in the nursery. She stared at the yellow ducks on the wallpaper border against the pastel blue walls, and at the stuffed teddy bear sitting on the refinished, painted dresser. *I am really a mother,* Julie mused, with a contentment not experienced after the births of both daughters. Endless days were spent in the house playing dolls with Christina and Emma as they watched their new little brother make faces and smile. Sometimes Julie's daughters wrapped their protective arms around Tom-Tom and her heart flooded with a new love for all three of these blessings. *I can do this mothering thing in a family unlike what I had. Words will be kind and love*

226

will fill the rooms. Tom came home every night for dinner with a light in his eyes and a hug for all of them.

A March thaw left muddy ruts behind slogging tires. Mounding snow melted into clumps of grass, road sand, candy wrappers, and fast-food containers. Julie's joy was buried under piles of diapers and unpaid bills – *both stinky.* A nagging feeling of uselessness gnawed around the edges of her contentment.

Tom's attentiveness also waned as he was drawn back to the bar and his buddies. An April Fool's Day trip to town for a quick beer ended three hours later with Tom barreling into their backyard riding a John Deere tractor.

A John Deere cap? Forget about it! Julie had the trap baited when Tom entered the mud room, bent over, and untied his boots.

"I quit work to stay home and take care of our kids. How much did you pay for the tractor? How can we afford it? Why wasn't there money for me to go to beauty school?" Julie shifted her baby in her arms and patted his back with the intensity of her rising anger.

Tom hurled his boots into the corner, rose, and glared at Julie. "I make all the money. I can do anything I want with it! I'm not going to stand here and listen to any more from you! I'm hitching a ride back to the bar where I left my truck. Don't wait up for me."

Julie turned in time to see her daughters peeking around the corner at her, eyes filled with tears. She reined in her rage, wanting desperately to protect her children from the anger and abuse that had defined her childhood. Setting Tom-Tom in an infant seat, Julie told her girls to find their dolls. She ran into the kitchen and pulled the church directory out of a drawer, picked up the phone with trembling fingers and dialed her pastor's home number.

"Pastor." Julie was getting good – *too good* – at skipping small talk. "Tom bought a tractor and we have absolutely no money to pay for it. We're up to our eyeballs in debt." Julie wasn't sure what pastors were used to hearing, but she didn't figure this was a time for sanitizing the truth. The vultures were circling.

"Julie." Pastor Hines cleared his throat. "Tom was the one who bought the tractor. It's up to him to figure out how to pay for it. It's his responsibility. God will make a way through this for you. You can trust Him on behalf of your whole family."

I wish I could tell you that my faith has replaced my worry. I'm afraid worry is winning this battle. "Okay, well, thanks." Julie hung up as her girls came into the kitchen dragging plastic crates full of dolls and doll clothes. *After seven years of marriage, our house is still cluttered with second-hand furniture, and the only reason our kids have decent clothes is because I sew everything. And yet we own a new tractor and chain saw. Something is messed up somewhere. God, are You still paying attention?*

The fierce storm howled over Lake Michigan, bringing gale force wind and rain that pounded against trees, houses, and cars. The temperature dropped to thirty-two degrees, icicles transformed trees and power lines into chandeliers, and Mother Nature became a diamond-bedazzled, treacherous woman. People stood at their windows watching branches crack and topple – sometimes in slow motion – and it was another twenty-four hours before they ventured out to view the damage. When the temperature rose, falling ice chunks littered the ground like shattered glass.

Power was restored to most homes within a week, and Julie's anger melted with the ice. When Tom suggested a five-mile drive to visit his Aunt Lucille and Uncle John, Julie jumped at the chance for a family outing, thinking maybe this was God's way of giving Tom the soft heart she so desperately wanted for herself.

Nothing as epic as a tractor purchase stayed a secret in Kale. John and Lucille knew about the tractor without knowing how angry Julie had been because of it. When she showed up at their door with dark circles under her eyes, they assumed the cause was full-time mothering fatigue. John's foolproof cure for all ailments was a glass of his homemade plum wine. Julie hadn't had any alcohol for a long time and was ready for something sweet and maybe a bit spirit-numbing.

Julie consumed wine and a glass of homemade German beer by the end of round one of small talk. She was so starved for adult conversation and her husband's attention that she was oblivious to glass after glass set before her – piña coladas, Brandy Sevens, and wine. It had been a long time since she felt this good, laughed this much, and had Tom's arm around her. Julie stayed glued to the couch while Tom regularly got up to check on the girls, who fell asleep on the rug in the den; and on baby Tom-Tom, who slept in an old playpen, last used by John and Lucille's children.

It was after midnight when Julie tried unsuccessfully to read the numbers on her watch. "Tom, I think it's time to go, don't you?" Julie laughed uproariously.

Tom was barely tipsy. "Yeah, it's almost one. You stay here and I'll get the kids settled in the car."

"Okay, José." Julie smiled and fell back on the

couch while Tom's aunt and uncle tiptoed out of the room. Tom brought Julie's jacket to her, helped her into it, picked her up, and got her settled in the car. Another storm had dumped heavy, wet snow on fallen trees not yet cleared from the ice storm. The ten-minute drive home took forty-five minutes. By the time they pulled into their driveway, Julie had passed out. Tom shut off the engine and left the keys in the ignition, got out and raced around to Julie's side, lifted her out and carried her into the house and upstairs. He plunked her down on the floor outside the bathroom. He then quickly ran back down and out to the car, cradled a girl in each arm and fought the wind as he took them into the house and left them on the living room sofa. He ran back out again, unbuckled Tom from his car seat, and heard his daughters screaming even before he opened the front door. There, at the bottom of the stairs, lay Julie in a heap, hood pulled over her head, mumbling and groaning. Tom handed his son to Christina and knelt beside his wife.

"Tried to crawl ... bathroom ... wrong way ... dark ... stairs ..." Tom checked for signs of broken bones, sprains, or bruises. Julie tried to sit up, rubbed her elbow, hiccupped, belched, and went limp.

"Listen, Gumby, you're not going anywhere." Tom gently lifted his wife and carried her back upstairs.

"I'm notta rolla sod."

Tom laid Julie tenderly on their bed, then went back downstairs, calmed his daughters, and tucked all three children into bed. As soon as he collapsed into bed and fell instantly asleep, Julie got up and stumbled to the bathroom, which is where he found her when he awoke to the wailing of his son an hour later. Tom coaxed Julie awake long enough to nurse their baby while he helped her sit up on the cold tile floor. The girls awoke when the sun was high in the sky; Tom-Tom had slept twelve hours. When he needed to be nursed again, Tom brought him to Julie, who had managed to crawl back to bed. She was in a state of near panic at the thought of killing her baby with all the alcohol he had absorbed through her milk.

The next three days were a blur. Vaguely aware of being spoon-fed soup, Julie wondered, as consciousness gradually returned, how skin could hurt so much. When her mother showed up to help with the kids, Julie thought she was hallucinating. *I must be looking in a side view mirror, since my mom is closer than she usually appears.*

CHAPTER 23
STORM CLOUDS

The alcohol burned out of her system, leaving a residue of loneliness in Julie's spirit. Women from church were kind and encouraging, but none had been let into the vault of her soul, a place largely unknown even to her. Julie had not returned to work and deeply missed June and the others from the Friday morning prayer group. Tom's attentiveness faded within a week of Julie's drinking episode; and as much as she loved her children, a connection was still missing.

Jamie Anders. I'd forgotten all about her. I would never have made it through my senior year without our daily home room talks. Marriage and jobs and babies had led Julie and Jamie in different directions; but Julie thought they could easily reconnect. Julie needed it, even if Jamie didn't.

A quick call to Miriam Evans to arrange an afternoon of day care, a hasty gathering of toys, extra clothes, and a diaper bag, and Julie was on her way. Three kids were settled in the car and dropped off at Miriam's, after which Julie's car seemed to know it was destined for Jamie's house. She had nothing to lose.

Deep purple thunderclouds heaped on the horizon. There was no time for a side trip to K-Mart to buy a purse-size umbrella. *That is a next time trip.* Julie pulled into Jamie's driveway twenty minutes later as her windshield wipers swiped at warp speed. Lightning flashed around the darkening sky in spontaneous outbursts of power. Julie had always been mesmerized by thunderstorms, strangely calming during her childhood, as if they overpowered the chaos in her family.

Julie opened her car door against horizontal, driving, hot sheets of July rain. Anticipating instant drenching, she tilted her head back and yelled, "Bring it on!" She walked to the front door, flung it open, hopped inside and closed the door behind her, rain cascading off her clothes over the tiled entryway.

"Yo! Jamie!" Julie shouted above the storm. "It's me, Julie Dietrich – Julie Sandford! Are you home?" Julie stood still and listened, feeling foolish for not calling ahead.

A television set clicked off, and a tall gal wearing cut-off denim shorts and a t-shirt that said, "If a Finn marries a Greek, you have a Freak," entered the room. All Jamie's friends knew they had an open invitation to come into her house without knocking or ringing the doorbell. Jamie reached back to tighten the rubber band around her high ponytail, her face lighting in recognition.

"Julie! Julie Sandford! How have you been, friend?" She ran up to Julie and wrapped her in a hug. Both girls laughed as Julie's clammy, wet clothes stuck them together.

"Get down with your bad self, girl!" Julie rattled off the line the two of them had always thrown at each other. They had been really tight for a short time, even discovering that Jamie's mom and Arlene were childhood friends.

"Jewel, let me find you dry clothes. As soon as I get back, I'll make coffee, and we'll raid the pantry for Mallow cups, like old times!" Jamie ran out of the kitchen, through the den and up the stairs.

Julie watched the rain beat against the kitchen

window and thought about the time she and Teddy had driven his Firebird through a car wash. *There must be a hole in the ozone – too many memories are getting through.*

Over the sound of the driving rain, Jamie heard a knock at the back door at the same time it pushed open. A man burst into the house like she had ten minutes earlier, with water dripping off his raincoat and puddling around his feet. His umbrella had lost a battle with the wind; the nylon dropped in defeat and the metal frame looked like spokes of a broken wheel. The man pulled down the hood of his jacket to reveal a full head of dark, wavy hair. His face was gentle, his complexion ruddy, and his eyes the deepest brown Julie had ever seen. He looked about six feet tall; his broad shoulders and full chest reminded Julie of one of those handsome heroes in the old war movies she loved to watch.

The stranger made a valiant effort to wipe his face with a soaked sleeve. As though the weather was of no consequence, he casually said, "Excuse me, is Jamie here?"

"Sure, hang on a minute and I'll go get her." Julie skipped out of the comfortable kitchen and into the living room to dig her bare toes into the shag carpeting. Despite the heat outside, she began to shiver from her wet clothes. She quickly ran upstairs, spotted a closed door, and took a chance that this was Jamie's bedroom. Knocking on the door and shouting, "Girlfriend, some man is here to see you," Julie sailed back downstairs, plopped onto a kitchen chair, and waited. The stranger stayed in the entryway; Julie ignored him and absentmindedly thumbed through a pile of magazines on the corner of the table.

Coming in armed with a pile of folded clothes,

Jamie stopped and stared, first at Julie, then at the man. Her eyes grew huge, and her normally light complexion turned several shades of red.

Glancing up from her magazine, Julie grew alarmed. "Jamie, what's the matter?"

Unaware of any unfolding drama, the man looked at Jamie and said, "How's it going with you, Jamie? And what about this weather? Barbie sent me over to ask if you'd like to go to dinner with us sometime this week."

"I'm not sure," stammered Jamie, as she collapsed onto a kitchen chair and hugged the clothes. She looked again at Julie and then at the man. "Have you two met?"

"We were waiting for you to do the formal introductions," joked Julie.

Struggling to keep her voice calm, Jamie introduced the man to her girlfriend. "Julie, this is Elliott. Elliott, this is Julie." Elliott muttered a hello, ducked his head, threw aside his useless umbrella, pulled his wet collar up to his ears, shrugged his shoulders, and opened the door. "Barbie and I will call you later, Jamie," he said as he was swallowed up by the storm and closed the door behind him.

Putting her head down on the table, Jamie choked back tears. "Oh, Julie, I am so sorry. I didn't know what to think, or say—"

"About what?" Julie was befuddled.

Jamie raised her head, looked at Julie through a blotchy, tear-streaked face, and yelled, "That was Elliott!"

"I know. You introduced us."

"You don't understand. Everyone calls him Elliott because his last name is Ness. You know, like

Elliott Ness in 'The Untouchables,' who chased Al Capone."

"That's funny. Why are you so upset?"

"Because his real name is Eugene – Eugene Ness, your biological father."

Julie's pulse exploded in her ears.

Jamie plunged ahead. "Don't you remember when I used to tell you about Eugene and Barb Ness, how they would come over and take me out to dinner, and how they would buy me presents for my birthday? They've been friends of my family for years. Eugene has always treated me like a daughter. I thought ... I thought ..."

Julie jumped out of her chair. "What? You thought *what*? You thought I knew this guy was my father? How the heck would I have known that? No one ever told me his last name!"

"You remember when we were at that YFC meeting, and I said, 'I'm sorry he abandoned you?' I was talking about Elliott. Eugene. I'm so sorry."

Julie grabbed her purse, hung the strap over her shoulder, and headed for the door. "Look, James, I've got to go. Let's stay in touch, OK?"

"Please don't be mad at me."

"I feel a lot of things. Disappointed. Bothered. Confused. Betrayed." She blew out a long breath. "But I'm not mad at you. It was never your responsibility to tell me about Eugene. I need time to figure this out. See you later." Julie opened the door and walked out into the storm, a perfect picture of her life. *How could that man stand in the kitchen and look at me and not tell me who he was or try to make any connection with me? And why has he treated Jamie like his daughter all these years?*

During the short drive to the daycare, Julie's

mind drove backwards to the first time she, her mom and her brother had made their midnight escape to Michigan. The day after they arrived, Grandpa and Grandma Cerbé took them out to Burger King with two old people who were introduced to Julie and Dan as Grandpa and Grandma Ness. Every Christmas in Michigan, the Sandfords, Cerbés, and Nesses were together. *How could my mom have done that to herself and to me? No wonder she always looked so uncomfortable. I figured she was comparing her clothes to the other ladies and didn't think she measured up. But this – I don't understand this at all. Where was Eugene all those times? Where were Eugene and Barbie? God, please help me.*

The kids were in bed and Tom had gone out looking for his drinking buddies. Julie collapsed on the couch and listened to the rain tap a steady rhythm on the roof. It was strangely satisfying to have the weather reflect her emotions.

Julie picked up the morning paper and flipped through the local news section, eventually reaching the obits at the back, where she experienced the second shock of the day. Teddy Tannenbaum had fallen asleep at the wheel and been killed by a grain truck driver.

Lord, please let this day be over.

CHAPTER 24
"GO WEST, YOUNG MAN"

Maybe she could kill her past if she choked the life out of it. Julie longed for the coming Christmas holiday to be different from her childhood; and as far as she knew, different from anything Tom had known, as well. A joy-robber typically rifled through her memories, leaving the collateral damage of sadness heaped across her spirit from mid-November to mid-January. This year, she needed to rob the robber and break its power. If Danny Sandford could act like a reasonable father and grandfather, then Julie would do the normal thing and invite her parents over for Christmas dinner. Since returning to work in September, Julie had worked whatever shifts she was given, and what loomed ahead was working graveyard on Christmas Eve. She would be home Christmas morning to pop a stuffed turkey in the oven and make all the fixings for a perfect holiday meal. Wrapped presents for her children were under the tree. Neither person nor gift would be abused in her home.

Tom sat at the kitchen table three days before Christmas, watching Julie put a hot dish into the oven. "Julie, that dad of yours – or I should say *Danny* – is a drunk."

Pot, meet kettle.

"I don't want him in my house. If you want him here, I'm gone."

Why am I pulling for the dark horse? Julie's wobbly voice exposed her confusion. "I'm not sure why I want to do this. I guess I feel like our kids deserve a grandpa like Grandpa Richard was to me. Or like Grandma Emma was – and still is – to you." *I will not let him out of my sight with our kids. One of these days I need to tell Tom what Danny did to me.*

Tom stared at the wall clock and breathed evenly. "Then I guess maybe I could stay. I've always gotten along okay with your mom. I sure can't figure out why she remarried that creepy guy, though."

Julie rolled up a dishtowel and threw it at Tom's head. "Heck if I know!"

"Hey!" Tom got up and grabbed Julie's shoulders, spinning her around. Julie threw her arms around Tom, the man who had promised to spend the rest of his life taking care of her.

"Come here, you." Julie led Tom back to the table and motioned for him to sit down. "I want to tell you a story I heard from my cousin Vicki."

"I didn't know you had a cousin Vicki."

"She's about twenty years older than we are. I haven't seen her since the first time we moved to Michigan. I forgot about her until she called me out of the blue last week."

"What'd she want?"

"I don't know – I think she just wanted to reconnect."

Tom got up, went to the fridge, popped open a can of beer and sat back down at the table.

God, please help him to stop drinking.

"So?"

"My family lived in houses and trailers that should have been condemned. Until we lived near the Andersons, I thought everyone lived like we did."

"This house must seem like a palace to you!"

"I am really grateful for it."

239

Tom drank the rest of the beer in one gulp. "I like it too."

"My mom always told me that we had to move because Danny was offered a better job somewhere – but Vicki knew that we moved because of evictions."

"That will never happen to us."

"It gets better. Apparently, Danny has a half-sister, Pat, who married a guy named Mac when she was only fourteen and he was fifteen!"

"No way!"

"Way! Pat and Mac divorced and remarried each other four times. Mac eventually made his fortune in construction, and then he and Pat bought a Caribbean island! Their finances probably helped buy Danny a get-out-of-jail free card a bunch of times."

"That's freaky. You got any more interesting relatives? How about rich ones?"

"I wish."

"Did Vicki say there would be any money coming our way?"

"Nada."

Christmas dinner was the first of many meals shared between the Sandfords and the Dietrichs during the next months. Christina, Emma, and Tom-Tom loved their funny and charming Pop-Pop. Arlene – Nana – usually distanced herself from Danny and her grandkids, saving her energy to stockpile her relentless criticisms of Julie's parenting and housekeeping for the day-after phone call.

Would Danny ever apologize for his hurtful words and grotesque actions during Julie's childhood? She knew there were times when Tom said or did something that triggered horrific memories in Julie; her response was a lashing out at him, until they both ended up confused and hurt. *The real target should be my children's grandfather.* Julie searched for ways to close the early chapters of her life.

"Julie, Danny's gone!" Arlene sobbed over the phone.

"What do you mean, *gone*? You were both here for dinner last night." Julie was rolling out dough for cinnamon rolls, and helping Christina with math homework, only half-listening to her mom over the sound of Pac-man coming from the living room.

"I mean, finnito. Vamoosed. When I got back from the mall, his clothes, his work boots – everything was gone."

I didn't even like the man, yet he managed to abandon me anyway, just like Eugene. "I'm sorry, Mom, but I need to go. Talk to you later." Julie hung up before being dragged into another conversation about what a wonderful husband Danny was.

She was not superstitious. But just to be safe, Julie considered climbing into bed and pulling the covers over her head on April Fool's Day – *another forgotten birthday.* It had been a year and change since Danny disappeared, and her mom seemed not only to accept it, but to enjoy the freedom of supporting herself. When Julie told her kids that their Pop-Pop was out on a grand adventure, they, too, accepted it with a resilience Julie had never felt as a child.

Julie promised her kids a fun, trick-free day at Nana's house and told herself that she would once-and-for-all let go of her ridiculous and irrational fears. As soon as her kids were settled with their toys and games,

241

Julie joined Nana at the table for a cup of coffee and a slice of homemade banana-nut bread. The ringing doorbell did not pull the women out of their comfortable state of lethargy until the persistent visitor rang three more times.

"I'm coming!" Arlene got up and stepped around several pairs of shoes on her way to the front door.

"Open up, Arlene. It's your old friend, Doug."

Arlene opened the door and smiled. "As I live and breathe, I never thought I'd see you again. Where's your partner, the Pillsbury Doughboy?"

Julie saw a worried look on Officer Seaver's face. "I wish I didn't have to do this." Doug gingerly placed an envelope in Arlene's hand.

"You want some coffee?" Arlene's voice trembled slightly.

"No, I've gotta run, thanks anyway." Doug turned and walked down the sidewalk.

Arlene opened the envelope, unfolded a thick pile of papers, stared at the top sheet, and dropped everything on the floor. "Doug, wait!" Officer Seaver turned around just as Arlene ran and vaulted herself into him, threw her arms around his neck and hugged the living daylights out of him. "Thank you!"

Julie ran to the front door, bent down, and picked up the papers. The top page was a summons for divorce proceedings.

"Mrs. Sandford," Doug gushed, "I've been doing this kind of work for twenty-five years and no one has ever thanked me!"

"At least I know that that worthless man is in Wyoming. I hope he stays there until he falls into the Grand Canyon."

It's time to find him. Julie tired of shouldering a hundred-pound burden of anger. The only way to get rid of it was to confront Danny. *"Do you know what you did to me all those years ago when you were drunk, or did you black out and forget everything? I wish I could black out. I've had to live with these memories for too many years. One of us must lay them down, and I'm willing to. I know you're not my biological dad, and I'm trying to forgive you for what you did."* Julie was ready to throw off the victim identity and pick up a new one – if only someone would tell her what that was.

Julie's plate was full of her children, her husband, and her job. When the frenetic activity slowed down, her anger towards Danny came up for air, followed by migraines. Sleep brought relief from the pain, but also brought nightmares in which she was trapped in a burning building, waiting to be rescued by Mr. O'Keefe or Mr. Thomas or Mr. Koski, or sometimes a dragon-like creature. This cycle of fighting and fleeing lasted a year and hijacked the energy Julie needed to pursue Danny out west.

May entered with a stretch of beautiful, clear mornings. Julie willed herself to recuperate quickly from a pulled back muscle so she could go back to work. A lilac-scented breeze drifted through the open windows; it was a day that made her simply glad to be alive.

Julie was startled out of her thoughts when a large man in a dark uniform filled the space in front of her screen door. She painfully rose from a reclining position on the couch and recognized the county sheriff.

"Oh, no," Julie muttered. "Did something happen to my husband?"

The sheriff spoke in an efficient and unemotional tone. "I'm looking for Julie Sandford."

Julie fought to keep her breakfast down. "That's me, but my name's not Sandford. It's Dietrich."

"Is your father's name Danny?" the sheriff replied in the same monotone.

"Yes, he is my adoptive father."

"I'm sorry to be the one to tell you this, but your father died March twenty-second, and you're the only next-of-kin we could track down."

"Did you try to contact my mother?" whispered Julie.

"Yes, we tried, but we did not have an address for her."

Julie sought refuge in trivia. "No, I guess you would not have known that after marrying and divorcing Danny for the second time, she changed her last name back to her maiden name, Cerbé."

"Can I come in?" Without waiting for a reply, the sheriff walked in, and over to Julie. He handed her an official-looking certificate and said, "I'm sorry to add to your grief, but your father is being cremated today."

Julie used information gathering as a shock absorber. Before the sheriff was out the door, she had picked up the receiver from the phone sitting on the end table and called four-one-one. The sheriff's last words were that Julie might be able to get some answers from the chief of police in Casper, Wyoming. *I wonder how much this call is going to cost me. Seems like I've spent my life paying the price for Danny's mistakes.*

Several different connections and thirty minutes later, Julie found Sergeant John Mollen. "My name is Julie Dietrich. I live in Michigan. My father, Danny

Sandford, died somewhere in Wyoming in March. Can you help me?"

"Hang on a minute. It's here somewhere." Julie heard rustling papers. "Here it is. Seems your dad was married to a Native American woman named Chondra."

"Does your report say when he was married?"

"Record show it was about a year and a half ago."

He was not legally divorced until a year ago. "Any idea where he worked?"

"Seems he worked construction jobs until he fell off a roof on a job site and broke his back. He got a two-hundred-thousand-dollar settlement."

My mom certainly never saw a dime of that money. Julie took a deep breath. "What happened to Danny?"

"He and Chondra were in some seedy motel—"

"Spending two-hundred thousand?"

"Who knows? You can blow through that kind of money fast if you want to. Anyways, the manager was doing his rounds to collect the week's rent. When he couldn't get an answer from Danny and Chondra, he opened the door with his key and found Danny lying on the floor next to the bed. The manager freaked out but still called nine-one-one. Ambulance got there in ten minutes. According to the M.E., Danny died twelve hours later in a local hospital. Autopsy showed acute alcohol blood poisoning resulting in septicemia and pneumonia. Report also says he looked like a concentration camp survivor."

"What happened to Chondra?"

"No one knows. I hope I don't see her name on another report from the M.E."

"Me either."

"Do you want the ashes sent to you?"

"No." Julie expressed her thanks and hung up. She lay back down on the couch and stared at the ceiling. *Living with an alcoholic father was like being handcuffed to a rattlesnake. I spent my life trying to avoid its bite until one day it slithered out and attacked itself with its own venom.* Julie pumped her fist in the air. "Yes, yes, yes! That creepy, horrible, despicable, nasty, awful man is never going to hurt me again. Ever! It's done! It's over!" Julie then sobbed uncontrollably as the sky tore open, drowning her house, her yard, and her soul in a flood of sympathy.

CHAPTER 25
CLOSED DOORS AND
UNOPENED WINDOWS

Depression moved in and lived in Julie's heart. Her friends assumed she felt vindicated by Danny's death, the ultimate what-goes-around-comes-around. She even used that phrase so she wouldn't disappoint them. *But I am still out of control. His death was the last one-upmanship. How am I going to win now?*

Julie arrived at work by six-twenty on Fridays to talk to June before prayer time started. When June shared how much her pastor had helped her deal with anger towards her father, Julie considered seeking the same kind of help. *I've been going to EV Free for a long time – past time to move out of the pew and formally meet Lance Johnson.*

Julie sat in an easy chair in the pastor's study early Saturday morning and measured her comfort level. One wall had built-in shelves holding unadorned hardcover books, a scale model of a red, classic Corvette convertible, a framed picture of a petite, blonde woman with a small boy, a sealed box of animal crackers, a stack of cassette tapes, a carved, wooden cross on a stand, and a pair of Sony headphones. The paneled walls displayed framed diplomas and certificates, and crayon drawings of praying hands, trees, and people. An older typewriter perched atop a metal desk defied modern technology. Julie relaxed and looked openly at her pastor.

"Pastor Lance, I have a friend who got help from

her pastor, and I was hoping you could do the same for me."

"I'm glad you came."

"You won't feel that way by the time I unload."

"My feelings won't matter; the Bible says we're supposed to help carry each other's loads."

"Mine've been weighing me down for too long." Julie rubbed the vinyl on the wide arm of the chair.

"Which load is the heaviest?"

She continued smoothing out invisible wrinkles. "The bucket of blame I've been lugging around since I was about eight."

Lance cupped his chin in his hand as his eyes opened wider in sympathy.

"And shame. Blame and shame."

Silence.

"Go on."

"My father hurt me. For years."

"How so?" Lance spoke softly.

"He called me ... bad stuff." Julie stared past Lance out the window behind him. *What if Mom finds out I'm here and accuses me of betraying the family?* "I'm not sure I should say any more."

"Everything you say here is confidential."

Julie shifted her focus back to Lance, who dropped his hand and rested it on his desk.

"I haven't had many men in my life I can trust."

"I'm sorry."

"I am, too." Julie crossed her ankles and looked down. "My father abused me ... and then left me."

"Was that a relief?"

"Yes." She shifted in her chair. "No."

Pastor Lance folded his hands on his desk.

"I've been damaged goods most of my life." Julie

248

uncrossed her ankles and straightened her sandal strap.

"Take your time."

"If I smoked, this would be a good time for a cigarette." Julie and Lance chuckled together.

"How about a cup of coffee?"

"Great."

"Be right back." As Lance walked around his desk, past Julie and out the door, she fought the urge to flee. *What if I'm opening a box I'll never be able to close again? What if I don't like what crawls out?* She leaned her head back, closed her eyes and remembered the time she sat in a chair like this in a waiting room, right before she got news that she was pregnant again. That was a frightening time for her but having Emma was a joy, and maybe something good would come of this time, too.

Lance came back with two Styrofoam cups. "Is black okay?" He handed a cup to Julie.

"That's the only way I like it. Thank you."

Lance sat back in his chair, took a sip of coffee, and turned sideways to look out the window. "June's a great month. Do you have a busy summer planned?"

"Working, raising kids, gardening, farming. 'Do it and get through it,' like my mom always said."

Lance swiveled his chair back around and faced Julie.

"Do you ever—"

"I feel like I'm trapped in a room with no inside handle on the door, no windows, and it's getting hard to breathe." *Maybe I'm saying too much. He probably just wanted to know if I take vacations or something. Stick to the questions, Julie.*

"I'd like to talk about your father."

"The … abuse?" Julie felt her face burning.

"Not if it's too hard for you."

249

Julie curled a section of her hair around her ear.

"I found out in high school that he wasn't my biological father. He adopted me when my mom married him."

"How old were you when that happened?"

"My biological father deserted my mom and me when I was three months old."

Lance wrinkled his eyebrows.

"You were abandoned by your real father, and then abused and abandoned again by your stepdad?"

"Yeah. Then my *adoptive* dad divorced my mom, remarried her after I got married, and left a year later without a forwarding address. Then I got news that he had died in Wyoming. I never had a chance to confront him about what he did to me, so I guess what was really abandoned was my hope for closure."

"This is a tangled story."

"Got that right."

"What did – what's your adoptive father's name?"

"Danny."

"What did Danny do to you?"

"What didn't he do?"

"Emotional abuse, verbal abuse, sexual abuse?"

"Yes, yes, and yes."

Lance released a loud sigh.

"Was there anyone who tried to protect you?"

"My mom's parents helped me out of some trouble. If they knew what Danny was really like, they never talked about it."

"Anyone else?"

"Danny's mom lived with us for a while when I was a kid, but she had all these confusing behaviors. I learned a few years ago that she was an alcoholic and suffering from some type of dementia."

Julie finished her coffee, tore off little pieces of Styrofoam, and dropped them into the cup.

"Julie?" Lance finished his coffee and waited for Julie to look at him. "How does your mom fit into the puzzle?"

Julie erupted in a derisive laugh. "That's a joke!" She crushed the rest of her cup and pitched it in the wastebasket. "I don't think I should have said that."

"There aren't any shoulds here. Please go on."

"My mom was – *is* – the most self-absorbed and co-dependent person I know."

"How so?"

Julie got up, walked to the door, grabbed the knob, and stared at it. She continued to talk while her back was turned to Lance.

"The first time Danny molested me in my bedroom," she whispered, "I told my mom about it, and she said, 'Oh, he was just in the wrong room.'" Julie turned around and yelled, "The wrong room!"

Lance shook his head.

"I've been in this profession a long time and heard many stories of abuse, but none that involved an excuse like that."

Julie walked over to the bookcase and picked up the model car.

"There were so many things I never told Mom." She set the car down and walked back to the chair. "When I was a senior in high school, I drove down to Detroit with a couple of friends so that we could visit our boyfriends. I was a victim again ..."

"Of—"

"Rape. Date rape."

"Oh, Julie."

251

She plunged ahead.

"When I got back from Detroit a day sooner than I was supposed to, Mom never asked me why I was home early or if anything happened. I used to think that if the water wasn't rocking her boat, she could pretend she was the only one floating." Tears rolled down Julie's cheeks as Lance handed her a tissue.

"Julie, are there books, or friends, or anything that's helped you work through some of this?"

"I had one really close friend in high school whose experience with her grandfather was like mine with Danny. We didn't know how to help each other except to create a world for ourselves that didn't include any males."

"Completely understandable."

"And then I had some messed-up friends, like this girl who introduced me to bulimia. She assured me that it would give me the control I wanted, but all I got were more migraines, so I stopped purging after about a month. A couple of different times as an adult I tried it again. Once, I had a blood vessel in my eye burst from repeated vomiting. That scared me. When I prayed about it, I knew God had taken away the urge, and I haven't done it since."

"It's astonishing you could quit without any help from anyone. It shows that you have great inner strength."

Julie looked at Lance with mascara-smudged eyes. "I've never thought of myself that way. All my life people told me I was too stupid to do anything."

"What people?"

"My second-grade teacher, who made me sit in the Stupid Chair and write my name in a Stupid Student Answer Book."

"No!"

"Unfortunately, yes. And there was my father – I mean Danny – who was never pleased with my grades or anything I did. And my husband, who once told me I was too stupid to pass a test for a job."

"Those words can tear holes in you."

"They can, and they have."

"Your husband—"

"Tom."

"Tom hasn't been in your corner?"

"He usually paints me into one."

"You're very articulate."

"I pretty much know to hit the nail with my own head!"

"And funny!"

"I moved so much growing up that I never had a chance to make friends as a little girl, and I really wanted this one special doll for a friend. When my mom wouldn't buy her for me, I started having inner conversations with her. I'm still doing it today."

"What would it take to get those conversations out where real people can hear them?"

"I don't know."

"Do you trust people to handle your words with care?"

"Not sure of that, either."

"Do you think your husband would help?"

"Heck, no."

"Does he know all the things you've told me?"

"Only a few." Julie pursed her lips tightly together.

He looked thoughtful. "What kind of childhood did Tom have?"

"Better than mine, because he wasn't sexually

abused, at least as far as I know. He wasn't any better in the emotional department. After his dad died his mom married a guy who hated him."

"Have you and Tom tried marriage counseling?"

"I wish."

"Would it be okay with you if I prayed for you?"

"Now?"

"I'd like to."

"Out loud?"

"Only if you're comfortable with it."

"Sure."

Pastor Lance folded his hands and bowed his head. "Dear God, I'm amazed at how honest Julie's been here. We want her to get healthy in every way, and to deal with traumas of her past. We know that You are the best Father, the heavenly Father who has watched over her and protected her, even when it didn't seem like there was much protecting going on. Give us wisdom to know how to best help her and thank You for loving her with an unconditional love. Amen."

Julie and Lance lifted their heads. "Julie, I wish I were the one to help you. I believe in honesty as much as you do, and I know someone who's immensely more qualified to help you than I am. He's a colleague of mine, Lars Olson, who's a very gifted psychologist. He has an office in Grand Rapids. I've known him for many years. I would be glad to give you his number so you can set up an appointment with him. Call me whenever you want and let me know how things are going." Lance got up and walked around his desk.

It feels like I'm being dismissed again. But if there's a chance that Lars could really help me, then I should try.

"And thank you for trusting me. That's a big first

step for you, isn't it?"

"I guess it is."

"You bet it is. You may not have arrived yet, but at least you've left the station."

"Really?"

"Absolutely."

Julie shook Lance's hand and left.

Lars Olson's office was more functional and less homey than Lance's. Julie doubted she would have felt initially comfortable in a place where she suspected she would have to take care of some serious business. She had spent years on an arid road with few watering holes, which left her feeling like a tumbleweed, bouncing through life without any direction or sense of value.

"Julie, before we get to the real reason for your visit, I need to do an intake."

"I spent several years working in a hospital, so I'm familiar with that."

"Great. I'll try not to take too long with it."

The intake flowed into a larger river of confession and catharsis as Lars gathered information on Julie's health, medications, family of origin, marriage, and work history. While she gave detailed accounts of the different incidences of abuse, the boyfriend triangle that preceded her marriage, her desire to find Eugene, her endless stomachaches and migraines, the feelings of abandonment, and a deep need to be loved – especially by a father – Julie saw her life playing on a big screen. Lars used the DSM-IV, along with his obvious intuitive skills, to hang a label of Major Depressive Disorder on her – not a label of crazy, or stupid, or inept. Her past had been a bulwark against any attempt to build a foundation of worthiness.

Weekly sessions with Lars helped Julie replace her need for comfort with the belief that, finally, here was a man who proved himself dependable and honorable. She settled into the upholstered armchair and waited for Lars to start.

"Julie, I'm a strong believer in the power of Christ in my life."

"If you had said that to me from the get-go, I would have been out of here."

Lars chuckled. "Why for?"

"I've been burned too many times by Christians convinced they're God's fingers pointing out my faults, His voice proclaiming my sins, and His arms folded tightly against my desire to be loved no matter what."

"I'm sorry that happened to you. Sometimes we're the ones most likely to shoot the foot soldiers instead of standing together against the real Enemy – the one who wants to rob you of your joy."

"That ship sailed a long time ago."

Lars sat back and looked kindly at Julie. "What's your main goal for therapy?"

"To find a way to heal the wounds of my past, so they stop ripping open and bleeding into my present."

"You have already done a lot of work by figuring out what you want." Lars scribbled some notes on his pad while Julie unzipped her down jacket. "I've never suggested this to anyone before, but because you're so thoughtful and articulate, I think this may work well for you."

"I'm listening."

"Have you ever been a journal writer?"

"I started keeping diaries when I was a little girl pretending to write to a doll named Thistledew. When I

256

got older, the diaries became journals – and sometimes I addressed those journals to God, or to my best friend, Chris."

"Then I think this will be perfect for you. I'd like you to write a letter to Danny Sandford and tell him how angry you are at being robbed of your innocence."

"My life has been damaged by emotional shrapnel from him."

"Don't hold anything back. No one – not even I – will read your letter. I should tell you that you're about to stir a pot that's had memories sticking to the bottom of it for a long time; and when those hardened, blackened recollections float to the surface, your life might seem worse than if you'd left the pot alone. I can give you tools to help skim off the debris of your past and dump it. I'll describe more after you get the letter written."

Julie heaved a big sigh. "I'll try."

Julie cancelled her appointment the following week so she could finish her letter. It was slow going and awkward, as she dealt with conflicted feelings of betrayal. The more she wrote, the more the dam broke open, words gushing out of her hand as quickly as she could write, finally finishing at ten pages.

"Here, Lars." Julie pulled a neatly stapled group of papers out of her purse back in his office.

"I told you I wasn't going to read your letter. I've given some thought about what you should do with it."

"Send it into orbit?"

"Close."

I should have waited for a warmer day! After

257

Julie's husband and children were gone, she bundled up and went outside, ready to follow Lars' last instruction about her letter. She laid the stack on top of a snowbank, pulled a lighter out of her pocket, and watched the flame quickly turn the letter into black ash. *Lars said God would add the ash to the compost already in my life to grow a bounty of forgiveness in my heart, and forgiveness toward Danny, toward God, and toward myself; and He would heal the wounds.* Using the end of a stick to dig a small hole, Julie scooped the ashes into it and buried them.

CHAPTER 26
HUMPTY DUMPTY

Lars has always been honest. He never promised that all my memories would stay buried. Julie's sense of smell resurrected some of them. Every time Tom made sexual advances while he was drunk, the sour smell of alcohol on his breath flooded her brain with images of Erik and of her father, and she'd end up running to the bathroom and emptying her stomach. When Julie mentioned this to Lars, he suggested that it might be time to open as much of her past to Tom as she felt able to do, a little at a time. He also said that bringing her story out in the light would take away the power it still held over her in the form of guilt. The thought of talking to Tom was far scarier than writing the letter, but she knew Lars was right, and she could no longer carry the weight of secrecy about the molestation and abuse she had suffered from Mr. Thomas, Mr. Koski, Mr. Bittner, Erik Martin, and her father.

By the end of six months, Julie was ready to be done with therapy. If Tom had been willing to go with her ... but that wasn't something she ever expected to see. As she said goodbye to Lars Olson, she remembered the verse Pastor Lance often quoted to her: "The lovingkindness of the Lord is from everlasting to everlasting; His mercies are new every morning; great is Thy faithfulness."

It was the eve of their ninth wedding anniversary. Julie had spent six months thinking about Lars' last homework assignment and decided this was a good time to start unlocking her carefully guarded shame. Tom's sobriety – normally hidden as well as Julie's past – wore down the last of her excuses.

Julie finished loading the dishwasher and casually said, "Tom, let's go for a drive. It's such a beautiful night. We could ask one of your cousins to come over and watch the kids for a while." *Maybe it'll be easier to spill my guts to Tom if I don't have to look at him.*

"Yeah, sure." Tom folded the newspaper, dropped it on the floor and got up to find their kids.

With warm air blowing through the truck's windows, Tom seemed content to look out at the neat houses and farms and fields lining both sides of the highway. *Maybe I should create a tidy, sanitized version of my memories. Tom wouldn't know the difference; but I'm pretty sure Lars would say that I'm not going to unlock the chains of my past until I use the key of complete honesty.*

"I need to tell you some things I should have told you a long time ago." Julie turned her head to look out her window as Tom whistled softly. *He's not exactly encouraging me. At least he's not yelling at me, either.* "You know my dad was an alcoholic."

"Yep. No news there."

This is going to be messy. "There are some things you don't know."

"What – he was a thief? He did time for robbing a liquor store? That wouldn't surprise me, considering how much he drank."

Julie pushed down her anger towards Tom and concentrated on the confession-at-hand. "One time when Danny got drunk in my mom's café, he … raped me."

The whistling stopped.

"Another time ... actually, lots of times for a couple of years ... he got drunk, came into my bedroom, and ..." There was a knot in Julie's throat that momentarily choked her words.

She turned and saw Tom gripping the steering wheel tighter.

"When you've been drinking, and your breath smells like Danny's did, and then you come into the bedroom, and you want to—"

"Who do I look like to you?" Tom banged his fist on the dashboard, turned his head and glared at Julie. "If I'd have known ... I don't know what I would have done to him. But I'm not him." Tom turned back and squinted his eyes at the setting sun. "Don't you dare compare me to that horny—"

"Stop!" Julie swallowed the lump in her throat and leaned her head against the door, thinking this would be a good time for someone to reach across her and shove it open.

By the time they got back home and walked into their house, Julie had dried her tears and decided to hide behind a wall of functionality. If Tom didn't want to deal with her past, she would continue living in the present like a well-oiled machine – rise at six, make breakfast for him, do jobs around the farm until eight, return home and get the kids ready for school and daycare, and back to the farm to work until she showered and left for her full-time job at one-thirty. After work, she canned vegetables, made freezer jam, cleaned the house, washed the clothes, and collapsed into bed at three in the morning.

Meals were cooked to perfection. Children were raised with precision. Sex was given on demand and her stomach routinely emptied after each encounter. Intimacy was protected behind the wall.

A flat line was far worse than an erratic one. Julie needed something to shock her heart back to life.

Flowers and leaves shed their dormant state overnight, unveiling a technicolor world. Julie faced a rare Sunday afternoon with nothing to do and was anxious to put distance between her life at home and whatever she felt drawn to by the vibrancy of spring. Car trips – in the old days with boyfriends and in the new days with her husband – never ended well. She was ready for a solo flight and would maybe keep driving until she ran out of gas.

Outside the town limits of Kale was a mileage sign for Cross River. Forty miles sounded like a good trip, so Julie headed in that direction. *I need clear mile markers in my life. God, where am I headed?*

Last night's rain was still evident in the deep puddles on the highway. The bright afternoon sun made the air smell clean, unsullied. Julie loved fresh beginnings but felt like she was the second generation in a family of dream-recyclers. Nothing in her life held any promise of newness.

A farmhouse had a for rent sign in the window. *That's what I've been looking for. I'm quite acquainted with farmhouses. That one needs a facelift; bet I could do it.* Tom had fulfilled his promise to take care of Julie, which was the only way he covered all the bases in their marriage. His latest job was in insurance sales, where he rose quickly to the position of top salesman while continuing to work the farm. Both he and Julie lived life at the speed of sound, but only one of them was heard. *I have a voice. I am going to use it.* Julie pulled over to the side of the road, fished a pencil and scratch paper out of the glove box, and wrote down the phone number listed on the sign.

Julie called the number from home, arranged to meet the owner, and pay the first month's rent. *Tom can run the farm by himself for a while. I'm going to need time to get ready to move.* Every spare cent and minute were spent on the house, cleaning mouse droppings out of kitchen cupboards, scraping peeling paint, scrubbing walls and floors to a sturdy shine, painting all three bedrooms, the living room, and the bathroom. As soon as the paint dried, Julie borrowed Tom's cousin's truck, loaded some of their furniture, clothes, and the kids' toys, and she and her kids moved to their new house. After all her childhood moves – including the midnight flight from Danny – Julie had not expected to move again like this. At least with the other moves, there was a good reason behind them – eviction, job change, and hope of more financial security. This was different. Julie could not explain why she was leaving. *My friends would be shocked over me ditching a handsome husband and beautiful home.* Julie knew that some of those friends were in abusive marriages, and that they were guarding their adult secrets as she guarded her childhood ones.

What would Grandma Emma think? It felt like the days with Mama T all over again; Julie didn't mind losing the guy half as much as losing the mom. It was time to call Grandma; she had avoided it for too long, and the truth was that she missed the elderly saint far more than she was willing to admit.

"Grandma Emma? It's Julie." Julie pushed the

words through a golf ball in her throat.

"Julie? Mein Liebchen? Oh, how I haf missed you!"

Tears ran down Julie's face. "Really?"

"I haf vanted to call you, but I vas afraid you would tink I vas interfering mit you und Tom."

"This isn't the old days anymore, Emma. You can cook for me anytime!"

Emma's chuckle was raspier than Julie remembered. *She's getting older. I can't think about losing her.*

"I know you und Tom haf been getting along nicht so much."

"No, Grandma, Tom and I have been separated for quite a while."

"My Tom vill always be my junge, but he is not vell in his head und heart. I haf prayed for him every day since he vas small, und I vill keep doing it. But you, Julie, I haf loved for all dese years, und you vill always in my heart be."

"Emma, you are my special grandmother. You were there for me when no one else was. Did I ever tell you how much I love you?"

"Ja, but I haf short-term memory loss!"

"Then I will just have to remind you often!"

"Vat do you kids alvays say? 'It's a deal!'"

"Can I come see you sometime?"

"Anytime. My door is open for you alvays."

"Danke, Emma."

"Guten nacht, Liebchen."

Julie hung up the phone and hugged herself the way she knew Grandma Emma would. She started into the kitchen to get a cup of coffee when the phone rang. *Emma must have forgotten to tell me something.*

"Hello, Emma."

"No, it's Tom."

One of these days, I will yank the phone cord out of the wall. "Tom, I'm headed for bed."

"What? It's only ten o'clock. You're never in bed before three."

"Things are different now." Julie slid the pot out of the Mr. Coffee maker.

"I've heard."

Julie ignored the sarcasm, poured herself a cup of coffee, opened the microwave door, slid the cup in and carefully shut the door before answering Tom. "What's going on?"

"I want you to come home."

"I *am* home."

"Why should you live in an old farmhouse? I thought you had enough of that in your life."

"I thought so, too. But it's peaceful here."

"I could pay more attention to you, and it would be peaceful here, too."

"Goodnight, Tom."

The conversation was a verbatim of the previous night, and the night before that. *He's called me every night for weeks. Why do I keep answering the phone?*

The conversation took another route. "Tom, I told you I go to bed by ten."

"Yeah, whatever."

Is this how he plans to convince me he's going to be a better listener?

"Julie, my Uncle Jack invited me to come out and visit him in Kansas City. I really want you to come with me. You didn't get a decent honeymoon, and we've never had a vacation. Please come home and we'll talk.

265

I know we can work things out."

Julie's heartbeat increased. "If I agreed, who would take care of the kids?"

"I've already talked to Emma, and she is willing."

"For how long?"

"Four days."

"And the farm?"

"My cousins will feed the critters for us."

"I don't know, Tom—"

"Please, babe."

"I've never been on a plane."

"Me neither! It's time for some adventure in our lives."

"You mean more than living with you?"

Tom chuckled. "I deserved that. But if you come home, I have a surprise for you."

Not another tractor. "I'll think about it."

Julie walked into her bedroom in the Kale house the next day and saw a white pants suit spread out on the bed, along with sandals, purse, and a gift certificate for a manicure. Even though she didn't see a new dress, she suddenly felt like a happy little girl and hoped there were two more wishes left in her bottle.

Uncle Jack and Aunt Suzanne met Tom and Julie at the airport, and the four of them hit the pavement running for the next three days. Their itinerary included a Royals game, Boyd's Bar-B-Q, the City Market, and jazz clubs on Eighteenth and Vine. Julie did not know married people could have this much fun together; and she never expected Tom to be this attentive to her. She was an eighteen-year-old newlywed who had been rescued, swept up by a romantic guy, unable and unwilling to catch her breath.

On the return flight to Detroit, Julie sank back into her seat in happy exhaustion. Looking out her window on a checkerboard of farms and wheat fields, Julie wished for a life as ordered as the landscape. She turned and looked at her husband, a man who was transformed during these last three days. He casually reached into his jacket pocket, pulled out a small velvet box and flipped open the cover.

"Julie, you launched this at me when you left. Please take it back and come home. I'll go to counseling. I'll do anything. You know we're meant to be together."

My friends warned me about this. Julie smiled at Tom, leaned over, kissed his cheek, and let him put her wedding ring back on her finger. Tom laced his fingers in Julie's, and the two leaned back and closed their eyes.

First Free called a new pastor. Julie both liked and trusted Pastor Lance Johnson, rare with the men in her life. But if Tom were serious about going with her to counseling, she was willing to check out the New Guy.

Pastor Tim was a recovering alcoholic, the only credibility he needed to earn Tom's respect. By the end of their first counseling session, the men were talking and joking like old friends, even after Tom gave his homework assignment to the couple, which was to go on a date once a week.

Tom and Julie laughed their way through corny movies, ate at nice restaurants, rode snowmobiles around their land, and held hands. Often. When Julie told Tom she'd like to go to school for her nursing degree, he squeezed her hand and told her she was smart enough to do anything she wanted to do. *My second wish.*

Tom came home every night for dinner, playtime, and story time with his kids. Julie climbed into bed and waited anxiously for him, rarely suffered headaches, and felt better in every way.

Tom missed dinner and stumbled into the house at eleven. Julie was willing to give him a chance to be human. Things were going so well for them that Pastor Tim ended their counseling sessions. When it happened again a week later, Julie flipped back through her journal and read the pages where she had pleaded with God to give Tom the desire to be with her and the kids. It was a timely reminder that Tom had come such a long way, and that everyone deserved a second or third chance.

The same thing occurred three more times the following week. Tom's drinking put a chokehold on Julie's dream. *I will stay until Tom-Tom graduates from high school, but then I'm leaving even if I only own the clothes on my back.* The earth outside their door was ready for plowing and planting, but Julie's sad heart was stony and overgrown with weeds of disappointment.

Hallmark moments had not happened in Julie's marriage. She didn't expect a change on her tenth anniversary. During their months of counseling, Tom could have figured out that his wife wanted diamonds, or clothes, or books; but where did he get the idea that she wanted a manure spreader with a red bow taped to the top? *If this wasn't so pathetic; and if Tom and I had any hope of a decent marriage; we could laugh about this. I might even think he meant it as a joke. But I know he can't connect the dots, so I'm not going to say anything.* Julie's co-workers teased her mercilessly while she awaited the punch line to her story. As word traveled back to Tom, he reconsidered his gift and presented Julie with an actual anniversary card and a hundred-dollar bill.

"It's too late, Tom," Julie sighed. "I bought a sapphire ring and matching earrings, wrapped them in a box, bought a card to go with it, and signed it, 'Happy anniversary to Julie, from Julie, love Julie.'" She tossed Tom's card onto the kitchen table. "I feel a little bit like the stuff you spread with that contraption."

CHAPTER 27
"ANGELS WATCHIN' OVER ME, MY LORD"

Dentists with braces, ophthalmologists with glasses, and male gynecologists all confused Julie. Yet she worked at a state hospital for the mentally challenged while her own mental and emotional state made her an accessory to the crime of hypocrisy. *I could climb into one of the beds and pull the covers over my head or strip off my clothes and bark at the moon or have a heated discussion with a shadow on the wall. No one here would treat me like there was anything wrong with me.* A new position as Certified Nursing Assistant put Julie in direct contact with people who struggled to stay afloat in constantly churning water. And despite it all, this job was more satisfying than any she had ever had.

Everyone's favorite patient on the long-term care wing was Bill Bradford. Julie observed that the profoundly mentally disturbed could look anywhere from twenty-seven to seventy-seven years old. Bill's slight paunch, stooped shoulders, and graying hair suggested a forty- or fifty-year old man. He had free rein to roam the halls as his padded slippers made a flapping sound when he shuffled. Bill was a normally passive man who experienced psychotic episodes only when frightening voices echoed in his head – and that had happened only once in her six months there. Julie was protective of him and grew to love the caring man, who was happily oblivious to socially acceptable behavior.

Marissa was agitated. A full moon brightened

her room; Julie had learned not to overlook the effect of lunar phases on her patients. *I hope I leave here in one piece tonight.*

"¿Qué pasa?" Julie made eye contact with Marissa as she approached her bed. Marissa lacked verbal ability, but her eyes were sophisticated communication devices of love and appreciation. "La luna es bonita esta noche." Marissa nodded slightly, then turned her head to stare at the moon. All the staff honored Julie's gift for calming the patients.

I wonder what's going to happen to my marriage. Julie grabbed a bottle of lotion from the bedside table, flipped the top, poured a dab into her left hand, and set the bottle down. *What if I end up like this, in a hospital, unable to tell anyone where I hurt?* Julie carefully rubbed lotion into Marissa' arms and legs. *Am I capable of telling anyone where I hurt? I still can't get Tom to hear me.*

Bill came around the corner, peered into Marissa's room, tipped his head forward, yelled, "Leave me alone!" and ran full tilt at Julie, whose back was to the door. Ramming the top of his head into the middle of Julie's back, she catapulted over Marissa's legs into the opposite wall and crashed to the floor. Bill backpedaled, turned, and shuffled down the hall a little crookedly, after leaving one of his slippers in Marissa's room. Marissa stared at Julie, whimpered, and visibly shook while everything around her was quiet. Most of the staff was in a meeting on restraints. Julie waited for an eternity of minutes, then carefully stood up and waited for the pain to hit. *I need to fill out an accident report and get home!*

Julie hobbled down a flight of stairs to the

nursing supervisor's office on the first floor. Inside the office were two desks, a metal file cabinet, an old mimeograph machine, a worn, upholstered armchair, a large fish tank on a food cart, and a framed picture of a lighthouse hanging on the back wall. A small meeting room off to one side had the door flung open to reveal a round, brown table, dingy, yellow plastic chairs scattered in disarray, and a narrow counter with a microwave and Styrofoam cups perched on top of it.

Julie tried to ease into the chair. She began to sweat while the room spun. The lighthouse left the frame and whirled around her blurred eyes. Just before she passed out, a nurse walked in, looked at her in alarm and reached for her arms.

A small, bright room was the next thing Julie saw as she felt a table underneath her. Bells, beeps, and alarms competed with voices shouting for tests and x-rays. *If I die from the pain, at least things will quiet down.* A prick in Julie's arm muffled the noise, like she was underwater, and the room went black.

Julie stirred, opened her eyes to bright sunlight pouring into her room and heard clear, quiet voices.

"Blood clot lodged between her spine and sciatic nerve ... size of a baseball ... right sacral iliac ... poor kid ... terrible pain ... Valium will help ... three months of complete bed rest ... probably never walk again ..."

Stop! I'm here! Please talk to me! Julie focused on Tom listening intently to the doctor; she did not understand the words. Her own thoughts drowned them out, whispering, you cannot walk away from your marriage. *How can I depend on Tom to do everything for us? He never did anything when I was able-bodied. I'm not sure he knows how to do anything around the house, with the kids ...*

The injury was not Julie's fault, not by a long shot, not ever. But she felt guilty, especially when Tom turned and drilled her with a look of inconvenience. *I need to assemble a Dream Team: Grandma Emma, Sharon, Miriam Evans, and maybe even Mom.*

Anxiety over a potential Valium addiction increased daily during the following weeks, especially after Julie left the hospital and the careful monitoring of the nursing staff. *I am* not *doing drugs and I* will *walk again. If that doctor knew how my husband treats me, he would realize I love a challenge.*

Physical therapy shot hot bullets down Julie's back with each labored step. Resolve won the battle, until she could walk the quarter mile down to her mailbox – her recovery road.

Julie awakened to a glorious summer morning; not even arguing blackbirds dampened her joy. The large numbers on the alarm clock displayed four-twenty, giving her another half-hour of sleep before needing to get up for her first day back at work. She had agreed to fill in temporarily for someone on maternity leave, day shift. After twenty minutes of staring at the ceiling, she decided she was ready to get up with the birds. Julie saw thin clouds streaking across the sky, piercing the rising sun into a spectrum of pink, orange, and lavender. *This is the day the Lord has made.*

A hot, soothing shower was the perfect way to start the day. Julie dressed in her white pants, blue uniform smock, and comfortable shoes. She unwrapped the towel around her head, bent over and shook it out. Loosely permed auburn hair was her favorite pick-and-go style. Low maintenance had worked well during her recuperation and rehabilitation, so she decided to keep it. After applying very light make-up – eyeliner and mascara around her deep brown eyes – Julie did a quick mirror inspection, turned off the bathroom light, peeked into each child's bedroom, and walked to the kitchen. She often heard her pastor quote the verse, "His mercies are new every morning." Today was a day of gratitude for the mercy of a completely healed back, functional legs, mind and spirit intact.

Julie punched the on button on the coffee maker, stepped outside the back door and walked her recovery road to the mailbox for the paper. She reached her arms toward the sky, whispered words of thanks, spun a circle, and laughed out loud. This was, indeed, an awesome day.

Julie enjoyed a leisurely cup of coffee and a banana nut muffin. The Dream Team had all returned home, leaving Tom to get the kids up at seven, feed them muffins and cereal, and make sure they were ready for Kids Kare before he left for work. He had learned how to meet their basic needs and curbed his drinking during Julie's down time, while she had learned to appreciate miracles in all their forms.

Dew-covered grass glittered like diamonds as Julie eased into her car at five forty-five. Pulling out onto the highway, she saw the temperature sign on the Farm and Fleet store: seventy-nine degrees, unusually warm for this time of the morning, even in July. By mid-day, the thermometer would read close to ninety-five again, like it had all week. That, combined with ninety percent humidity, would turn her car into a movable sauna. She was glad she'd be in the air-conditioned hospital for the next several hours. When she returned home in mid-afternoon, she would change into shorts and a tank top and sit in front of an oscillating fan with an icy glass of tea.

Walk and work were possible. Julie was empowered to feed her family and her self-esteem, both of which were a bit thin.

Bill still lived at the hospital. Julie started out somewhat cautiously around him but relaxed after that first day. All the patients were relatively calm, and she rejoiced every day she walked into work. *The jury is still out on my mental health, but one out of two ain't bad.*

As Christmas drew near, Julie was caught in the same frenzy of activity that had everyone in its grip. Patients and staff alike loved the excitement of decorating the units, listening to carolers, and watching their confined world transformed into a kaleidoscope.

Her shift was almost over. Julie had an hours'- worth of shopping and other errands to do, and then get home and hide some of her purchases before the kids got off the bus. *I'll check on the few patients still in their rooms. There shouldn't be too many, since it looks like almost everyone is out in the main hall listening to the carolers. Then I'll grab my purse and coat, and I'm outta here!*

Tommy Jones was a favorite of everyone's, but he usually stayed in his room when there was a lot of excitement. He was at least sixty years old, which made Julie think about the wry sense of humor his parents had in naming their son. The name fit his destiny; he was soothed by Tom Jones' music. The staff made sure Tommy's eight-tracks were in good working order.

Julie peeked in his room and saw Tommy pulling the tape through the slots of the eight-track and wrapping the tape around his neck. The tape probably wasn't strong enough to do any real harm, but staff were instructed to use the four-point restraint when necessary. Julie dumped her jacket and purse inside the door, ran over to Tommy's bed, and lightly touched his arm. Normally placid and able to refocus his attention with touch, he decided today to let out a shriek, raise both arms, and push against Julie's chest. She hurtled back against the wall, air gushing out of her lungs, and passed out.

The lights and noise of the Emergency Room at St. Michael's were, sadly, all-too familiar to Julie. *I am logging frequent flyer miles.* When the test results showed her back free of breaks, she cried in relief and in disappointment that she was in this place again. Julie heard she would not be dancing out of here; she had a severely sprained muscle that would require complete bed rest for several days. *I wanted to make Christmas traditions for my family beyond the violent ones of my childhood. How am I going to do that now?*

Julie returned to work by late January. She was a team player; Workmen's Comp had covered her bills and she was determined to make this job work for her. Church friends and coworkers questioned why she did not quit her obviously dangerous job. None knew the only way she could walk out of her marriage was on the financial stability road, which this job would provide. *Besides, I really like my job. The patients are far less violent and abusive than what I lived with growing up. That was a family of buggers, as Grandma Emma would say.*

Julie re-injured her back four more times in less than four years. *God, I don't believe that You want me to be hurt or are somehow allowing me to get hurt ...*

unless You're trying to get my attention. Is it time for me to find a new job? Is there some reason for me to be somewhere else? Trying to walk Your path for my life is still new to me. Please, please help me find a new job!

Years of molestation and difficult childbearing exacted a silent toll on Julie's body. At thirty-two years old, she had a hysterectomy, followed by strep throat and a staph infection just six weeks later.

Someone had uncrossed her fingers.

CHAPTER 28
"TIL DEATH DO US PART"

Bodies in protective mode stage rigorous protests against grueling physical demands and constant injuries. Julie loved her job and had assumed it would be her life's work but was ready to embrace something new, something safer.

She was also ready to discard her marriage. She had assumed she would be married for life; but the likelihood was that she and Tom would seriously injure each other worse than they already had if they stayed together through all three children's high school graduations.

Where ... how ... am I going to find a different job? I'm trained to work with mentally challenged people ... and I know restraints ... but is there a market for that outside of the hospital?

Julie wanted to unload her burden on church friends and ask them to pray for a new job for her during the prayer and praise time of the Sunday morning service. It was a stretch for her to trust, both in God, and in people who had the chance to use her vulnerability against her. *God, these people have been kind to me and to my family for so many years. What am I afraid of?*

Julie rebooted her attention back to Pastor Tim.

"There is a prayer request here from a teacher who desperately needs an aide for an autistic boy in her seventh-grade class."

I never thought about a classroom. Kids with autism or Down's can sometimes cause harm to themselves or to others. I could be that aide. Julie was impatient for the service to end so that she could seek out the teacher.

Julie agreed to be a substitute Sunday school teacher for the younger kids. With her small group, the sermons, the love of the people, and the bible study at work, she was steadily growing in faith and confidence. There was still the sensation of walking too close to the edge of the cliff, but Pastor Tim had said that God loves a dangling Christian.

The Sunday school classroom was ready for Julie at eleven o'clock. She was a little nervous and slightly out of breath but forgot both of those things when she saw a tall man crouch down to kiss his little boy goodbye. Both father and son had flaming red hair—

"Erik! Erik Martin!" The man stood, turned, and with recognition lighting his face, made it to Julie in two steps and wrapped his arms around her, lifting her off the ground.

"I heard you were subbing today. I wanted to see you, but I was afraid to." Except for more smile lines and fewer freckles, Erik looked the same as Julie remembered him. When she was no longer airborne, she looked at Erik and smiled.

"What—how—tell me how you got here."

Erik laughed the familiar laugh of the guy who just told the punch line of a lame joke. "Julie, it's only by the grace of God that I am here and not living a druggie life somewhere. All the time I was trying to get off the hook, God wanted me on it, dangling and depending only on Him. I should have been dead six lives ago." Erik grabbed Julie's elbow and gently pulled her towards the corner away from the door and spoke softly. "I honestly cannot believe what I did to you … how I treated you. I know it doesn't sound like enough to ask your forgiveness, but that's all I've got. I really hope you can give it."

Julie didn't hesitate. "It is so good to see you here. Of course, I forgive you. That horse is dead, and we aren't going to beat it anymore." Julie smiled. "And where is your wife?"

"Sue is waiting for me in the adult class. And that little guy over there is Kenneth, my pride and joy. My family is everything to me." Erik smiled and waved to his son. "If God took me today, I'd thank Him for them and for all the second chances He gave me to find Him." His eyes filled with tears.

Julie was in a state of joyful shock. "Erik, say hi to your wife for me. And maybe our families can get together sometime."

"Okay, see you." Erik walked through the door, turned, and said, "Read it if you got it! It's the only thing you need!"

Julie's heart filled with an almost forgotten sense of elation, remembering a verse from the book of Joel that Pastor Lance quoted – a verse that had not made sense to her until now: "Then I will make up to you for the years the swarming locust has eaten." Lance explained that God was like a farmer tilling and reclaiming ground. It took fifteen years for God to redeem her time with Erik, a time Julie thought she would never forgive or forget. Facing the darkness in her own heart made her overwhelmed with gratitude for God's forgiveness – and she found it freeing to extend that forgiveness to a guy who had caused deep hurt in her past.

A sleepwalking dream that night began with a motorcycle ride to her wedding with Teddy-Boy, with Julie holding her veil down against the wind. When the wind became too strong for her to fight, she tumbled off the bike and lay on the ground, arms splayed out at crooked angles, as Teddy stood over her, laughing a hideous laugh. Suddenly Erik stood behind him, pinning his arms behind his back and threatening to break both. As Teddy's face writhed in pain, Erik morphed into Tom, who released Teddy's arms, pulled a gun out of his belt, and held it to Teddy's head. Julie found a gun next to her, picked it up and shot Tom, who shouted, "No, Mom!" and became Tom-Tom before he slumped to the ground. Julie had shot her son.

Julie awoke screaming Tom-Tom's name while standing in the kitchen. She ran to the front closet, threw on her winter jacket, slid into her boots, and left the laces flopping as she grabbed keys off the hook near the door. *I need to get out of here.*

The highway outside Kale city limits held a terrifying beauty, as it followed the top of a ridge dropping to a ravine of glacier-formed rocks. The drive was eerily quiet as snow-muffled tires led Julie's car into soul rest. *Driving off the shoulder would be easier than waiting for my car to stall on train tracks. I can slam on my brakes; skid and drop into nothingness; and everyone will assume I hit a deer or a patch of ice.* A lone bald eagle soaring high in the gray sky kept an eye on Julie's death wish.

A ten-point buck froze in mid-leap directly in front of the car. Julie hit the brake pedal and fishtailed across snow-covered ice, screaming as her car careened toward the edge of the road and then stopped suddenly, as though held back by a giant hand. When Julie's heart

281

settled to a normal rhythm, she opened her door, climbed out of the car, and plodded all over the road looking for deer tracks. *Where's the buck? Where are the tracks?*

Back in the car, Julie heard a voice through the sound of chattering teeth: "You need to trust me. I love you." *My car engine is off. The radio is off. Is that God's voice? Does He care what happens to me?* Julie patted her frozen tears and drove slowly home with an awakening sense of what it meant to be humbled before a powerful God.

"Melissa? This is Julie Dietrich. We go to church together and I heard that you put in the prayer request for a classroom aide."

"I absolutely did."

"That was three or four weeks ago. Has your school filled the position yet?"

"No, they haven't. My before-school prayer group has faithfully prayed every week."

"Well—"

"Are you interested?"

Julie took a deep breath. "I think I am."

"What is your experience?"

"I don't have a teaching degree, or any experience with kids outside of raising my three. I've spent the past several years working at Fairview State Hospital. I have a lot of experience working with people with mental and emotional challenges. I have compassion for those people. I also know first aid and restraints."

"Why don't you stop by the school and fill out an application?"

"I forgot to ask where the school is!"

"It's in Allen Park."

Twenty-five miles from home? How could I afford the gas money for that drive every day? "Okay, I'll think about it."

"Please do. I need someone … yesterday."

Miss Julie's low-heeled shoes clicked against the tile floor at Martin Luther King, Jr. Middle School in Allen Park, Michigan. She had been hired as a teacher's aide within one week of applying for the job. Unsure of whether she was good enough, they were just desperate enough, or some of both, those musings were forgotten in the flood of memories brought on by the smells of the school hallway. Wax, magic markers, stale milk, tater tots … Julie was back in third grade with Miss Meyer. *How do stupid people become aides? Will I be sent to the office if I'm not strict enough?* A slender woman with stylish blonde hair walked towards Julie. There was something so familiar—

"Glo! Gloria Gustafson! You're so—"

"Skinny! And I'm Gloria Peterson now!" The early-arrival students stopped and gawked at the women whose hugs almost knocked each other down in the middle of the hallway.

"What—"

"How—"

"You first!"

"Glo! I can't believe it's you! You look fantastic! The last thing I heard was that you were living somewhere out east with your husband."

"We were. After Jim and I graduated from Michigan State, we married and found jobs in New Hampshire. I taught school and he worked as an engineer. We loved it out there; but we really missed our families, especially after Stephanie was born. We moved back last year, and I was blessed with this job. Let's go to the lounge." Glo linked her arm with Julie's. "We can sit down with a cup of coffee. I didn't even ask what you're doing here."

"I'm the new aide in Melissa Jenkins' room for a boy with autism."

"You will love Melissa. She's a new teacher, energetic, creative, kind, organized, and a totally cool Christian gal."

"I for sure know the last. We go to church together."

Gloria opened the door to the lounge, directed Julie to a chair and headed for the coffee pot. "*You* go to church?"

Julie laughed. "Don't sound so surprised! You and Bret and some others had a bigger influence on me than you realize. I'm finding God's way for my life."

Gloria set steaming Styrofoam cups of coffee on the table. "This is suddenly a dejá vu – you and me drinking coffee in the lunchroom at Fairview, and me asking you about your weekend with Erik Martin."

"I was just thinking the same thing."

"Julie, I'm sorry. That sounded judgmental. I know I was very hard on you then. I had some maturing to do." Julie took a sip of coffee. "I was so afraid I'd hurt you, but I didn't have enough courage to ask your forgiveness."

Julie touched Gloria's hands as tears spilled from her eyes. "Glo, you were my best friend, and the only one who shot straight with me. I had no business driving down to Detroit."

"So, you didn't keep dating him?"

"I actually did, for a long time."

"And?"

"And, he proposed to me, along with Teddy Tannenbaum and Tom Dietrich – all on the same night!"

"No way!"

"Way!"

"Which one did you marry?"

Julie stared into her cup. "Before I answer that, you need to know that I never thought you owed me an apology. You did nothing that needed forgiveness. I wish I had gone back to the YFC meetings with you and heard more about how to live the kind of life God had planned for me. I was angry and hurt."

"Julie, 'If wishes were horses' ... you're here, we've found each other again, and I can't wait to introduce you to the other Christian teachers who meet once a week before school for prayer and support and encouragement."

"I can't believe we're together!" Both women got up, hugged again, and opened the door to what Julie hoped would be a fresh start, at least as far as her job was concerned.

Marriage was not as easy to change as a job. Julie agreed to let Tom live in the basement for three months until he saved enough money to find an apartment. One month, two months, the last week of the third month – and Tom had not made any moving-out progress. He usually came home late and staggered downstairs to turn the TV volume up full blast, which was Julie's signal that it was safe for her to fall asleep. Occasionally he returned earlier when Julie was still meticulously cleaning every inch of the kitchen. She knew confrontation was inevitable and did not have anything to do with her input; Tom was hard-wired for verbal abuse and made it work without any trigger.

This cannot go on any longer. Tom should be gone by now. This is the night I will be up waiting for him, whenever he returns, early or late. We need to work this out. Julie was completely unprepared for his arrival that balmy, spring night as he burst through the door, face and arms covered in blood and smeared across his t-shirt.

"Tom! What happened to you?" The amount of blood on Tom's body and shirt made up for the lack of blood in her face.

"Need. My. Gun." Tom panted. "Rocky. Gotta go."

"Rocky? Your deranged cousin? Why?"

"Gotta kill him." Tom grabbed a dishtowel hanging from the stove handle, wiped his face, tossed the towel in the sink, ran outside, and jumped into his truck. Julie dialed nine-one-one. *This is one thing I know how to do.*

With the speed of an ambulance, police officers arrived at Kale Bar and Grill and found Tom spouting obscenities and waving his gun around, safety off. As soon as he saw the officers, Tom ducked out the back door and sped home, arriving just ahead of a car with lights flashing and siren blaring. Tom fell getting out of his truck, got up and swore, stumbled to his house, unlocked the door, opened it, walked in, pointed the gun at his wife and children huddled together on the couch, and passed out on the floor still gripping the gun.

A Restraining Order is worthless in this county. It's too big an area for the sheriff to reach my house in less than forty-five minutes. By then, if Tom were here, I would be dead. An RO never worked with Danny. Julie

286

did not trust a person or system or order to protect her. She banked on Tom's unwillingness to keep her in his sights with the probability of jail hanging over his head. She had underestimated the strength of Tom's anger – again.

It took ten months for the divorce to become final – ten long months for Tom to defy the Restraining Order almost every day, showing up at the house to play use-the-kids-to-blackmail-the-wife. *This will never end unless I take the kids and leave.*

"I need to tell you something, Julie," whispered Mari Larsen one Sunday after church. "When I lost my husband, Ebel, almost a year ago, you wouldn't believe the friends I lost, as well."

"For crying out loud, you're the church organist!"

"Doesn't matter. They were convinced I was a husband stealer since I was single. They shut me out of their lives. Don't be surprised if it happens to you."

"Did people think you wanted to remarry?"

"Heck no! Everyone knew I was married for forty years to a mean, ornery alcoholic. Some even knew I felt this huge weight lift off me when he died. Speaking of weight, I lost it and started doing my hair the way I wanted to and going places I wanted to visit – and people thought whatever they wanted to think."

What collateral damage will come from my marriage disintegrating? Tom's cousins – he jokingly called them the full catastrophe – were their neighbors and closest friends. Julie thought of them as brothers and sisters, especially during birthdays, weddings, and graduations. The gathering place was Tom and Julie's, where Julie cooked enough food for two battalions of

287

cousins. Every event was an excuse for a party. Cutting wood to heat homes ended in a hot coffee and gooey cinnamon roll feast at their house. Julie faced losing her extended family, one of the best supports for her self-esteem.

Bills were paid on time but without enough money left over for heating oil. Julie's salary was too high to qualify for fuel assistance. The divorce was not yet final, so Julie didn't receive alimony or child support. *I will not go back to eating Spam.*

Tom's last act of homeownership before he disappeared was cutting a fallen oak into huge chunks still in the woods. Julie knew that any of the cousins living on either side of them would be willing to help haul the wood back to the house, leaving her a heat source for another three or four weeks.

The girls played in the woods while Julie put on one of Tom's Carhartt bibs and found a lightweight ax. She was angry at herself, at him, at the world, and at God. Every swing of the ax intensified her anger. *This is going to take me hours to do! What happened to Tom's promise to take care of me? I don't want to do this. What if I injure my back again?* After two hours, Julie's muscles were screaming. She dropped the ax and trudged into the house, tears frozen to her eyelashes.

Tom's cousin Gary lived a quarter mile down the road. Within minutes of Julie's phone call, he and his three kids pulled into her driveway in an old Chevy pickup hauling an open trailer. Julie's kids and their second cousins played football and buried each other in the snow while she and Gary loaded wood into the trailer.

Work was finished in time to resurrect the

family tradition of pie and coffee. In thirty minutes, hands and feet were completely thawed, the pie tin was crumb-clean, and the kids played games in the family room.

"Gary, I can't thank you—"

The back door burst open. Gary's wife Jayne stomped into the kitchen.

"Hey, Jayne, join us for coffee. Sorry the pie's all gone."

Glaring at the offending plates and cups before directing her venom, Jayne ignored Julie and hissed, "Gary, where have you been?" Gary and Julie stared at Jayne from opposite ends of the table.

"We just finished stacking wood and had dessert." Gary sounded confused, and Julie noticed a decrease in noise from the family room.

Jayne's body visibly shook with the effort to maintain control as she clenched her teeth. "I called and called, and no one answered."

Please God, no. Tell me Jayne does not suspect us of fooling around. A few of the older kids wandered into the kitchen. Gary's older son Eric took one look at his mom's face and slowly backed out of the room.

Julie negotiated a hairpin curve. "Jay, we've been sitting here. The phone hasn't rung." Gary eased out of his chair, walked to the phone, lifted the receiver, held it out so that everyone heard the dial tone, hung the receiver back up and walked over to his wife.

"Jaynie." A telephone ring shattered the tension while Jayne's eyes bore holes in Julie's stricken face. Turning sharply, she threw open the door and slammed it so hard that the only framed family portrait of Julie's family fell off the wall and crashed onto the floor.

Gary is a sweet, lovable, gentle soul – all safely

hidden behind a homely face. If we were stranded on a desert island, population growth would cease. Gary and Julie looked quietly at each other, ignoring the phone still ringing in shrill vindication.

"Is what happened what I think happened? Did Jaynie think something was going on here?" Gary spoke gently.

"Yeah, I think so."

"I'd better go."

"I am so sorry. If there's anything I can do, please let me know. I can talk to Jayne and explain things if she's willing to listen."

Julie never felt so completely alone. *I am dead to Tom's family.* She got up to put the phone out of her misery.

Gary dropped his kids off at Julie's to play in the fresh snow of a new morning. With Gary and Julie staring awkwardly at each other, Eric yelled, "Hey, Aunt Julie! Boy, was Mom mad at Dad when we got home! First, she threw a carton of eggs at him, then she baptized him with a gallon of milk. After that, she screamed and ran upstairs. Dad had a gross mess to clean up!"

I should make my life simpler and tattoo a scarlet L for Leper on my forehead. It was her first Sunday at church after the Jayne incident. Julie assumed she would find two groups of people at church: those related to Tom who felt a sense of loyalty to him, even though he had stopped attending at the end of their marriage counseling; and those threatened by Julie's divorcee label. Either way, she was untouchable by the same people who had spent several years embracing her with love and affirmation. If Grandma Emma could still drive, there would be at least one person in her corner.

No one volunteered to help drive Julie's kids home from school after soccer practice or piano lessons. If her car broke down, she would have to have it hauled to a junk yard. There would be no hand holding to lessen the throbbing ache of her divorce. She still had her job and house repairs. And three angry kids. *Note to self: never divorce the hometown boy.*

The loudest echoes in the empty house came from the newer bedrooms Tom had added on after Tom-Tom was born. *This was supposed to be my dream house. Now it's going to be someone else's dream. God, what went wrong? Tom and I were so young when we got married. Did either of us know what we were getting into? How many times did I tell Tom I loved him, while inside I was screaming, "Please love me more!"* Julie walked through the living room, across the thick carpeted floor into the tiled kitchen, and ran her hand along the side of the sage green, dual oil and wood burning stove – one of her prize possessions, and one of the few things Tom bought for her that she truly valued.

Tom and I were broken-winged birds when we married, each hoping the other would find a way to help us soar above every hurt and betrayal that defined our childhoods. It would have made sense for at least one of us to figure that out and say it. We were clueless about how to talk to each other. We cussed in stereo, but it didn't help us communicate love, or compassion, or trust. I still don't know the best way to cry for help.

Julie made one final sweep of the house, turned off lights and checked for closed windows. *For five years, I inhaled and held my breath, waiting for this*

291

house to be built. After I exhaled, I still wasn't in the place I sought – a place where I could withdraw more love than I invested, and where there would still be a surplus in my home account.

CHAPTER 29
FLAT TIRES AND INFLATED DREAMS

First Evangelical Free Church had a small but vocal, moderately influential group of people who used the Apostle Paul's description of the Bible – the sword of the Spirit – to sharpen their weapons of judgment. They interpreted verses in Matthew as a condemnation of divorce, even those fueled by adultery. They fulfilled Mari's prophecy by thrusting sharpened words into the hearts of those already in pain.

Julie's heart bled – not from being liberal, either politically or theologically – but from the barbs in her marriage. She avoided the Judgment Clan and clung to the people who embraced her with gentle arms of love.

An attractive, thirty-something, single woman was a rare species in her church. Julie found herself in demand for after-church lunch dates. Sean Mills was tall, lean, and blonde, with a whimsical, soft-spoken nature, the opposite of Tom. After a half dozen dates, Julie was held by his interesting stories. She had never known anyone who lived in Alaska and worked on the pipeline; and for a long time, she ignored almost everyone else to spend time with Sean.

The first dinner date was pleasant. In the middle of the night, Julie awoke from a dream where she was running away from Sean. He reappeared at every corner and tried to throw a big net over her that she barely escaped. Julie shook off the dream, went to the kitchen and warmed up a cup of coffee. When her brain started firing on all cylinders, she realized her relationship with

Sean had reached the tipping point. He showed every sign of a marriage proposal, while Julie battled between the need for intimacy and an equally strong aversion to it.

The congregation had followed the whirlwind romance between Sean and Julie. The sword-sharpeners quoted verses against remarriage, while many others let them know they were praying for the leading of a Wise God. When battle fatigue showed on Julie's face, a discerning, older woman suggested Julie spend time focusing only on God without making any decisions about Sean, who made it clear to Julie that he had waited thirty-two years to marry the right woman – and she was it. Julie explained to Sean that she had been in the wrong marriage for fifteen years and wasn't sure who or what was *it*.

Without a goodbye to Julie or anyone else at church, Sean disappeared. Word around town was that he had moved back to Alaska.

What's wrong with me? I broke this guy's heart and mine isn't in such good shape, either. I can't play the game the way I did in high school. I'm older and have more at stake, especially my kids' emotional safety. I need to get some things figured out or stop dating. For the here and now, I have children to raise and a job that needs clear headedness.

The fifty-mile roundtrip from Kale to Allen Park became easier and cheaper when Julie found Butch Lane and Jim Newman, two teachers looking for a third to carpool. Because she had had very little experience or success with guys who were just friends, Julie was surprised when Butch and Jim became exactly that. The teasing banter made the drive pass quickly. It reminded

Julie of the first staff meetings at Lakehaven. She ribbed the guys every time they folded their lanky frames into the back of her Toyota Celica. Six months of carpooling made her thankful not to be driving alone.

The teasing took on a different tone on a beautiful morning in early September.

"Jule, you need to meet Danny Lewis," Butch declared.

"You mean the history teacher?"

"And soccer coach," added Butch.

"He's a great guy," echoed Jim.

"Isn't Nancy your cousin? I heard she dated Danny after her husband died, and she says he's fantabulous!" Butch snickered.

"Uncle!" Julie laughed.

"He's six one, and has one of those wide-open, honest faces that I bet everyone loves." Jim puckered his lips in Julie's rearview mirror.

"Why don't you date him, then?" Julie raised her eyebrows and did her best Groucho Marx imitation.

"I'm already spoken for." Jim put his arm around Butch.

"Ain't we cute together?" Butch laid his head on Jim's shoulder.

"You guys are morons."

"At least we're more *on* than off."

"Double Uncle!"

"Do we win?"

Yeah! Leave me alone."

"Then drive on, Jule, oh faithful chauffeur."

Winter had the chilly October evening in its vice grip when Julie left school and headed for her car. Butch and Jim stood next to the car, stomping their feet, and swinging their arms to hold the cold back.

"You have a very flat, right-front tire," they spoke in unison.

"Who are you guys – Martin and Lewis? Cut the comedy." Julie was not ready for bantering until she was in a warm car.

"We're not teasing," Butch said. "It's as flat as most of Jim's jokes."

Julie looked at the tire in the gathering darkness and wailed. "What am I going to do? I don't have any money or credit cards."

"Danny Lewis could fix the tire for you," said Jim, making a poor attempt at keeping a straight face.

"I won't owe any man anything!" Julie's voice was as taut as piano wire. "Sue can give us a ride home, and I can figure out something tomorrow. I'm quite sure things will get worse before they get better," she added ruefully.

Jim and Julie got in the backseat of Sue Kendall's vintage Dodge Dart. Butch said offhandedly, "I need to run back into the building – I left papers I need at home tonight. Be right back."

"Hurry up – it's freezing out here!" yelled Julie.

Once inside the school, Butch took a few deep breaths, slowed to a saunter towards Danny's room and wandered in casually.

"Hey, Dan."

"Hey, yourself." Danny flipped his pencil in the air, caught it and stuck it behind his ear. "What's up?"

"Butch and I've been carpooling with Julie Dietrich, and she gave us extra car keys in case she ever locked herself out. And lucky you: Her Toyota has an acute case of flat tiredness. Wouldn't she appreciate it being fixed—" He tossed the key to an unsuspecting

Danny, who instinctively reached up and snatched it.

Sue and company pulled into the school parking lot the next morning right next to Julie's car. Julie steeled herself to get out of the car, walk over to hers and inspect the damage in the light of a new, but rather unpromising, day. In total shock, she saw a new tire on a newly washed car.

What gives? She looked up as her posse headed into the building. *Maybe one of them called triple A and had it fixed without telling me. Those people are amazing. I'm lucky to have them for friends and coworkers.*

Some of the teachers shared lunch break together in the teacher's lounge.

"I hope you don't mind that I washed your car while I was at it."

"You?" *Danny Lewis has clear, hazel eyes.*

"Guilty. I'm a handy guy."

"What do I owe you?" *Listen buddy, your eyes are beautiful, but I got nothing to give.*

Danny took a sip of coffee. "Nothing. It's on the house."

"Oh."

"Bye." Danny set his mug on the counter and left.

What an idiot. "Oh?" That's the best I could come up with? Would it have been so hard to thank him?

On the commute home, Julie tried the casual approach. "Butchie, what could I give Danny to thank him for fixing my car?" Julie kept her eyes focused on the road.

"Buy him a bag of Oreos and tell him that's the way a modern woman bakes," replied Butch, a smile dancing around his eyes.

The next morning, Julie walked into the lounge armed with Double-Stuff Oreos, figuring that exaggerating the thanks would include her in everyone's joke. The room erupted in laughter while the Oreos vanished. After Julie thanked Danny, he worked hard to keep his face a normal color.

After all I've lived through with men, I can't trust my instincts. I need to maintain caution here. Julie felt like a giddy teenager every time she saw Danny. *My teen years disappeared without knowing that feeling. Maybe this is God reclaiming more ground for me.*

Marriage had taught Julie to grit her teeth and bury her hopes on Valentine's Day. It was early February and time for Julie to start flexing her coping muscles. She sat in her cubicle in the back of the classroom with a fresh cup of coffee, stashed her purse in the back of her file drawer, and powered up her computer. While waiting for the computer to boot, she attacked her ever present pile of mail and separated it into three stacks: Urgent, Useless, and Unbelievable. After sorting twenty sizes and shapes of envelopes, she came to a large manilla one that was not a candidate for any of her efficient categories.

Julie unwound the string on the clasp, flipped up the top, reached inside and pulled out a large, red, construction paper heart with a white ruffle material glued around the border. In neon green marker were the words: "I've been watching you – and what I see is nice." Julie turned it over and did not find a signature. On the third floor, Danny Lewis was organizing his desk for the day. He picked up a pile of yesterday's tests and discovered the same homemade Valentine underneath.

Curiosity trumped her resolve to skip lunch as

298

Julie walked into the lounge. "Sue, do you know anything about someone sending me a Valentine that looks like it was made by a third-grade boy?"

Sue flashed Julie an innocent smile. "Uh-uh."

"You'd talk clearer if you hadn't swallowed the canary."

"Umm ... Danny Lewis?"

"Negative. We're not anywhere near that in our ... friendship."

"Well, then, I guess it will remain one of America's Unsolved Mysteries."

"Very funny!" Julie picked up a stale donut and launched it at Sue's head. As it missed and landed on the floor, both women linked arms and walked out the door.

Julie swallowed a large serving of pride as the school day ended. She walked down the long hallway to Danny's classroom, pounding pulse in her ears drowning out every other noise. A large group of students was huddled around Mr. Lewis' desk, along with Sue, Butch, and Jim. *Why are they here?*

Waving the Valentine over her head, Julie announced, "Does anyone know who sent this to me?"

Danny's face turned beet red from embarrassment; the other faces turned equally red from laughter. Brandishing his Valentine over his head, Danny said, "Maybe the same person who sent me this one!"

Julie pointed her Valentine at Sue, then at Butch, then Jim. "Okay, you louses, 'fess up."

Sue reached into her purse and pulled out a folded newspaper. "Here." She opened the paper and pointed to a circled paragraph in the classifieds.

Julie dropped her Valentine on Danny's desk, grabbed the paper, and read the paragraph out loud. "Danny, thanks for all the work you've done for me. I really appreciate your help. Love, Julie."

"Ooh-ooh." The middle schoolers poked each other in the ribs and made no attempt at being quiet. Julie looked at the sea of faces and knew she should feel mad and incensed; but to her surprise, she felt excited and flustered.

"All right, citizens, return to your lives." Butch patted Julie on the shoulder as he followed the others out the door.

Growing attraction replaced skepticism and fear for Julie. Danny was kind and solicitous. He volunteered to change oil in her car. He explained there was an air filter that needed changing, but basically, the car ran well. When Julie offered to pay him, he refused to accept it. He acted like a sport when a bag of Double-Stuff Oreos magically appeared once a week in the teacher's lounge.

"But enough about cars," Danny said one day during lunch. "What do you like to do? Hunt? Fish? Bike? Garden?"

Proceed with Caution, Julie, so that no one is injured in the making of this friendship. "I'm not into hunting and fishing. I mostly work and take care of my kids."

"Who are your kids?" Danny leaned forward and looked openly at Julie.

I can see through those eyes down into your heart. "Christina's fifteen, Emma's fourteen, and Tom-Tom's nine."

"Divorced?"

300

"Yes, not long ago." *Am I giving too much information? What are the conversational rules for divorced people?*

"I've been divorced ten years."

"Kids?"

"I have eighteen-year-old twin boys, Sam and Yam."

"Yam?"

Danny's laugh was full of unselfconscious joy. "When the boys were four, I started reading 'Green Eggs and Ham' to them. There's the line that says, 'I am Sam, Sam I am.' Sam picked out his namesake, but Jeff thought I was saying, 'Sam Yam', so he started pointing to the page and saying 'Yam'. It stuck, and I've called them Sam and Yam ever since.

"They don't mind?"

"They have great senses of humor, plus they're both over six feet tall and big, tough football players. Who's going to mess with them?" Danny's eyes twinkled.

The conversation lapsed into companionable quiet.

"Danny." Julie ventured. "Our friends went to a lot of trouble to get us together. Why don't we go out once, and then they'll leave us alone? Besides, I'm getting fat eating Oreos!"

"Me too! Sounds like a plan. How about a movie?"

"When?" Julie's hands shook under the table.

"This Friday?"

"Great."

"Bye, then." Danny got up and walked out of the room.

Real great. I've got nothing to wear but fancy

The Mistake Has a Name

clothes – not good for sending a casual message on a casual date.

Julie called Danny at home, on the chance she could torpedo their date.

"Hey, Danny, it's me – Julie."

"Hi."

Is it a mistake to call him at home? Is that a more than casual message? "Ummm ... about our date—"

"Yeah?"

"I know this sounds silly, but I only have dressy clothes and they wouldn't be right for a movie. We probably shouldn't go on Friday." *That sounds so lame.*

"Would you go if you had the right clothes?"

"I'm not—"

"I don't mind going shopping. How about if we shop this Friday and we can catch a movie next weekend?"

Julie giggled. "A man-sighting in the mall!"

"Boggles the mind, doesn't it?"

"Lewis, have you crossed over to the Dark Side?"

"Luke, I am your father." Danny's pitiful attempt at imitating Darth Vader made Julie laugh out loud.

"Oh, man, you've been hanging around Butch and Jim too long. They got to you!"

Danny laughed. "I'll see you at work tomorrow."

"Night." Julie hung up. *You're too nice for my own good.*

Walking into the darkened movie theater, Julie thought back to their shopping date. It had taken an hour for Danny to convince her that he liked being with her, and that he enjoyed watching her pick out a pair of boot cut Levis, a pale green turtleneck, and a black fleece vest. Afterwards, they drove to Big Boy's and ordered breakfast at eight o'clock at night. They reluctantly left the restaurant at eleven. Julie was hooked. *This guy is handsome and a gentleman. Where's he been all my life?*

Danny guided Julie toward empty seats in the middle of a row at the back of the theater.

"Do we have to wait until after the previews to dig into the bucket?" Julie didn't want to look greedy, but half the fun of any movie was the hot, buttered popcorn, a huge cup of Dr. Pepper, and a box of Junior Mints.

"No way! Put it right between us."

Julie giggled as she and Danny took turns holding their snacks while taking off their jackets and fitting them around the backs of their seats. By the time they were settled, the credits were rolling for "Look Who's Talking Too."

"I don't get it, Julie," whispered Danny.

"What?"

"I'm confused."

"Seriously?"

"Yeah."

Julie decided to have some fun and be coy.

"How many kids do you have?"

"Two – you know that."

"How did they get here?"

"Whaddya mean?"

I'm probably enjoying this more than I should. But it's too much fun!

"You need the egg, the sperm ..."

Danny's eyes got big as he laughed. "I can't believe how dopey I am!"

Julie put her hand on his shoulder. "No, you're sweet." She had never met a man embarrassed by anything and found it endearing.

"Don't tell anyone about this!"

"I'd never *conceive* of the idea."

Danny slumped down in his seat, tipped his head back and moaned. "I deserved that!"

"Sorry – I couldn't resist! Butch and Jim and I have pun-offs every day – makes the long drive to school go faster."

"I'll have to get some tips from them if I'm going to keep up with you."

"Don't mess with the master."

By the time Julie and Danny had finished their lighthearted bantering, Julie wasn't sorry she missed some of the movie.

Julie walked in the door after midnight and called Sue.

"Hi, Sue. I hope I'm not calling too late."

"Not at all! I want a full report."

"I'm free-falling without a safety net."

"You had a good time?"

"I loved it!"

"Knew you would."

"I feel dizzy ... nervous ... excited ... my heart's racing ... and I'm really scared."

Silence.

"Sue?"

"I'm here. I'm deciding whether I should tell you something."

Uh-oh. "Like …"

"Like – did you know I dated Danny?"

"I heard that."

"It was a long time ago. He's been divorced ten years, and we dated after he'd been single for maybe a year."

"Okay."

"I think I know how you're feeling about him because I felt the same way. I proposed to him, but he said he could never marry anyone; that he had been burned once and would never put himself through that again."

Julie sighed.

"Please don't be mad at me." Julie heard the tremor in her friend's voice.

"Not mad at all. Now I know we can go out and have fun."

"You're sure you aren't mad at me?"

"Heck, no! You helped me get some balance back in my life."

"Yes?"

"For sure. Our next date better be bowling. No more movies for a guy who doesn't understand conception."

"Whaaat?"

Julie giggled. "Never mind. It's a long story."

"Danny, thanks for another great date. I know it's only midnight, but you've got a long drive back home. I'll see you at school on Monday." Julie stood at her door, whispering so she wouldn't wake her kids, and blushing like a teenager over her infatuation with this wonderful guy. *When was the last time I felt awkward around anyone? I don't want to blow it with him. He's*

305

sweet and kind, and everything about being with him feels right.

"I'll be there. Catch you at lunch time?"

"Yeah." Julie didn't trust her voice. Danny turned around, walked out her door and closed it behind him. *Why didn't he kiss me on the cheek? I like him!* Julie absentmindedly wandered over to the kitchen, where she saw Danny's hat sitting on the table. She grabbed it, ran to her door, and raced outside to the driveway.

"Danny! You'll need this."

"Thanks," he whispered.

Julie reached up with both hands, put the hat on his head and leaned in to kiss him. His warm lips made her forget how much the rest of her body shivered. She pulled away and ran backwards, shouting, "Be careful!"

"It's too late for that!"

Julie started crying and turned to run to her front door before Danny saw her tears. *I'm not sure I could explain the tears to him. I haven't shed many happy tears in my life – barely enough to identify these.* Julie dried her eyes on her sleeve and picked up the cordless phone.

"Mom? ... I'm sorry, I know it's late ... yeah, I'm fine ... I'm more than fine. I think I met the man I'm going to marry—"

"Lord, no!" Arlene shrieked.

Julie slammed the phone down. *Why did I think she'd be happy for me?*

CHAPTER 30
FATHER KNOWS BEST

The greatest irony of life knocked on Julie's door. She was determined to find the father who had abandoned her as a child so he could give her away again as a bride. Someday.

Locating Eugene became a game of Clue. Motive was everything, kind of a whydunit. *Why did Eugene leave Mom and me? Why didn't he ever try to find me? Why didn't he know me when he stood next to me that day at Jamie's house?*

The first move was easy. Julie knew that Grandpa Richard and Grandma Rose were still friends with Eugene's parents, and they gladly gave her his Washington address. Julie didn't know when he and Barbie had moved back, but she would find him first and ask questions later.

Julie drafted a simple, one-page letter, explaining everything she knew about Eugene, and making it clear that she wasn't interested in his money or cars or house or possessions, only his presence. She dropped the letter in the outgoing mail at work and spent the next week focusing on her job, her kids, and Danny. She desperately wanted Danny to know what she was up to; maybe he would encourage her to break the chain of deceit that had imprisoned her for most of her life. *All he knows is that my dad did some bad things to me and that he died in Wyoming. Danny promised me that the new Danny in my life would trump the first one; that he would love me and be gentle; and that all random acts would be only ones of kindness. I'll get this figured out,*

Eugene will come here, and we can get to our wedding and a new life. Pastor Dan quoted a verse from First John about the evil deeds of darkness exposed to the light. There will be time for all that once I find Eugene.

The letter might have been lost in the mail. Julie double-checked the address with her grandparents and wrote another letter. *I will start with Dear Eugene this time instead of Dear Dad. And I will leave out the paragraph about what my mom did after he left us.* Julie finished the letter, dropped it in a mailbox on the way home, and counted on the same diversions to keep her thoughts clear. If either letter was returned with a no forwarding address stamped on it, there would be closure.

Julie looked out her window at the spring rain pummeling the timid flowers and remembered when Connect the Dots had been her favorite pastime – a sad substitute for girlfriends and dolls. *I wanted a family like the Cleavers. I hope finding Eugene will give me that family.*

Neither letter was returned unopened or stamped undeliverable. Julie wished she had let Danny in on her scheme. Would there be anything to tell him?

Julie mailed six more letters to Eugene. The first was typed on her computer; the remaining five were copies. Julie thought he only deserved typed letters since he had abandoned her.

"Grandma, it's me again."
"Hi, Julie. I'm always glad to hear from you."
"Thanks, Grandma—"
"By the way, did you ever hear from Eugene?"
"That's kind of why I'm calling. No, I haven't."

"Did you try talking to Chuck and Nancy?"

"Who?"

"Didn't your mom tell you about them?"

"No." Julie's heart beat harder.

"I don't understand her."

"Me either. I don't expect to."

Rose let out an exasperated sigh. "Chuck is Eugene's brother."

"You're kidding!"

"No, I'm not. He and his wife Nancy live in Coldspring."

"This is too much. They've lived here—"

"All their married lives."

Julie shook her head. "It would be nice to get all the clues."

"I'm sorry I didn't tell you sooner. I assumed you knew about them."

"Grandma, don't assume anything."

"Guess not."

"Do you think I could call them?"

"I'm sure you could. They're very nice people."

"So are you, Grandma."

"Right back 'atcha."

"Later."

Julie pushed the off button on her cordless phone and pitched it on the bed. *Do I chance a face-to-face, or should I call these people? What if they don't know about me? Anything's possible with this family, especially where my mother is involved. Thing is, I can't ask anyone except her or Jamie. What happens if I open Pandora's Box?*

"Hi, James. It's Julie. Is this a good time to talk?

I'm calling from school." Julie's hands were sweating.

"Oh, Jewel, I was really hoping you would call. How long has it been since you were here? I wanted to call you, but I was afraid it might hurt you worse to hear from me." Jamie's gentle voice brought tears to Julie.

"James, I have a lot to tell you. And I need to ask your forgiveness for running out the way I did. So much has happened in my life since then."

"Girl, you're kind. No forgiveness is necessary."

"Thank you. Thank you so, so much."

"You're welcome and worth it."

"We definitely need to get together. I've missed your friendship. But for now, I have a quick question for you."

"Shoot."

"Do you know Chuck and Nancy Ness?"

"Yeah."

She's probably dreading the other shoe dropping, since I already kicked her with the first one.

"I've been sending letters to Eugene for the past couple months, and I haven't heard back from him. I just found out about Chuck and Nancy, and I wanted to contact them to make sure I have the right address for Eugene. Do you think it would be all right for me to do that?"

Jamie sighed in relief. "Absolutely! I've been with them a few times; they're cool people and I'm sure they would shoot straight with you."

It was Julie's turn to sigh. "Thank you, friend. You've taken a huge burden from me. I will call them today."

"Go for it! Call me soon, okay?"

"Roger that." Julie hung up, ready to jump back into the deep end.

Julie verified Eugene's address with Chuck, printed another letter and mailed it. *I wonder if Barbie intercepted the letters; after all, Eugene's past is not hers.* Julie didn't want to fret needlessly. She needed to wait a little longer.

No letter ever arrived from Washington.

"Julie?" Nancy had a naturally soft voice, especially on the phone.

"Yes?"

"This is Nancy. Nancy Ness, your aunt."

"Hey there."

"Have you heard from Chuck's brother yet?"

"No, no I haven't. I hit a brick wall."

"I hope you don't think I've been too forward, but I decided to call Barbie yesterday. You sounded anxious, so I thought I'd call and do a little digging. Turns out Eugene spent several months recuperating from hip surgery, then knee surgery. The second one brought an infection that went through his whole body. Barbie said they thought they were going to lose him a few times."

Before I had a chance to talk to him? "How is he now?"

"He's much better, and Barbie said she's finally able to give him your letters."

"Nancy, you're amazing. I can't thank you enough for doing this for me."

"Please do me a favor?"

"Anything."

"Let me know what happens."

"Done."

Julie folded and unfolded and refolded the letter

311

from Eugene so many times the past three days that it was starting to tear on the crease lines. It didn't matter because every word was permanently etched in Julie's mind and on her heart.

"My dear Julie," Eugene began. That could have been the beginning and end and been enough. Julie had never had a father call her dear. The love packed in one word erased years of heartache; of abuse and violence from Danny, the only father she had known until now.

"You are a beautiful woman with a beautiful family. I would never, ever have willingly given you up for adoption. I think your biological father was a Navy man from Pennsylvania."

The dysfunctional world of her childhood shattered with that one sentence. Eugene's matter-of-fact words came from his belief that this was old news for Julie. *Someone dropped the ball.*

"When people assumed I was your father," the letter continued, "I never corrected their thinking, because I wanted to save your mother any further embarrassment. When we married and moved to Washington, I never told her the mumps I had as a twelve-year old left me sterile. That was wrong of me."

The constant rereading of the letter lessened some of the shock.

"Barbie and I never adopted children; I guess that's why we treated Jamie like our daughter. As far as my parents, brother and wife knew, you were my biological daughter. I don't know why none of them ever learned that most men who had mumps as boys ended up sterile. I guess we're all guilty of creating our own reality. I'm glad I have the chance to finally tell you the truth. Maybe you can put an end to the lies that dogged me for so long."

God, are there any more bombs? This is like "The Price is Right." Do I look through door number three for father number three? I probably shouldn't be bargaining with You – but if You help me find my father, I promise I'll spend the rest of my life following You.

Julie reached up to the top shelf of her closet and pulled down a box her mom had recently given her. Most of it was filled with report cards, including the one she had wanted to tear to shreds. There were also artwork and other school papers. Julie tossed the report cards in the trash, pulled out everything else and plopped down on the floor, then retrieved her birth certificate from the top of the pile. *Why didn't I connect these dots sooner? Dan and I are sixteen months apart; if Mom's initial explanation about Eugene had been true, she would have had to divorce him, meet Danny, and get pregnant, all within one month. Maybe it was God's grace that clouded my understanding until I was old enough to absorb the truth about Danny and Eugene. What will I do with the truth?*

CHAPTER 31
A LITTLE GESTURE

Arlene was getting an unannounced visitor. *I'm not giving her any time to concoct another fairy tale.*

"Hey, Ma." Julie poured herself a cup of coffee, sat down at the kitchen table, stretched out her long legs and kicked off her flip-flops. "The lilacs are beautiful, aren't they?"

Arlene lifted her hair off her neck, undid the top button of her blue-striped blouse and glared at her. "You're the only person I know who notices flowers in this heat! You should pay more attention to your kids. Why don't they come to see me? Is Tom in trouble again? You know if you stayed home more often—"

"Ma, I didn't come here for a parenting lecture."

"I can see that."

A tense silence fell over the room while Arlene fanned herself with a folded newspaper. *Will she ever stop harassing me about my kids? Does she have any idea the reason they don't visit her is because of how nasty she treats them? I'm not dealing with that right now.*

"Mom." Julie wore her innocent face. "I wrote a letter to Eugene a few months back."

Arlene's face turned ashen. "What?"

"I needed some questions answered." Julie pulled Eugene's letter out of her purse. "Imagine my surprise when he told me he isn't my biological father."

With trembling hands, Arlene dropped the paper, picked up a package of cigarettes from the table, pulled one out and attempted to light it. She could not stop her hands from shaking and threw the pack and disposable lighter across the room. "Why can't you ever leave things alone? Even when you were a child, you could never," she pounded on the table, "never, never leave anything alone! You always asked, 'why, why, why!'"

Julie looked calmly at her mom with a mixture of anger, humor, and pity. "Eugene obviously told the truth."

Arlene exhaled a plaintive sigh. "I guess there's no reason to keep anything secret anymore." Holding her head between her hands, she choked out her story in a muffled voice.

"When Eugene – Elliott – and I moved to Washington, there was no house, no job and no money. When I found out that he could never give me a child, it was the last of a string of lies and deceptions. He was offered a construction job in Hawaii, and I knew I absolutely would not go with him."

Arlene lifted her head, got up slowly, walked out of the kitchen, and was gone for such a long time that Julie thought she was being dismissed again – the expected outcome every time a subject got too close to the bone. As she grabbed her purse and got up to leave, Arlene came back into the room cradling an old Florsheim shoebox. Mother and daughter sat down as Arlene set the box on the table, lifted the lid, dropped it on the floor, and began sorting through the contents of the box. *I've seen that box for years; didn't it just have another pair of shoes in it?*

"Here. If you're so hell-bent on discovering the truth, you might as well have these." Arlene pulled out a stack of black-and-white photos and pitched them at Julie, who laid them out in front of her.

315

Arlene spun the photos around and pointed to one of them. "That's Elliott and his buddies in the Navy, during the Korean War." She tapped the other picture with a sharply manicured, red nail. "This is Elliott and his mom, taken the morning he shipped out."

Julie could not believe what she was looking at. "Why didn't you ever—"

"He was a handsome guy, wasn't he? Everyone said we were the perfect couple. We were elected homecoming king and queen our senior year."

"You mentioned you were homecoming queen when I was in high school."

Arlene got up, walked to the refrigerator, pulled out a can of Diet Coke, flipped the top, took a long drink, and returned to the table. "Like I said, after Elliott left, I got a job at a restaurant-bar called Coasters. Mostly servicemen came in there." Arlene ran her finger around the rim of the can.

Do you realize you're picking up a conversation you started twenty years ago?

"I was very lonely, and I wasn't about to sit home twiddling my thumbs while Elliott swam in the ocean in Hawaii. I was twenty-seven and ready for some of the fun he promised when we moved out there."

Julie stared at the photos.

"I was working the night shift at Coasters when this guy, Andrew, came in. He spotted me, walked up to me, and said, 'Has anyone told you that there is a mysterious beauty about you?' Who could resist a line like that? He came back every night after that, and soon we were dating. By the time I found out he was only nineteen, I was carrying you."

Julie thought back to when she was eight, and her mom tried to explain how Grandma Philips was

316

married twice, so that her last name was no longer Sandford. It was way too much information for Julie then – and she felt the same way now.

Arlene was on a roll. "Andrew was at Puget Sound for another nine months after you were born. When he was discharged, he assumed I would marry him and the three of us would go back to his home. I think it was in Charlottesville, Virginia."

Julie was a lonely, abandoned girl. "Mom, why didn't you and I go with Andrew?" she whispered.

"Because," Arlene suddenly wailed, "I hated coloreds. I hated the South. I hated the heat!"

"And you were still legally married to Elliott?"

"That too."

"What did Elliott do when he got back and found out you were pregnant?" *I can't believe I'm asking you these questions.*

"He was angry – but he was always even-tempered – not like Danny. He was not like any of the other men I've known, either before or since then. He seemed resigned to whatever I wanted. He did not fight for me. He never asked who the father was. When I demanded a divorce – well, that was fine by him. The only thing he asked was that I agreed to give you his last name – Ness."

Oh God – I wish you had stayed a single mom. "And when did you marry Danny?"

"I met him after Elliott moved back to Michigan, and Andrew to Virginia. By the time Danny proposed to me, I was carrying your brother. Danny legally adopted you, and I didn't care about keeping my promise to Elliott. I didn't think he deserved it."

The web of deceit that trapped you for so many years also trapped me. "Did Andrew expect you to tell

317

me about him someday?"

"I figured since he was in the Navy, I could tell you he'd been killed in some kind of accident at sea."

Julie's heartbeat was louder than the ticking wall clock. "So, all you know is that Andrew is from Charlottesville, Virginia? You don't know anything else?"

"It was the fifties. I was embarrassed. I was never going back to Michigan. No one would ever know about Andrew. I don't know why I ever moved back here; it was a big mistake."

Seems your secret stopped several years short of the grave. This was the last time Julie could press her advantage. "Mom, can you please tell me everything you remember about Andrew? Like, what's his last name?"

"Little." Arlene finished her soda.

"Don't make me play twenty questions." Julie focused all her emotions into what she hoped was a direct hit on her mom's guilt.

"And he had brown hair and brown eyes. I think he was about five-ten." Arlene tossed her can into the garbage. "He was stationed at Puget Sound Naval Shipyard for three years, from fifty-four to fifty-six. My friend Charlene from Bremerton is the only person who knows about him. Could be she remembers more than I do." Arlene got up, picked up the shoebox, and stepped on the lid as she left the room.

I'm amazed it took you this long to leave.

CHAPTER 32
CLOSE ENCOUNTERS AND
TANGLED BLISS

I should have kept the box closed. Julie sought relief from her churning thoughts in the security of familiar people – her coworkers, her children, and Danny. Throughout that summer, she and Danny took all five children to the zoo, restaurants, and drives to the Upper Peninsula. Butchie had a large boat and invited Julie and her full catastrophe – his favorite phrase – to join him and his wife on their boat to watch the Fourth of July fireworks on Lake Michigan. The beautiful, starlit night, with the moon rising over the water as the fireworks began, redeemed Julie's early years of unpredictability and deprivation. *I could get used to this. Christina and Emma and Tom-Tom like Danny and his boys, and Sam and Yam like us. This is my second-chance family.*

Danny invited Julie and her kids to his parents' house for a picnic on July fifth. Julie knew she should be past the point of nervousness – but the last time she cared about impressing anyone was Chris' parents in high school. *God, what if Danny's parents are like my parents? Or worse yet – what if they're nice, but they don't like me? I wonder how much of my life Danny shared with them.*

Georgia and Daniel Lewis had playful respect for each other. It was sweet and encircled everyone around them. Julie forgot about herself and entered the dynamics with happy abandon. By the end of the picnic, Julie knew her love for Danny was the wrapping on a

319

delightful family package.

Danny, Sam, and Yam made the drive to Allen Park every Sunday morning to go to church with Julie and her kids, usually spending the afternoon together until it was time for everyone to return to church for supper, Kids' Adventure Club, youth group, and small-group Bible studies for the adults. Danny was comfortable and well liked at Free. Julie stopped thinking of him as a visitor in *her* church.

The thirty-somethings planned a cross-country skiing outing for the first Saturday in December. The day would end with hot chocolate and a warm fire at Kale Chalet.

Julie glided across the new-fallen snow, thoughts centered on how many bad things had occurred on an endless loop in her life during the winter and especially around Christmas. She was hard-wired for pre-Christmas to mid-January depression, although sincerely hoping something would break that loop.

"A dime for your thoughts." Danny skied behind Julie, talking freely to her as they dropped back behind the others.

"I thought they were supposed to cost a penny."

"Your thoughts are worth more than that."

The sun dipped lower on the horizon, just past mid-afternoon. A sliver of moon made its quiet appearance in the opposite sky. Julie was incredibly grateful for the guy behind her who embraced silences and who genuinely cared about her.

"I was thinking about something Pastor Tim often says – that God chooses not to reverse consequences in our lives, but instead chooses to redeem them." The trail led out of the woods and into a clearing; Julie waited for Danny to pull up beside her.

"I've thought a lot about that, too."

"Some things that happened to me were just that – they happened without my consent or control." Julie stopped, laid her poles on the ground, and zipped up her vest. "That fire in the chalet is going to feel wonderful!"

"You bet!"

Julie picked up her poles and started her easy glide again. "But some of the things were my doing, and they became my undoing. Do I have the right to ask God to work those things out for good in my life?"

Danny slowed his pace to stay even with Julie. "When I thought my first wife was serious about kicking her alcoholism, I went to AA meetings with her. At first, I was so wounded, I couldn't think about anything except being an expert victim. Then, when I thought about the wrong choices I made in my life, I didn't figure God wanted anything to do with me. If He didn't have a magic wand, I was doomed to spend the rest of my life continually suffering the consequences like Scrooge and the Ghost of Christmas Future."

"I love 'A Christmas Carol!' I cry every time it gets to the end!"

"Me too. But if you tell anyone, you'll regret it!" Danny grabbed a clump of snow from the high bank bordering the path and hit the center of Julie's retreating back.

"Danny, we need to catch up to the gang!"

Danny and Julie were surrounded by puffs of exhaled air as they skied a fast clip over the carefully groomed trail. When they were within shouting distance of the chalet, they slowed down, and Danny picked up the thread of their earlier conversation. "What turned things around for me was a verse from Psalms that talks about God redeeming our lives from the pit. I figured whether I was thrown into the pit, fell in accidentally, or jumped in on purpose, He could lift me out of it. It took a long time to realize that God does not pull me out grudgingly and then suspend me over it again, threatening to drop me if I step away from Him."

Oh, the love Julie had for this man skiing next to her, a man who might be willing to spend the rest of his life always at her side. "Danny, have I told you that you're the one for me?"

Danny made a noise that sounded like a half-laugh, half-cry. Julie stopped skiing, suddenly alarmed.

"Danny, what's wrong?"

Tossing his poles into the air, Danny threw his arms around Julie, enveloping her in a massive bear hug.

"Last week, I asked my dad how I would know if you were the right woman for me. He answered, 'She will tell you!' And he was right! And you're right!" Danny pulled off his gloves and took Julie's hands.

"Julie Marie Dietrich, will you marry me?"

The first time I met you, I looked through your deep brown eyes into your heart. "On one condition."

Danny lowered his head.

"That it happens before the end of this year."

Danny lifted his head, let out a war whoop, raised his fist and yelled, "Hey, guys, we're getting married!" The group gathered outside the chalet broke out into wild cheering.

The church was filled with garlands, pine wreaths, candelabras, red satin bows, and white, glittery lights. It was Christmas Eve; Julie stood outside the double doors at the back of the sanctuary. She thought a Christmas Eve wedding would bring a small gathering,

322

with most of their church friends at home celebrating the holiday with their families. As much as she wanted to share her wedding with friends who were true family, she would not be disappointed with them for choosing their biological families over a Christmas Eve wedding. *If I had a loving family during any Christmas growing up, I would have chosen to be with them at any cost.*

After Julie told Danny about all the times her adopted dad had destroyed their Christmas tree and presents during a drunken rage, Danny convinced her that God would redeem those memories with a Christmas Eve wedding. Julie was initially hesitant; her mom would scoff at how unconventional it was, and just plain wrong. *My mom will find something to complain about anyway, and Danny is the sweetest man I have ever known.* It turned out to be easy for Julie to agree to the wedding date.

For the past three weeks, people sent Julie emails saying, "Who are you kidding? We would *never* miss your wedding!" One of her friends slipped through the sanctuary doors and whispered, "The place is packed!" Grandma Emma, Georgia and Daniel Lewis, Grandma Rose and Grandpa Richard, Danny's grandparents, Arlene Sandford – all family who were there with love and encouragement. Christina and Emma stood at the front; Tom-Tom ushered everyone to their seats; Sam and Yam stood on either side of Julie. Stephanie Peterson skipped down the aisle, spreading rose petals from her basket onto the floor, oblivious to Gloria's smile. If ever there was a magical evening in Julie's life, this was it. *God is good – all the time.*

Still, Julie struggled to lock and load her thoughts on the ceremony. Joy had been an unfamiliar emotion most of her life. The hesitations in her first wedding ... marriage to an alcoholic ... mistakes she had made ... empty places in her spirit she tried to fill by controlling all the outcomes ... none of these things mattered here. She was marrying a man who promised to draw her closer to a second-chance God – not a God of seconds or leftovers, but a God drawing her to a continual feast at His table of redemption. Danny said it was God's extravagant grace, and Julie was more than ready to taste it.

"Tonight's message to Julie and Danny is The Back Side of Christmas and Marriage." Danny squeezed Julie's hand as they turned and faced Pastor Tim. "We are standing in a building filled with poinsettias, sparkling lights, lit candles, and the fragrance of pine. We also know that the tables in the Fellowship Hall are filled with every kind of cookie and baked good imaginable. And let's hope there are a few fruit cakes there!" The congregation laughed at their beloved pastor's fruit cake obsession.

"I suspect our homes are decorated to the nines. We want to show only the good sides this time of year. If a batch of cookies is burned, we might rescue them, but we don't waste icing or cinnamon candies on them. If there is a crooked side on our Christmas tree, or a side with gaps in the branches like missing teeth, we turn that side toward the wall and don't waste ornaments on it.

"At our family gatherings, there might be a drunk Uncle Joe who becomes the elephant in the living room. We ignore his behavior, step around him, and hope he will wander to a place where he can pass out alone.

"There is often depression, discouragement, and a blind hurtling towards a new year filled with hopelessness. We ignore that side of our spirits for the sake of the season.

"There is the precious, infant Jesus in a sanitized and stilled stable, worshipped by tame animals which, if we believe the crèche scenes, know exactly where to stand around the manger.

"What is the back side of Christmas? It is the back of the baby Jesus, ripped open by a leather whip, the price for our forgiveness. It is the side the world needs to see.

"In the same way, there is a back side to marriage. Danny and Julie have each experienced the back side in their first marriages: alcoholic spouses; emotional and mental abuse; days and months and years of hopelessness. They are bringing God into their marriage as one strand of the three-fold cord not easily broken. They know there will be trials – times when they see only the back side, like the knotted side of a needlepoint, and they may be tempted to despair." Pastor Tim looked at the couple before him. "Remember the back side of your marriage is the same as the back side of Christmas: It is the torn back of Jesus, the only One who is able to bring you forgiveness and strength. The book of Lamentations says, 'His mercies are new every morning.' Hallelujah!"

The congregation broke into spontaneous applause. Julie was surprised that it took so long for her eyes to spill over with tears of joy. Real, deep, God-giving joy.

Rings and vows were exchanged. Danny and Julie were announced as Mr. and Mrs. Daniel Lewis, and Julie floated through the reception, a life-size doll with the perfect dress.

325

CHAPTER 33
THE CHARLESTON TWO-STEP

A new house in Allen Park was perfect for Danny and Julie, with their commute to school less than five miles. Far more importantly, Julie was deeply grateful to her husband for understanding her need to start fresh in a place without old memories. Their house was a simple, three-bedroom ranch, built in the nineteen-seventies and obviously well-maintained over the years. Sam and Yam were at the University of Michigan in Ann Arbor. Christina, Emma, and Tom-Tom were busy with school and extracurriculars. Almost a year had passed since their wedding; although content with her husband, job, and family, Julie had not stopped thinking about her biological father. She had desperately wanted him to walk her down the aisle but never had time or courage to look for him.

Sitting in their cozy kitchen on a Saturday morning, looking over her Christmas shopping list and marveling over Danny's willingness to shop with her – even after they were married, and he had nothing more to prove – Julie thought about what it would be like to have her real dad spend Christmas with them. Unless records were tightly sealed, it should be easy to confirm that Andrew Little was stationed at Puget Sound sometime in the mid-fifties. Arlene had either lied to Julie or misled her so many times and for so many years, that it was difficult to trust that she had the right name for her bio dad. But it was a jumping-off place. Monday during her lunch break, Julie would use her cell to make a long-distance call to Washington.

It was twelve-thirty Eastern time, nine-thirty Pacific time. Julie hoped the base office opened before ten.

A very short phone call and a very helpful clerk at Puget Sound showed no record of any Andrew Little. *Have I hit a wall already? I've waited to find my real dad since high school when I thought I would someday meet Eugene Ness. It can't end this way.*

If Danny wondered why he never saw Julie in the lounge, he did not mention it, other than the occasional comment that she was losing weight. It was easy for Julie to answer with, "I'm just making sure I fit into a special dress." Danny seemed okay with that. The truth stretched farther than the dress: Julie began using all her free time to stay in her classroom and surf the Internet for addresses and phone numbers for the International Adoption Agency, the United States Adoption Agency, and agencies in Virginia. Julie drafted a simple letter giving her name, date and place of birth, her home phone number, and the reason for her letter – to locate her biological father stationed at Puget Sound Naval Shipyard from nineteen fifty-four to fifty-six. After mailing five letters, Julie switched her focus to work and her family, using only spare time to daydream about her real dad.

Julie received letters expressing sympathy for her search but stating that her request was denied. Undeterred, she called the agencies, got different contact names, and remailed the letters. *Maybe the left hand doesn't know what the right hand is doing.*

After each rejection letter, Julie broadened her search – to the Vital Statistics Office in Bremerton; to the base historian who looked through yearbooks of the USS Missouri; to other base personnel; to anyone and everyone who would listen to her story. Phone calls and letters had a common thread: nothing could be done without either Julie's real birth certificate or Andrew's social security number. Julie wrote to Eugene and asked him to mail her a letter granting her permission to obtain her original birth certificate.

Julie left a paper trail over the next months. She bought a large plastic bin to store the weekly letters she received. On Good Friday, she walked into her kitchen in time to catch the phone before the answering machine took over.

"Hello, is this Julie Lewis?" The voice sounded young and hesitant.

Julie dropped her keys on the counter and distractedly shuffled through a pile of yesterday's junk mail. *I wonder what she wants. A donation for St. Michael's? A promise to vote for her favorite democratic candidate? Money for new vests for the local police force?* "This is she."

"My name is Sheila, and I work in Military Records for all the naval bases in Bremerton."

Julie dropped the mail. "I didn't think you would return my call. I've gotten used to riding the red tape express."

"I know how that goes."

"What can you tell me?" Julie closed her eyes and knew everything she valued was tied up in the answer.

"Probably not what you want to hear."

"Andrew Little is dead."

"No. I mean, I don't know." Sheila let out a big sigh. "This is hard."

"Whatever it is, I need to hear it."

"Seems like someone could have easily told you

this months ago."

"Yeah?"

"Absolutely. Back in seventy-three, there was a fire in our building, and all the files with last names ending in K through Z were destroyed."

"Which includes L for Little."

"Uh huh."

"Why didn't someone tell me sooner?"

"National security, privacy, incompetence – who knows?"

"Well, Sheila, thank you for telling me. I don't know what I'll do next, but at least I know what I don't need to do anymore."

"Good luck to you, Julie."

"Luck, prayers, I'll take them all."

Julie crawled into bed with a weighted heart. *I should have told Danny before now because it looks like I was trying to keep something from him.*

"Hon?" Julie turned on the nightstand lamp, propped her pillow against the headboard and sank into it.

"What, babe?" Danny put one arm under his pillow and used his other hand to rub Julie's arm.

"There's something I need to tell you."

"Now?"

"I should have told you a long time ago."

"You're not sick, are you?"

Julie heard loving concern in her husband's voice, which increased her levels of both comfort and guilt. "No, not physically. My heart is sick."

"Whaddya mean?"

"Do you remember me telling you about my biological dad, Andrew Little?"

329

"Sure. You said you would like to find him someday."

"Actually, I've been trying since Christmas. I want my kids to have another grandfather, and I want something I never had – a father who loves me."

"What have you done so far?"

"I've written tons of letters, made phone calls, and surfed the Internet. Today I found out that Andrew's military file burned in a fire at Puget Sound Naval Shipyard."

Danny kept rubbing Julie's arm. "Maybe you could call Arlene. She probably knows more than she's told you."

"Tomorrow." Julie reached over and turned out the light. Confrontation with Arlene would wait until she was intimate with this loving, tender husband who shared her heart.

"Happy Easter, Mom."

"What's happy about it? You couldn't bother to bring your family over."

Julie bit her lip. "I told you, we've been invited to Danny's parents' house. You are also invited."

"And I told you that I don't enjoy myself over there. I always feel like a fifth wheel."

"It's not just a couples thing. Your grandkids will be there."

"They don't have time for me."

What if you made time for them? That's the way it's supposed to be. It's what I wanted all my life. I don't think you get it. "Maybe you'll want to come some other time."

"Not likely." Julie heard the door of her mom's heart slam shut.

"Can I ask you something?"

"It seems to be what you're good at."

Julie ignored the sarcasm. "What was your friend Charlotte's last name?"

"Hoffman."

"Where is she living now?"

"Brother, here we go again." Julie thought her mom sounded more tired than annoyed.

"I promise it's the last question."

"Charlene Hoffman lives in Corbett, Oregon."

"Great. Goodbye."

"Why do you want to know?"

Julie took secret, rare pleasure in withholding information. "Just curious."

"Figures." Arlene hung up before Julie could say anything else.

I will give her that one.

The Lewises had four weeks of accumulated vacation and a honeymoon on deck. Julie suggested that she, Danny, and his mom, Georgia, fly to Oregon to visit Georgia's sister Pearl. Georgia was thrilled at the idea but hesitated to be a burden, until Julie explained that she and Danny would leave her at Pearl's, go off for a week of sightseeing and romance, and then return for her. Georgia offered to book the flight and pay for three roundtrip tickets to Portland.

Julie had enough adrenalin to fly to Portland in her own power. As soon as they settled in their plane seats in Detroit, Georgia put her head back and fell asleep. Danny was lost in "Field and Stream." This was Julie's first trip back to the Pacific Northwest since she left at eight years old; she was not going to sleep or read and take a chance on missing anything.

Planning for the trip had been a whirlwind. Everyone at school gave Julie suggestions for what to see and do in Corbett, twenty miles east of Portland. She and Danny had reservations at the Brickhaven Bed and Breakfast overlooking the Columbia River Gorge. They also planned to see Multnomah Falls, the Washington Park Rose Gardens, Mount Hood, the Bonneville Dam, and anything and everything else fun and interesting. And of course, they would pay a visit to Arlene's friend Charlene.

Maybe Andrew – my dad – got tired of Virginia and moved back to Washington. If Charlene kept in touch with him, we could contact him and go see him! I know I shouldn't get my hopes up, but I can't help it.

The flight attendants collected lunch trays before Julie realized she had ignored both the food and the view outside her window. Her mind was occupied creating a scenario of a reunion with her father.

Brickhaven Bed and Breakfast topped Julie's expectations. Built in the nineteen fifties, it was constructed of recycled bricks and with a conscious effort to copy the designs of Frank Lloyd Wright. Every room was decorated in English country décor; several of them overlooked the Columbia River Gorge. Michigan was home and had the beauty of inland lakes and miles of magnificent shoreline; but this part of Oregon was wild and spectacular. *I could live here. I wonder if Danny would be willing to move.*

The Triple A directions were neatly folded in Julie's purse, although not needed after she memorized them during the flight. Danny drove their rental car up into the Cascade Mountains, while Julie tilted her head back and felt the cool, foggy May air caressing her face.

Danny's voice broke through her reverie. "You got the directions?"

"We're looking for Summit Road. We should see a sign in about a mile."

The car was shrouded in a haunted desolation. Danny drove the last mile and pointed to a sign for Summit, mostly hidden behind overgrown branches. They turned on a gravel road and saw a beat-up trailer partially enveloped by a growth of bramble.

I didn't expect Charlotte to live in a trailer. I should feel comfortable here.

Danny glanced at Julie. "Is this the right place?"

"We followed the directions." Julie opened her door as a large, mangy dog limped over and stared at her with glassy eyes.

"Maybe we should go," whispered Danny as he got out and stood next to Julie. A woman wearing jeans and a pink t-shirt appeared at the screen door. Her silvery hair fell in thick waves on her shoulders, pulled back from her face by a pair of glasses propped on top of her head.

"Julie! Is that you? Darn if you don't look like Arlene forty years ago!" Charlene pushed the door open and ran down three steps in a pair of blue flip-flops. She embraced Julie, then turned toward Danny and flashed a brilliant, guileless smile. "And who is this handsome guy?"

"Charlene, this is Danny, my husband."

"No one has called me Charlene since I was a little girl and in trouble. My name is Charlie. We don't need to stand on formalities. I need both of you sweeties to call me Charlie." Julie and Danny each hugged

Charlie. "I hope you can stay for lunch." She spun around and stepped carefully toward the trailer. Julie made sure she stepped in Charlie's footprints.

A comprehensive thesaurus lacked the words to accurately describe the assault on her senses when Julie walked into Charlie's kitchen. A large cage in the corner was home to two yellow-faced cockatiels with orange cheek patches, squawking like their spiky hair was styled against their wishes. The bottom of the cage was covered in a layer of carrot pieces, broccoli tidbits, soggy spinach leaves, and congealed rice. Dogs of unknown breeds wandered in, in a quest to stake territory away from cats of various sizes and colors. Charlie casually mentioned that the other rooms in the trailer – bedroom, bathroom, and small sitting room – were each filled with a box, bowl or cage, home to a ferret, tropical fish, guinea pig and turtle. Swarms of flies landed everywhere.

"I know people think I'm loopy, but these critters need a home, and they're like my family."

Julie wished she had worn enough perfume to mask the smell of Charlie's menagerie.

"But enough of that. I hope you brought your appetite because I got a real good lunch made."

Standing behind Charlie, Danny looked at Julie and shrugged his shoulders. Julie half-smiled. *At least I won't embarrass myself by overeating.*

"Make yourselves comfy at the table, and I'll be right back." Charlie pushed aside a large dog and disappeared into the bedroom.

Julie trusted neither her thoughts nor her voice as she dug around her purse for a tissue and wiped off the seat of a vinyl chair. An uncovered casserole sat in

334

the middle of the table, looking like it had already been tested by one of the cats walking around it. *God, please tell me that this trip was worth it ... was worth this.*

Charlie came back carrying a large shoebox. "Do you mind if we wait to eat until I show you something?"

"No!" Danny and Julie answered in unison.

Charlie laughed. "How long have you two been married?"

"Long enough to know that we can wait to eat until we've seen whatever you have in the box." *I hope it's not another animal.*

Charlie set the box down on the table and took the casserole to the stovetop, returning with three cans of soda. "I don't think these had a chance to get cold yet, but I thought you might be thirsty."

"Thank you, Charlie. It was really nice of you to invite us."

"I'm tickled pink" – she pointed to her t-shirt – "that you found me." Charlie set the cans down and opened the box. "I haven't looked at these pictures since your mom and I lived in Washington." Charlie pulled out a black-and-white photo. "These young bucks are my husband and your daddy. They were on the Missouri together. Unfortunately, your daddy is the one looking away."

Julie choked down disappointment.

"I wrote to Arlene every year after she left Bremerton. I always asked her if she told you about Andrew, and if you ever met him."

A yellow lab walked up to Julie and nuzzled its nose into her elbow. Julie reached down to pet the dog and looked up at Charlie. "What do you mean, every year?"

Charlie's face wore an unfamiliar hurt expression. "I'm sorry I missed a few years. I think she got mad at me when I pushed too hard about Andrew, because she didn't write back. I stopped writing and called her at your grandma's house, but Rose wouldn't let me talk to Arlene. Not for a long time." Charlie's eyes pooled in tears; some of the dogs walked gently to her and laid heads and paws on her lap.

"Charlie, have you felt guilty about this?"

"Yes, I have. I've waited for Arlene to bring it up so I could apologize, but she likes to bury her head in the sand when anyone gets too close."

Julie was overcome with affection for this kind woman and ashamed of her unwillingness to look past the filth of the trailer. She sprang out of her chair and hugged Charlie tightly. "You've got nothing to worry about, at least with me. As for my mom, you have her pegged. I've spent my life looking for her good side and stay on it. I'm no longer sure she has one."

"Julie, I still feel—"

"Listen to me. Mom lied to both of us. She told me she hadn't heard from you since she left Bremerton. After her stroke a few years ago, she has a hard time remembering details about those years, except your last name and where you live.

"What did she tell you about Andrew?"

"Only that he was from Charlottesville, Virginia."

"Julie! He was from *West* Virginia!"

"West?"

"Oh, dear, I should have told you the truth myself a long time ago."

"Do you keep in touch with Andrew? Did he move back here?"

336

"No, and I don't know. I never heard from him or saw him again after your mom turned down his marriage proposal. He may have finished his time and headed back home. I never figured out why Arlene married that no-good, drinking, street-fighting man. What was his name?"

"Danny."

Charlie looked at Danny. "Do you ever resent his name?"

"Never thought about it."

"Good, because you don't look anything like him, and you sure don't act like him."

"At least he's out of my life," said Julie.

"Why?"

"Long story." Julie began spilling the highlights – *lowlights* – of her life and realized Danny probably hadn't heard all that she was sharing. By the time she came up for air, the dogs and cats were all sleeping in different spots around the room; even the birds were quiet.

Shadows were falling across the walls when Julie and Danny hugged Charlie one more time and left for the winding drive back to the inn.

Julie's enthusiasm ebbed during the rest of their sightseeing. All she wanted to do was go home and look for Andrew. Again.

A high-ranking naval officer in Military Records in Georgia got intel about Julie's search and did some digging. He reached Julie by phone and told her that he hit a wall without Andrew's social security number. When he suggested Julie hire a private investigator, she politely thanked him for his help and hung up. *Money may be no object for him, but it's the object and subject for me – and I'm sure for Danny, too. It wouldn't be a problem for rich people or celebrities, like Oprah Winfrey.*

Sam and Yam called the summer weather splendacious. Julie set aside the search for her father and focused on the blessings surrounding her every day. She and Danny had several free weekends without the demands of seminars or teaching-related activities. Their jobs were secure for the fall. Before they married, Danny promised Julie they would spend their summers on house projects, short daytrips with whichever kid was home, and being together. When the temp climbed into the nineties, they headed for the town beach. During cooler evenings, they had barbecues for their combined kids and a gaggle of their friends. On the Fourth of July, Christina and her boyfriend Stuart, Emma and her boyfriend Dusty, Tom-Tom and his posse, Sam and his girlfriend Josie, and Yam and his girlfriend Janice all converged at the Lewis home for a picnic. It was a raucous good time and reminded Julie of the years with Tom's cousins, minus the alcohol. As Tom-Tom said, they were high on life, and it was a healing, refreshing season for Julie's spirit.

When the return of fall sent everyone back to one school or another, Julie's thoughts returned to her father, the one missing factor in the equation of her life. The idea of contacting Oprah – an idea that seemed so absurd in May – suddenly seemed in the here and now. It would be easy to cut and paste parts of her various letters and compose one for the producers of "Oprah." Hers was a compelling story of three fathers, with the hope that the third one would be the charm. *While I'm waiting to get a response from the producers, I can lose a few pounds and be prepared for a television experience.*

Since there was no apparent protocol against receiving personal mail at school, and Julie wasn't ready to spring her new plan on Danny, she used the school address on the return labels. She experienced nail-biting tension over the weekends before she got back to school Monday mornings, looking for letters about her father.

Julie denied any power of discouragement over her, even though a month passed with no responses. She was an expert in the long shot and decided to send another copy of her letter to the producers of "Unsolved Mysteries." *I would love to meet Robert Stack! In the meantime, I might still hear from "Oprah." Then I would need to decide which show should get my story!*

Just before Thanksgiving, Julie accepted the reality that either her letter to "Oprah" was buried in a stack of junk mail on someone's desk or had long ago become fodder for the circular file. She would check her mailbox once more before leaving for the four-day weekend and make time over the holiday to tell Danny what she had done these many months.

"I'll catch up with you in the parking lot. I'm going to check my box before we leave."

"Are you expecting a dinner invite from the president?"

"Maybe! Why not?"

"Why not, indeed? Thing is, you're too classy for the White House!"

"A girl could get used to you."

"That's the plan."

Danny jogged toward the front door of the main entrance as Julie pushed open the door to the office, greeted the cheerful, over-qualified secretary, and pulled out the papers from her box. There was a monthly newsletter for aides who worked with autistic kids; the December school lunch menu; a sheet of announcements for all the holiday festivities; and a plain, brown envelope with a return address from "Unsolved Mysteries." Julie's hands shook as she opened her large canvas bag, shoved everything inside and headed out to the car.

Wednesday night tradition was set aside for a romantic, quiet dinner before the cooking-and-eating Thanksgiving marathon began. Julie couldn't focus on either Danny or the elegant restaurant fare. She wanted to go home, eat a piece of leftover pizza, get the ingredients for rolls into her bread machine ... *I wish I knew what to do.* If the letter in the big envelope was what she'd been hoping for, she could shred it, or pursue it. She needed to talk to Danny. If the letter was a rejection, it might not matter whether she talked to her husband.

On the drive home from school, Julie easily convinced Danny that she had too many preparations and house cleaning chores to have time for a dinner out. He graciously understood and offered to help Julie with whatever she needed. Together they spent the evening vacuuming, sorting through teenaged clutter, and washing the china and serving dishes for the big day.

Julie sat on the bed close to midnight, listening to Danny hum in the shower while she held the brown envelope. She looked at Danny's side of the bed and thought she knew what he would say if she asked him whether to open the letter. "You do what you want" – the most loving, maddening response she could imagine. *I was attracted to him because he had no desire to control me, but a little decisiveness now would help.*

When the shower water stopped, Julie put the envelope back in her purse and tossed it on the dresser. *Tomorrow.*

Regardless of the outcome of the sealed letter, Julie needed a break. She had spent the past ten months actively searching for Andrew, losing weight and sleep, and gaining a bin of letters suitable for wall-papering her house. It was time to see whether this letter would join its cousins in the bin.

The producer of "Unsolved Mysteries" informed Julie that the show was about to become history, and therefore, they could not explore any new cases. Julie's train of thought headed for mental derailment.

Julie was never close to Jim, one of Tom's distant cousins. When she heard his funeral would be the first Sunday in December, it gave her the chance for catharsis – to cry out her anguish over her lost father, while everyone assumed her grief was over Jim.

Settling into a pew near the back of First, Julie was surprised and relieved to see Grandma Emma walk in. She approached Julie with the same look of stubborn love that had won over Julie's heart so long ago. The two women hugged and sat back to listen to the contemporary piano music.

Pastor Tim must have another commitment today. There's a new man walking to the pulpit. Where have I seen him before? Waiter? Salesman? Insurance agent? That's Darrell Larsen from Channel Ten! I heard he was an ordained minister, but I didn't know he officiated at funerals.

"The Lord is my shepherd; I shall not want." Julie recited the familiar words during the service, listened to Grandma Emma's broken English, and hatched a new plan. *Darrell Larsen is on TV, and probably has a crew and money. His station could search for Andrew Little as a human-interest story. It's worth a shot!* "Yea, though I walk through the valley of the shadow of death ..." Julie was ready for a shepherd to lead and guide her to her father.

The mourners quietly stood in line waiting to extend their sympathies to the family. Julie considered introducing herself to Mr. – *Reverend* – Larsen, but decided there would not be a way to hold back from presenting her plan. This was not the time or place for it. She slipped out of line, hopped in her car, and raced home, firing up her computer before taking off her coat. For once, she was glad Danny hadn't come with her, although he was concerned that she would be ostracized from the family. After her reassurances that she could hold her own, he followed through with his original plans to go bow hunting with Tom-Tom. The house was empty, in ironic contrast to Julie's over-filled head.

With a little tweaking of one of her many form letters, Julie composed what she hoped was an informative, clear, and interesting letter to the news producer at Channel Ten. *Cross my heart, hope to die.* Julie printed the letter, put it in an envelope, found a stamp in the desk drawer, and decided that a brisk walk to the mailbox across town would be good for her racing heart. *Lord, I can't put off telling Danny any longer. Please give me the strength to approach him tonight. I don't want to walk this journey alone any longer.*

One long week later, Julie received a letter with WNBI in the return address. This time, she had a clean conscience, after telling Danny about the rejection letter from "Unsolved Mysteries," and about her latest scheme. She was no longer using her school computer's computer and address, having decided that her home – a home shared with a loving husband and family – was the best place to chase her dream.

"It is with great joy and anticipation," the letter began. Julie threw it in the air and danced around her living room. "Yes, yes, yes!" She shouted and sobbed in relief, months of accumulated work and stress cascading off her shoulders and decomposing at her feet. "I finally have help!"

"Gloria! Do you have time to stop by my room after school?" Julie replaced the plastic lid on her food container as Glo walked into the lounge. "I have some great news, but I have to get back to give Repete a test while the other students watch a video in history."

"He's a great kid."

"I love his nickname. When I met his father, it was obvious why they nicknamed him Repete. Pete and Repete have the same hair color, same crooked grins, same funny personalities. I know I'm supposed to be the one watching out for Repete, but sometimes I think he's the one blessing me."

"Every time I see him," Gloria mused, "he asks to come to my classroom to feed Rosie, our pet tarantula. Most of my students – especially the girls – admire Repete for his courage to hold Rosie. It seems like he and that hairy creature understand each other."

"I'll let Repete share that experience without

me, thank you very much!" Julie had an involuntary shiver, and Gloria laughed.

"So, what's the big news?"

"Can't tell you now – I really do need to get back to class. Catch me after school!"

"I'll be dying of curiosity the rest of the day!"

"You'll live!"

"Bye, Miss P!" Repete slapped Gloria's hand in a high-five as he broke into a run to meet his dad. Glo walked into Julie's room and stood quietly as Melissa Jenkins gave Julie a new book to be used with Repete tomorrow.

"Don't forget to lock the door when you leave."

"Thanks, Melissa."

"Thank you, Julie. You are amazing with Repete. His father is happy and peaceful, now that his son has someone with him all day."

I wonder what that feels like ...

Julie and Gloria settled into their chairs. Julie exploded, "Gloria, Channel Ten is going to help me find my real father!"

"What? How? Who?" I don't know what you're talking about!"

"About the time I met you in high school, I found out that the man I assumed was my father – the man who abused me and ground my self-esteem under his heel – was not my biological father. It took my mom twenty years to fill in the gaps for me, and for a long time I thought a second man was my real father, but it was actually a third man who fit the description."

"That's almost an unbelievable story."

"I have a hard time with it myself."

What does your dad – your first dad – think

344

about your search for your biological dad?"

"He died many years ago."

"Did you ever forgive him for what he did to you?"

"Yes. Or no. I tried. I think I have. I'm somewhere in the process of forgiveness, which may not be complete for the rest of my earthly life."

"Should I pray for the search?"

"Absolutely. I'm counting on it."

The producer's offer was more generous than Julie thought possible. Not only was he assembling a film crew to interview her at her house; he was ready to hire a private investigator. Best of all, he promised to air before and after segments, regardless of the outcome of the search. *I am going to need at least one new outfit for the reunion show. Since Andrew – my dad – is only five-ten, I'll make sure I wear flats on the show and let him enjoy his height advantage.*

It was difficult for Julie to wait for all the pre-interview details. She was ready for the crew to show up at her house the day she opened the letter, but there were legal matters and scheduling issues. And sometimes, just when things were set, the interview was preempted by a more important story. Finally, when the windows opened to warm spring air, the producer called and said the crew would be out the next morning. The secrets of the buds were ready to reveal themselves in daffodils, irises and tulips wrapping the house in a profusion of color. A lone figure sat inside, topped with auburn hair, and adorned in white pants and a peach shirt. Everything in Julie's world showed the promise of new birth.

The young man running the video camera did not look much older than Julie's son, which put her immediately at ease. He introduced himself as Leo and had a nervous habit of pushing a lock of wavy hair behind his pierced ear. He absorbed rapid-fire directions from the interviewer, an equally young-looking woman with hair color and a body build like Julie's.

Julie peeled back the layers of her story to Susan, while Leo looked like his mind was on the post-interview ham and rolls she baked and left sitting on top of the stove. She was surprised when Leo started talking to her as soon as he packed his equipment.

"Can I ask you something?"

"Sure."

"Why is it so important to find Andrew?"

"Because he's my real dad." *Weren't you paying attention?*

"I'm adopted, and I really love my parents. They are the only parents I've ever had."

"I'm happy for you." Julie collected her scattered, somewhat troubled thoughts. "Maybe because you have such a good, adoptive family, there's no gaping hole in your heart."

"What do your parents think about your search for your bio dad?"

"That is a long story, and not one you would be likely to tape."

"Oh."

"If you're interested, come back someday, and I'll tell you."

"Maybe I will." Leo thoughtfully pushed his hair behind his ear.

"I really am happy for you, but you might need to think about how many reasons there are for adoptions – and sadly, not all of them are about love."

"Why would a couple spend all the money and

time it takes to adopt, if it wasn't something they wanted to do?"

"In my case, I was adopted by the man my mom married – and I wish—"

"Is it okay if we eat?" Susan called from the kitchen. "This was so nice of you, but we have a busy schedule."

Leo held out a tissue to Julie, who didn't realize she was sweating. "Another time, Leo?"

"For sure."

The broadcast had a better-than-average chance of breaking a forty-year cycle of deception. Julie hadn't considered how people who knew the Sandford family would respond. It was not Julie's purpose to intentionally hurt her mom, but she was in for a penny, in for a pound – plowing ahead on her road of discovery.

There were more people who could be light shedders. Arlene's brother Johnny and his wife Caroline lived in Tennessee. Julie had spent a half dozen times with this aunt and uncle since childhood, but she knew that her cousin – *I wish I could remember his name* – was adopted and might be sympathetic to her search. Julie remembered hearing that Uncle Johnny was a retired high-ranking naval officer, and she was not about to turn down any offers of help.

E-mail was a good, fast, cheap way to communicate – somewhat personal, without being overly intrusive. Johnny and Caroline could collaborate on their advice, and one of them could email Julie when they were ready. Julie hit the send button on her email the day after the taping at her house.

"How *dare* you do this to your mother, after all she's done for you! How could you embarrass her like that? Don't you even think of running that on TV! Your father was good to you, too." Caroline's response – or Johnny's – the email response was unsigned – was combustible. Julie was never more relieved to have a fire extinguisher in the next room.

Thank You, God, that I didn't get that reaction from my family. I never tried to drive a wedge between my kids and their Pop-Pop, even though they don't remember much about him. I never sanitized the truth, but I didn't think it was necessary to give them the sordid details. They know he molested me. And Danny – bless him – knows that when I'm in a season of obsessive cleaning and organizing, I'm usually trying to make up for the lack of control I had as a child in Danny Sandford's house. He doesn't criticize me or dismiss me. He takes my hand, leads me to the couch, sits down next to me and asks how he can help. Maybe he can help me through this now.

"Julie?" Danny shouted from the kitchen.

"Hey, hon. Where were you?"

"I told you I was going out for a run."

Julie sighed. "I guess I forgot."

Danny walked into the den. "Are you okay?'

"Not really." Julie rubbed her forehead.

"Another migraine coming on?"

"No. That would be easier than dealing with this."

"What?" Danny stood behind Julie and massaged her shoulders.

"Look at my computer screen. Be prepared for spontaneous combustion."

Danny read the e-mail. "Let me guess – Uncle Johnny and Aunt Caroline?"

"Yep."

348

"You're probably not going to be on their Christmas card list anymore."

"Nope."

Danny swiveled Julie's chair around. "I'm sorry. I can't imagine how much this must hurt."

Julie tipped her head back and closed her eyes. "I try not to live like a victim—"

"I know that."

"But this almost feels worse than the abuse."

Danny tipped Julie's head forward and kissed the top of it. "Maybe you could try calling them," he whispered. "People tend to be less rude in person than when they have the anonymous cover of a computer."

Julie opened her eyes. "You think so?"

"It's worth a try. If you'd like, I'll sit next to you when you're on the phone."

Julie reached out and hugged Danny around the waist. "Thank you."

"Aunt Caroline?"

"Is this Julie?" Caroline's voice was impaled on barbed-wire fencing.

"Uh-huh. How's Uncle Johnny?"

"We're fine. But apparently you're not."

"I need to explain—"

"No, you don't. I'm so sick of hearing about abuse! Everybody I talk to has been abused. I watch the same shows they watch. *You've* been abused. *I've* been abused. You're forty years old. Get over it already."

"But Aunt Caroline—"

"Don't you dare embarrass your mother like this."

"*Me* embarrass *her*?"

"Exactly. She gave up a lot for you."

349

Drawing her words like a loaded gun, Julie aimed and fired. "I don't care what you think about me or my family—"

"Now just a—"

"You've never been there for us—"

"You can't—"

"You never helped us—"

"I expect you—"

And you've never been anything to me." Julie was more frightened by her boldness than she expected her aunt to be.

"You're a little—"

"It won't be necessary for you to hear from me again." Torn between the desire to slam the phone down or throw it through the window, Julie compromised by hurling it across the room, smashing it against the wall. *This must have been how satisfied my dad felt every time he destroyed our phone.* When Danny offered Julie the comfort of his arms, she pushed him away and wept.

"Mom?" Julie wiped her nose again and willed herself to stop sniffing.

"Who is this?"

"Julie." *I keep forgetting that her stroke did some weird things to her memory.*

"Is everything okay?"

"Yep."

"Kids fine?"

"Uh-huh."

"You haven't broken anything?"

"No, Mom. *No sense worrying her about my Achilles.*

"Why'd you call?"

"I need to tell you something."

"I figured you didn't call to ask how I'm doing."

"How are you doing?"

"Not good, but no one really cares." *We could be on this ride all night.*

"Listen, Mom, I did something last—"

"What? You're not pregnant again?"

Julie ignored the memory loss, or sarcasm, or whatever it was that made her mom ask the most over-the-top questions. "I'm going to be on TV."

"What did you do wrong?"

"Nothing."

"There's no good news on TV any—"

"Sometimes there is."

"Like what?"

"I was interviewed by—"

"What for?"

"Let me finish."

"Have it your way. You always do."

Are you kidding? "Channel Ten is going to run a story about me trying to find Andrew."

"Andrew who?"

"Andrew Little – my dad."

Silence.

"Mom?"

"Do you wanna find me dog dead in the car tomorrow morning?"

"What?"

"I said, Do you—"

"I heard you."

"Well?"

"Why are you doing this?"

"Why am I doing what? How could you do this to me?"

Did Aunt Caroline call her before I could? Julie

351

knew that, although the threat wasn't empty, her heart suddenly was. "No, ma'am, I wouldn't do that to you."

"All right, then."

"Goodnight."

The phone call to Darrell Larsen the next day was hard. Julie briefly explained that there were personal matters making it impossible for her to let the station run the story. Darrell sounded disappointed, but reassured Julie that they would still do it in the future if things changed for her.

CHAPTER 34
"YOU'VE GOT A FRIEND"

Emotional rigor mortis paralyzed Julie's senses. The May air, fragrant with the smell of lilacs; the draw of warm evening temperatures inviting walks without pesky mosquitoes; school doors ready to close for summer vacation; all these gifts made this one of Julie's favorite times of year. But she was incapable of seeing and smelling and embracing.

Why did I try not to hurt my mother? If the shoe were on the other foot, she would have taken it off and beaten me with it. I lost the only chance I had of finding Andrew Little.

"Glo? It's Julie."

"Do you have good news for me again? When is the show going to air?"

"It's not." Julie's eyes stung with salty tears – maybe the first sign she was emerging from emotional deadness.

"How come?"

"My mom."

"She put the kybosh on it?"

"Yep."

"Oh, Julie, I'm really sorry."

"Ditto."

"What're you gonna do next?"

"Nothing. I don't know. I'm tired of fighting everyone. I haven't even told you about a conversation with my aunt and uncle."

"What was that about?"

"They defended my adopted father's right to be

part of the human race."

"Ouch."

"It wasn't worth the effort trying to get them to see through their rose-tinted glasses into my childhood."

"They probably wouldn't have believed you."

"I'm sure of that."

"Julie, my practical, engineering husband is a problem-solver with the most upbeat outlook of anyone I know. He would say that you should go back to the drafting table."

"I can't afford a private investigator."

"No, but you own a computer."

"I tried the Internet for adoption agencies—"

"It doesn't have to be that complicated. You could type a flyer with your name, birthplace and date, phone number, e-mail address, and any info you have about Andrew. You could use the Internet to find addresses of Littles in Virginia and West Virginia."

"If I did that, I wouldn't leave Danny out of the loop this time. Private stuff would be in cyberspace, and it would affect both of us."

"That's a wise idea."

"Glo, what would I ever do without you?"

"Miss me!"

Julie needed Danny's practical side to consider the scary possibilities of her plan. She might anger her mother again. She could open a hornet's nest in innocent Little families. A creepy person could call the Lewis home or show up ready to extort money or threaten them. Worst of all, in Julie's mind, was not getting any response to the flyers.

"What about your brother?"

"I haven't seen him since the day of my first

wedding. He didn't graduate from high school – just took off and joined the army, then disappeared. He despised Danny Sandford as much as I did, but my mother says he's been drinking, married twice—"

"And Andrew Little is only *your* father."

"That's right. I'm willing to have my brother back in my life. Maybe Andrew could be a father to him, too."

"But first things first: We pray."

They talked and prayed about Julie's idea, enlisting the thoughts, prayers, and counsel of Pastor Tim, as well as church friends. Julie valued a simple verse from Proverbs – "There is wisdom in many counselors." Her children, and Sam and Yam, were also told about her idea. Christina and Emma were on board. Tom-Tom did not have an opinion, although Julie thought he might simply not want his mom to suffer any more pain or rejection. Sam and Yam said there was always plenty of food to feed one more relative. Julie chuckled over how everything for them came down to how much food was served at holidays and picnics.

With a green light from her family and the support of her friends, Julie searched the Internet White Pages for all the Littles in the United States. *Four hundred forty? Yikes!* She narrowed her search to Littles in Virginia and West Virginia and discovered seventy. *Still too many.* A further search of Andrew Little, Andy Little, or Drew Little ended in forty names. Julie printed forty copies of her flyer and mailed them out.

The waiting game was a familiar one, yet Julie was impatient for a response. She checked her mailbox, email and answering machine as often as she could. After just one week, she turned up the heat under the pot, got back on the Internet and printed out phone numbers for all the Littles who received flyers. *I'm glad I have a cell with unlimited long distance.*

Julie methodically called each number, introduced herself and explained who she was and what she was doing. The Littles methodically responded with anger and phone slamming. Julie hated to think that her phone calls might cause blistering marital arguments for some of the couples. *Deeds done in darkness are exposed in the light. Hopefully some good will come from whatever doors were opened when I called.*

Julie's usual excitement over the start of school in the fall was dampened by a dead end. She had had four responses from Andrew Littles, but none was the right Andrew Little.

"Hi, Miss Julie!"

"Repete! How was your summer?"

"Fine. I got to go swimming, find crickets, and play with Jimbo."

"Who's Jimbo?"

"My new friend who lives next door."

"That's great."

"Are you still my teacher?"

"I am. The school said I could stay with you this year."

"Yeah!"

"I think so, too." *It is very good for me, too, Repete. I can start focusing on someone besides myself.*

Mrs. Hammond, Repete's new classroom teacher, walked in and introduced herself. "I'm glad you're here, Julie. I want to tell you something before the students arrive."

Julie threw her purse in her bottom desk drawer and straightened her hair. "Shoot."

"I just heard about a statewide convention for parents, teachers, and aides of autistic children. It will be held in Grand Rapids at the end of September, and I'd love for you to attend."

"I would be happy to do it, but our finances are a little tight right now. My stepsons are in college, my younger daughter has a high-maintenance lifestyle of cheerleading uniforms, homecoming dresses—"

"The grant we got last year would cover your expenses for registration, hotel and food. I can't get away, but I'd really like for you to bring back information and tools that will help us both work with Repete this year."

"I'll talk it over with my husband and let you know next week. And thank you for the offer."

Julie was excited about the convention, even though most of her time would be spent in seminars. She needed something to steer her away from Andrew Little. She had dumped too much frustration on her family. Tom-Tom came home from school and asked her about her Little problem. Everyone tried to intercept the mail before she got home. *If I drive my family away trying to find my bio father who may not want anything to do with me, I have not gained anything, and I have a lot to lose.*

Danny wandered into the bedroom while Julie was packing her garment bag and suitcase.

"If you get a letter from Andrew Little, or Andy Little, or Drew Little, please call me on my cell."

"Julie—"

"Last week Emma gave me an unopened return to sender letter from an Andrew Little in Virginia." Julie zipped the garment bag.

Conversation was interrupted by a ringing phone. Julie pulled the receiver out of the holder and saw a long-distance area code on caller ID.

"Hello?"

"Yeah, hello. This is Andrew Little."

Julie heard a voice like Danny's – too young to be her father.

"I understand what you're trying to do; but there's no way my father could be your father. He was married during the period listed on the flyer."

"Well," Julie replied, not unkindly, "I don't want to make you feel bad, but my mother was also married at the same time."

The silence was potent.

"I'm in my forties," replied Andrew.

"So am I," countered Julie. "Was your father in the Navy during that time?"

"Yeah." Andrew hesitated.

"Was he stationed anywhere near Puget Sound?"

Another silence.

"Does your father have blondish-brown hair?"

"Yes." Julie heard air escaping from Andrew's lungs in a slow leak.

"Does your father have brown eyes?"

The remaining air was forced out of Andrew in one relieved, "NO! Thank God! They're blue!"

"Are you absolutely sure?" asked Julie.

"Yes, yes, they're blue, blue, blue!" answered Andrew triumphantly.

Julie sighed. "Thank you for being willing to talk to me. I hope I haven't caused any hard feelings between your parents!" Andrew good-naturedly wished

Julie luck in her search.

Julie met parents of autistic children and was truly humbled in the realization that she had never dealt with serious special needs in her children. The chaos and anguish of her first marriage would not have withstood the stress of raising a child with cerebral palsy, or epilepsy, or Down's, or autism. The parents she met were gracious, kind, and obviously loved their children – but they all wore the look of parents who hung on to slim threads of hope.

God, if I get home from the convention and there aren't any letters or phone messages, I'm done searching. This door will never be opened again. Julie was tired of attacking Little families with pepper spray and needed to refocus her life on her husband and children.

The convention was over. Julie was on a forty-five-minute drive to Christina's house and looking forward to the weekend with her and Stuart.

Tom-Tom absentmindedly answered the phone while watching TV.

"Yo."

"Hello?" A southern drawl stretched out the word to a length unfamiliar to him.

"Yeah?" Tom-Tom reached for his sandwich.

"Is Julie there?"

"Nope."

"Okay, I'll call back later."

"Wait—" Tom-Tom heard the dial tone, shrugged, hit the off button on the cordless phone, and pitched it on the couch.

Danny walked into the room. "Who was that,

T?"

"Heck if I know. Sounded like a country hick."
"Who did they ask for?"
"Mom."

Emma grabbed the ringing phone in the kitchen.
"Hello?"
"Is Julie there?"
"No, but—"
"I'll call back."
"But—"
Emma heard a click and stared at the phone.
"Was that a dude who talked like Gomer Pyle?"
Tom-Tom sat at the table eating popcorn and watching
a "Starsky and Hutch" rerun on a small TV in the corner.
"Yeah, it was."
"He called last night, asked for Mom and didn't
say who he was."
"Weird."

"Andrew," said Eunice with a steely glint in her
eye, "why don't you tell these people who you are when
you call?"
"Because" Andrew patiently explained,
"suppose Julie's mama and daddy, aunts and uncles,
brothers and sisters, husband and children – suppose her
family doesn't know she's looking for me? It could
cause problems for her."
Danny made sure he answered the phone when
it rang again the next evening.
"Hello?"
"Hi. Who is this?"
"Danny."
"Are you Julie's—"

"Husband. Who are you?"

"My name is Andrew. Andrew Little. I was born in Charleston, West Virginia. I've lived here all my life except for a short time when I was stationed in Bremerton, Washington. I have many reasons to believe I am your wife's father, and I'm anxious to talk to her. But I'd like to be the one to tell her who I am."

Danny sucked in his breath. "Andrew, she's staying in Grand Rapids until Sunday night. I'll try to get her to come home Saturday instead. It won't be easy, especially since I can't tell her why. I'll do my best."

Danny's sweaty palm almost dropped the phone before he could push the off button and toss it on the bed.

With windows up and radio blaring, Julie alternately pounded the steering wheel and shook her fist in the air. "God, you let me suffer through abuse for so long. I lived through a hell I can't explain to anyone. Why don't You let me find my real father? It's the only thing I want."

Julie dragged a defiant mood into her house late Saturday afternoon. She didn't know why Danny was so insistent that she come home a day early; he always had a long list of honey-do projects. Other than going to church without her, he was perfectly capable of feeding the gang, washing a couple loads of clothes, and making sure his soccer schedule was set for the fall. *It's not like him to be so strong with me. I hope he's not starting to show colors I didn't see before we got married.* Julie was seldom angry with Danny for longer than a few hours; it made her world feel off-center.

Julie tossed her keys on the couch, kicked off her shoes and walked over to the counter to glance through a high, uninviting stack of mostly junk mail. Her eyes lit on a return address from an Andrew Little in West Virginia.

"Danny," yelled Julie through the house, "why didn't you tell me about this letter from Andrew Little?"

"I'm sorry, honey, it must have been caught in the rest of the mail. I didn't see it."

Her usually meticulous personality traits set aside, Julie didn't bother hunting for a letter opener. She tore the envelope, almost ripping the letter in half in the process.

"Dear Julie,

My name is Drew Little. My father is Andy Little. He organizes Little family reunions in West Virginia every year. After receiving your flyer in the mail, he asked me to write to you and explain that he is not the man you are looking for.

Good luck in your search.

Sincerely,

Drew"

God, I promised that this would be my swan song. I meant it. Julie considered climbing into bed and pulling the covers over her head. *The world wouldn't stop revolving if I checked out for a while.* Going back out to the car to get her bags, she met Tom-Tom, who casually reminded her that his car was still in the shop, and he needed a ride to work in ten minutes. Julie decided it wasn't worth making an extra trip into the house; they would leave now, and she could deal with everything when she got back. Mother and son backed out of the driveway as the cordless phone chirped in the bedroom.

"Hello, is this Danny?"

"Yep."

"This is Andrew again. Is Julie home?"

"No, Andrew, but you could try calling back later tonight."

When Julie returned thirty minutes later, Danny said, "Some guy's been calling for you, and he said he'll call back later." Julie missed the snarkiness in Danny's voice.

It's probably Drew Little, calling to find out whether I got his letter. I can ignore him until tomorrow.

Tom-Tom was scheduled to work until ten but finished his shift an hour early. Julie was too restless to come in for a landing, so when he called home looking for a ride, she left to pick him up. As soon as she left, the bedroom phone rang again. Danny ran into the bedroom, kicking himself for not offering to get Tom-Tom. "One of these days I'm going to hurt myself from serious brain activity."

"Hi, Danny?"

"Yes?"

"It's Andrew again. Sorry I'm bothering you."

"No, you aren't at all. Julie had to leave again. I promise she'll be back within the hour."

"Is it okay if I call back?"

"Absolutely."

Danny met Julie at the door. "That guy called back for you. He's going to call again later tonight."

"Danny," Julie flatly responded, "I'm not talking to anybody. Whoever it is can call me back another time. All I want is a shower and bed."

Steam cocooned the shower as Julie was lost in a world impenetrable by the shrill noise of the phone. She heard the bathroom door open and Danny shout, "Yeah, she's here. I'll go get her." Extending his arm around the door, he said, "Julie, take this call."

"Get out!" screamed Julie. "I'm not talking to anyone – including you!"

"Take this call!" insisted Danny.

"Get out of here! What part of no don't you understand?"

"You *will* take this call," demanded Danny.

Julie stepped out of the shower, dripping wet and heaving with frustration. She was mad at Danny for his insensitivity and mostly mad at herself for being impatient with her kind husband. She grabbed two towels, threw one around her body and wrapped the other around her head. Grabbing the phone from Danny, she yelled, "Hello! Who is this?"

A small voice laced with a thick southern accent replied, "Hello, Julie, this is Andrew Little."

"I got the letter from your son."

"What son?"

"Drew."

"I don't have a—"

"Maybe you didn't know he wrote it."

"Wrote what?"

This guy tap-dances like my mom.

"The letter telling me you're not my father."

"But that's why I'm calling. I believe I *am* your daddy."

Julie sat on the bed and felt a faster heartbeat.

"But I thought you said you were not my father."

"Julie. Take a breath and let's start over. My name is Andrew Little. I got your flyer in the mail last week."

"That's what your son wrote in his letter."

"I don't have a son named Drew! My sons are Owen Lee and Ira Van!"

Another phone clicked on, and a genteel

southern voice said, "Well, hello, Julie, this is your Mama Eunice. I'm so pleased and proud that we finally found you. Andrew and I have been looking for you for a very long time."

Julie was glad she was sitting; her legs became molten liquid. All intelligible speech vanished.

"Julie, are you still there?" Andrew sounded alarmed.

"I am. I hope this isn't a hoax."

"It's not," said Andrew. "When you were born, I told Arlene I thought you were the most beautiful thing I'd ever seen."

Nothing on the flyers mentioned my mom's name.

"I've been trying to find you for a year. Actually, I've been looking for you all my life." Julie started to sob.

Eunice quietly asked, "Girl, how come you never came to West Virginia looking for your daddy?"

"How much … time … do you … have?" Julie choked out the words.

"As much time as you need."

Julie excused herself long enough to get dressed and unwrap her hair, then settled into bed and picked up the receiver. The time flew as she shared the highlights of her life with Andrew and Eunice. Andrew listened through steady breathing while Eunice laughed, exclaimed, cried, yelled, and focused on every word. By the end of the conversation, Julie was convinced that the best parts of Mrs. Ryczek, Mrs. Anderson, Mama T and Grandma Emma were all resurrected in Mama Eunice; and that finding her was almost as wonderful as finding her bio father.

Sleep eluded Julie. It was the most welcome

insomnia of her life.

Julie, Andrew, and Mama Eunice exchanged letters and phone calls. Julie's desire to fly to West Virginia filled every corner of her mind and heart. She could not afford the airfare but had learned some things about scheming, wishing, planning – and mostly about trusting a miracle-working God.

"Julie, we've missed you at our weekly prayer meetings."

"I know. It seems like every Monday morning I'm running late, or Danny's running late – and I hate for us to drive separate cars, even though we live so close."

"Understood. I'm just glad you made it today."

"Me too."

"Do you think Danny will ever come?"

"I'd like him to. He ends up with multiple responsibilities before school. His soccer players look to him for so many things – things that maybe their parents could handle."

"That's what makes Danny so great. He is much more than a coach, or history teacher – the kids all know it. You got yourself a good one there, friend."

"I know – he's a keeper because he's too big to throw back!"

Butch did a rim shot on the edge of the table. Julie felt her face turn red and was relieved when Mr. Hedstrom, an English teacher, motioned for everyone to pull chairs up to the table and be ready for a time of prayer and encouragement before the first-period bell rang.

"I'd like to ask a favor of all of you."

"Julie, prayers aren't favors, they're privileges."

"Good enough. I'd like to give someone the privilege of praying that I have the privilege of making a trip to West Virginia. I would like to meet my father and his family." Teachers and staff had rejoiced with Julie when she found Andrew Little – or even more incredibly, when he found her.

As others continued to share requests, Gloria whispered, "Call me tonight."

"Why?" Julie whispered back.

"Tell you later."

"I hate it when you do this to me!"

"You started it when you waited to tell me about Channel Ten running your story, remember?"

"No fair!"

"Fair!"

"Julie?"

"Gloria! I'm so sorry I forgot to call you! I went to Danny's soccer game after school, then dropped Tom-Tom at work—"

"Time out! I didn't send you on a guilt trip. I just couldn't wait any longer to spill my idea!"

"I need a cup of coffee."

"You're killing me here, girl!"

"I can listen while I pour."

"Sure?"

"Absolutely."

"Okay. Here's my plan. My sister lives outside Charleston, and she's begged me for a year to come and visit—"

"How nice for you." *Does she remember that my dad's family lives in Charleston, and that I've been trying to get there? I wouldn't expect Gloria to rub my face in it.*

"Let me finish! This morning, when you talked about praying that you could find a way to Charleston, I realized that you could come with me. I'm planning a trip to West Virginia during the Michigan Teacher's Convention at the end of October. It would be a wonderful four-day visit with Suzi."

"But Gloria – I still can't afford to fly down."

"Yes, you can, because I'm buying your ticket."

"You can't—"

"Can. My husband has a good job, and we've been talking about doing this for you ever since Andrew contacted you."

"Gloria," Julie sniffed, "thank you, and I love you."

How long has it been since we flew out to Oregon, hoping to find my father? Here I am on another plane. This time, it's really happening. I've been waiting for this for years. I think I'm going to be sick! Julie moved in slow motion, like so many of her dreams when she was being chased and couldn't run fast enough. This time, she was the chaser who could not reach a man walking slowly but always out of her reach. She was breathless, gasping and holding her side.

"Sorry. I didn't mean to elbow you."

Julie awoke with a start. "That's okay – these seats are small."

Gloria returned to her book, and Julie stared out the window, doubly amazed at God's provision. She had found her dad, and everything in her life telescoped to this precise point in time. She tried to picture meeting Andrew in front of a TV camera capturing every emotion showing through her eyes and smile. It was like a reunion show – but not really, because it was real life, and it was hers.

Julie pulled a small mirror from her purse and looked at her tanned face. She had never resembled Danny Sandford, which left her feeling like an orphan. Now, God's grace enabled her to disassociate from a man who had treated her like flotsam and jetsam.

Andrew and Julie had the same facial features, cheekbones, wavy, brown hair, and brown eyes. For the hundredth time that day, Julie pulled out her wallet and carefully removed the photo of Andrew and Eunice Little. Andrew wore a shirt, maroon tie with a gray paisley design, navy sport coat and slacks. Eunice wore a pastel blue dress with matching shoes and purse, and a pearl necklace and bracelet. Her brown hair was perfectly styled, makeup carefully applied. Andrew was only five-foot-six, which meant Eunice was probably five-feet-four. *Mom had a baby with Andrew and didn't even remember his height!* The day Julie received the photo, she yelled, "That's it! Now I know who I look like! I finally have an identity."

Willing herself back into Eastern Time, Julie felt the landing gear open, and the plane touch down smoothly. She watched the filled-to-the-brim cabin empty of passengers, feeling ready to enter the covered walkway, yet wishing she could stay seated a little while longer. *I am headed for the terminal. Feels like a gangplank. There's no going back now.* Julie stepped into a time warp, slogging through quicksand as people rushed around both sides of her, clipping her feet with their rolled baggage wheels. *I'm not sure I can walk.*

Gloria led the way to the terminal and spotted her sister. "Bye, Julie! See you back at the airport in four days! Call me at Suzi's if you need anything." Julie hugged her dear friend tightly, crying for what would be the first of many times that day.

As Glo turned and ran to her sister, Julie saw a couple standing quietly behind the ropes. Gasping for air, she heard, "Oh, my goodness, Drew, she looks like you!" Eunice yelled excitedly while Julie and Andrew stood face to face.

Julie had spent hours rehearsing profound words. All she could say now was, "Boy, you're short!"

"Boy, you're tall!" Andrew happily responded. And they hugged, while Eunice fussed with an uncooperative camera. Julie did not need a camera to capture a scene she would never forget. She wanted to touch Andrew's face like a blind person, memorizing every feature, yet felt compelled to act with restraint, not wanting to embarrass her new family.

The thirty-minute drive from the airport to the Little house was surreal. Julie's brain was saturated with the newness of this life. She tipped her head back, leaned it against the cool leather upholstery in her father's car, and closed her eyes.

When the car turned into a driveway, Julie lifted her head and saw a brick bungalow nestled among magnolias and dogwoods, rock gardens, flowerbeds, and carefully manicured grass. An unbidden and overwhelming sense of loss threatened her happiness. *Look at this house. Why didn't I grow up here?*

CHAPTER 35
PIVOTAL PEOPLE,
PIVOTAL TIMES

"Make yourself at home, dear. I'll get us some iced tea. Are you hungry? Supper won't be for a while yet."

"No, Mama Eunice. I ate a bag of peanuts on the plane."

"Goodness! Couldn't they give you real food?"

"I wouldn't have been able to eat, anyway."

"Well, you let me know if you're hungry before supper."

"I will."

Eunice disappeared through one door as another burst open, and a dark-haired, muscular, broad-chested guy bounded into the room wearing a black t-shirt and khaki shorts. *He's over six feet tall! How can be so much taller than his father? I wonder if he's Owen or Ira.* Julie was mesmerized by his dazzling white teeth and huge smile and was getting ready for a formal greeting when he walked over, said, "Hey, I'm Owen Lee, but everyone calls me Tiny!" and lifted her off the floor in a massive bear hug.

Julie laughed as she looked over his shoulder. Another guy with the same build came in with reddish-brown hair and a square jaw, and Julie assumed this was her half-brother, Ira Van, whom, she had been told, went by Pokey. As Tiny set Julie down, she waited for the same greeting from Pokey; but he simply said, "Hello," and sat down on the soft leather sofa across the room. *Okay, so maybe he wasn't looking for another sister.*

371

A youngish gal walked through the door swinging long, blonde hair across deeply tanned shoulders. Julie saw her own face and body shape about fifteen years younger. "Julie, this is your little sister Cissy," said Andrew, as the gal walked slowly to Julie, gave her a perfunctory hug, and sat down next to Ira.

"No one but Daddy calls me Cissy. I'm Francis Jane to everyone else."

Or maybe the Ice Queen. Julie felt as though she were standing naked in this room full of people who were alternately accepting and skeptical of her presence in their lives. *I'm sure they aren't all happy about setting an extra place at the table tonight.*

Owen – *Tiny* – grabbed Julie's hand and sat her on his knee in a large, easy chair. "C'mon, ya'll, let's catch Julie up on our family."

"If we tell her about the whoopin's, we'll be here all night!" Ira – *Pokey* – chuckled softly.

"Daddy was a believer in the Rod of Correction!" Everyone laughed as Eunice came into the room and sat down next to her husband, who had been a silent witness to the Rites of Introduction.

"Especially for you, Tiny," teased Pokey.

"The biggest rod was for you, Pokey," Tiny shot back.

"Time out!" said Julie, as she held up her hands in a t-shape. "Why Tiny and Pokey?"

"I was only four pounds at birth, so I was called Tiny by the end of the day."

"You definitely aren't tiny now!" said Francis Jane.

"Except for maybe that thing between his ears," said Pokey.

"And you," Julie pointed to Ira. "Why Pokey?"

372

"When Mama and Daddy brought me home from the hospital, Tiny looked at me and said Pokey. For some reason, the name stuck."

"You guys don't mind those nicknames?"

"Look at us: We're big enough to take on anyone we want!"

"You remind me of my stepsons, who go by Sam and Yam. They are also big bruisers, so nobody messes with them, either!"

"The four of us will be a great team!"

Julie glanced at Francis Jane, noticing an almost imperceptible scowl on her face. *I'm guessing she's not going to be a part of that team anytime soon – if ever.*

"My brothers are both full of it," muttered their sister.

"Cissified girl, watch it!" Pokey threw a pillow at Cissy, who ducked just in time.

"This is why we needed the rod," yelled Tiny and Pokey in unison.

I wouldn't have minded the rod from a loving father. Looks like you guys turned out okay. A mother, dad, and three siblings surround me. What else could I want?

Julie was whisked away to a different relative's house for supper late every afternoon and introduced like a debutante into Little society. Back at home with Daddy and Mama Eunice, Julie felt like she was living on Walton's Mountain, a peaceful place, the fulfillment of her every dream. She slept in Francis Jane's bedroom, beautifully decorated in French provincial furnishings. Cissy had her own apartment on the other side of the city; Julie hoped she didn't object to an interloper in her childhood bed. *A Goldilocks from Michigan.* Her first evening in the house, as Mama Eunice helped her settle in, Julie had tears splashing down her cheeks.

"Julie, what's the matter?"

"Oh, Mama, that Victorian dollhouse—"

"Should I move it?"

"No! I always wanted a doll growing up. I was going to name her Thistledew, and her dress ..." Julie sobbed as Eunice wrapped loving arms around her.

"Darlin', this is your home whenever you need it. I can't undo years of wrong, but I hope we can make good memories for you here."

"You ... already ... have ..."

Julie fell into her beautiful bed and into the sweet sleep that accompanies profound gratitude.

Andrew and Julie sat on the veranda during a pleasant fall morning, drinking coffee and watching hummingbirds sip from the red feeder hanging above the geraniums.

"Daddy, this has been a wonderful vacation for me."

"Glad you like it."

"At home, it would not be unusual for it to be snowing by now. And here I am, wearing shorts!" *God, give me strength.*

"I've always loved living here."

"I don't know when we'll have a chance to be together again."

"Hope it's soon."

"Me too."

Julie looked at Andrew and held his gaze. "Pop?"

"Yes?"

"Can I ask you something?"

"Yep."

"Actually, it's more than something. It's a big thing."

"Okay."

Julie took a sip of coffee and a big gulp of courage. "Can you tell me about your life after you left Washington?"

Andrew stared off for a long time, until Julie was sure she had offended him. *God, I asked for strength. Maybe I should be content that the family is starting to accept me.*

"Well." Andrew's eyes were clear, guileless. "I was discharged from the Navy at twenty years old. I wanted to marry Arlene – really wanted to marry her – but she didn't seem to want to have anything to do with me, my family, or West Virginia."

"She told me about that."

"When I came back home, I was confused and depressed over leaving my infant daughter behind."

Julie's eyes spilled silent tears.

"I went to college for a business degree and got my life on track – but I never stopped thinking about you. I tried to find you through a friend in Bremerton, but it seemed like you and your mom disappeared."

Julie sniffed. "I was already adopted by a man named Danny Sandford by then, and he had my name legally changed." *I don't know if Andrew knows about Eugene, but I'm leaving that one alone.* "When did you meet Eunice?"

"It was around my junior year, at a church social. I told her about you when we were engaged – and that I hoped to find you someday. She loved me, and reassured me that she would love you, too."

"She is a wonderful woman."

375

"Amen to that. We were married right around your third birthday – and I kept wishing you could be our flower girl."

"Oh, Daddy, me too!"

"But I began to have the feeling that you would never learn about me, and I didn't know any way to find you. Maybe I should have told my folks about you, and they could have helped me – but I didn't. I thought I would hire a private investigator, but the finances never worked out for us. After I graduated, I got a job with an insurance company, and I worked for them for many years."

Andrew stopped his story, got up and invited Julie to join him as they walked around the house admiring the exquisitely crafted and painted birdhouses, particularly the martin houses. *If he takes this much care with the birds, imagine how much care he would have taken with me!*

They settled back into their patio chairs and Andrew picked up the story thread. "When I was forty, my company had no money, and I figured the chance of finding you was long gone. Eunice and I often talked about whether you would try to find me."

"Believe me – if I had known about you, I would have looked everywhere for you!"

"And I still would have looked for you, but when I got into a new business … well, let's say everything went south." Andrew reached out his hand and gently touched Julie's. "I can't forgive—"

"Dad, this is a guilt-free zone. There's nothing we can do to change the past, but hopefully we'll have lots of time to reclaim what we lost. Deal?"

Andrew squeezed Julie's hand. "Deal."

Four days with the Littles gave Julie a road map

into the family's journeys and destinations. Relatives and friends expressed a genuine desire to have her visit again. There were quiet evenings, after the round-robin suppers, when the family – including Tiny's wife Lily and Pokey's girlfriend Cheryl – sat in the living room sharing stories and looking at photo albums. When they spent an entire evening looking through Tiny and Lily's wedding album, Julie wondered why Pokey was missing from the photos, not as a best man or even as an usher. *Maybe he was away at college, or in the Navy ... I don't feel comfortable asking on this visit.*

The return flight to Detroit was even more difficult than the flight to Charlotte. Julie loved the family she was leaving behind but didn't know when she would see them again; nor did she know how Danny would feel about the Littles. Tiny was a big, lovable teddy bear. Pokey began to soften his edges, after telling Julie initially that he "... ain't lookin' for no new sisters or friends." Francis Jane kept her emotional distance; Julie discerned signs of hurt and insecurity. *God, please make a way for me to see them again soon.*

I could trade lives with Repete. He lives in a world he creates and controls. If things get out of balance, he escapes until things make sense again. I would like to do that with the Littles, except that I'm not sure how I would know when the scales were tipping in my favor.

"Miss Julie?"

Julie shook herself out of her reverie. "Yes, Repete?"

"Can I feed Rosie after school?"

"Absolutely."

Danny and Julie walked out to their car after

school on the last day before the break. They were greeted with kids yelling at them to have a Merry Christmas. The holidays were a full-throttle time, preparing for a houseful of people, and hoping to find space to celebrate their second anniversary. Julie reached the place where horrendous memories of childhood Christmases were replaced with loving, joy-filled times. *Thank You, Father.*

Julie's mind raced the Indy track of all the things she needed to do – cooking, cleaning, and shopping. She wondered if the Littles would like the gifts she mailed. Her thoughts returned to their house as she and Danny walked into the kitchen.

"Mom! Phone for you!" yelled Tom-Tom from the living room.

"I thought you would be home late."

"I'm here for a forty-five-minute break, then back at work until ten." Tom-Tom strolled into the room balancing a peanut butter sandwich, glass of milk, banana, and cookie.

"Where's the phone?"

"I couldn't carry it – it's on the couch." Julie could never stay mad at her son, especially when he wore a silly, crooked grin, permanently etched on his face. He had all the charm of his father, minus the need to fuel that charm with alcohol. She was grateful beyond words that none of her children followed in their father's staggering footsteps.

Julie took off her jacket and scarf, hung them on a hook near the back door, and squeezed her son's shoulder as she passed him on the way to the living room.

"Hello?" Julie cradled the phone to her ear as she picked up a paper and pencil from the coffee table, prepared to jot down a to-do list while answering this call.

"Is this Julie?"

"Yes. Who is this?"

"It's Francis Jane."

Julie dropped pencil and paper, grabbed the phone, and stood up. "I'm sorry I didn't recognize your voice!"

"That's okay. I haven't exactly made a habit of calling you."

"Is anyone sick?"

Francis Jane laughed. "No! This isn't an emergency call."

"That's good." Julie wanted to say more but wasn't sure what was coming next.

"Julie, I think it's time we get together. I know I haven't been fair or open to you—"

"Oh, Francis Jane—"

"I want to start over. I'm flying into Detroit on a business trip on January third. How far would it be for you to drive down and meet me?"

"The drive is four hours, depending on the weather."

"I'll be staying at the Holiday Inn at the airport. My meetings will be finished by supper time Friday night."

"I teach Friday. If I leave right after school, I could be there by seven."

"What would you say to a late supper?"

"I'd say yes!"

"Thank you for being ... so gracious to me."

"Water under the bridge."

"Daddy told me he's amazed you're not bitter, after everything you've been through in your life."

"We'll talk when we're together."

"I'm looking forward to it."

"Me too!"

"I'll see you in a few weeks."

"Absolutely."

Julie punched the off button on the phone, placed it back in its holder, and yelled for her husband through a haze of happy tears.

Charlie's Chop Shop in the Holiday Inn was less than half-full when Julie walked in at six forty-five. When the hostess led her to Francis Jane's table, Julie was equal parts raw nerves and barely contained excitement. She wanted this time with her half-sister to go well; to be the start of a friendship, maybe even better away from the watchful eyes of the Little clan. Julie hoped for acceptance from Francis Jane without having to compromise her growing, healthy self-esteem, affirmed by her husband every day.

As Francis Jane stood, Julie slipped out of her coat, and both women burst out laughing.

"We obviously shop in the same stores!" said Julie, as she saw her mirror image in the woman standing before her. Julie and Francis Jane graced their five-foot-ten frames with a beige pantsuit and light pink blouse. The only difference was their hair – Julie's was short and auburn, while Francis Jane's was long, slightly wavy, and blonde.

The two hugged tightly. Julie relaxed.

"Julie, I know this is stupid to admit. Even though I was twenty-five when you came into our lives, I didn't want to be dethroned!"

"And I was forty – the queen of everything!"

The women sat down, lifted their water glasses,

and clinked them together.

"You're a hoot!" Francis Jane cackled. "Why was I afraid of you?"

"Lots of reasons. You assumed I was a gold digger. I wanted to claim some secret place in your dad's heart. I wanted to break up your parents—"

"Oh, Julie, let's be friends."

"We already are."

"And for heaven's sake, stop calling me Francis Jane. I can't stand that hoity-toity, stuffy name. It sounds like something out of a Brontë novel. I'm just plain Cissy."

"Cissy it is."

The sisters spent more time on conversation than on food, although Julie noticed Cissy eating slowly and then pushing half of it aside for later, as she explained.

"Cissy, do you mind if I ask you something?"

"Ask away. We've got all night. I don't need to check out until eleven tomorrow morning. You are staying with me tonight, right?"

"I am."

"So, what's the question?"

Julie took a sip of her Coke, put down the glass and played with the ice cubes, before looking up at Cissy.

"When I was in high school, I had some horrible experiences with my father ... at least, with the man I thought was my father."

Cissy pushed aside a crouton with her fork and stared at Julie. "You mean—"

"Yes. And I also had painful experiences with other men, with high school dates, with my first husband. I know our father was good to you, but did we

381

wear ruts in the same road when it came to … unspeakable experiences with guys?"

"What … do you mean?"

"When I was desperate to get control of my life, I experimented with bulimia. I got past that many years ago, but I recognize the signs and think I might be seeing them in you."

Cissy's eyes brimmed with tears.

"Ciss, I didn't mean to offend you! If I'm wrong, please forgive me."

"You're not wrong. I went through counseling and conquered it, but I find it easy to slip back into if I'm not careful."

"Can I help?"

"You already have, just by being so honest with me about your past."

"We would have to stay up all night for me to tell you even half the story."

"I am so sorry for you, dear Julie."

"Sometimes I am still sorry for myself. But I am not going to wear those memories like a pity sack. I'm learning about forgiveness and healing and unconditional love through my husband, my pastor, my church friends, and the middle-school boy I work with. I am not going to let my past have power over my present."

Cissy grabbed Julie's hand and squeezed it, "Thanks for coming into my life."

"I'm the one who's thankful for finding my sister."

Julie drove home the next morning fueled by three hours sleep, a quart of coffee, and with her intake valve open and overflowing with gratitude for her time with Cissy. *The scale is tipping in my favor.*

CHAPTER 36
"IF WISHES WERE HORSES"

"**I** would love for our family and the Littles to meet in Myrtle Beach for a reunion over spring break."

"When did you get that idea?" Danny was working on his snowmobile in the garage.

"Since Cissy and I were together in January. Christina and Stuart can afford plane tickets; so can Sam and Yam. That would leave Emma and Dusty, Tom-Tom, you and me."

"That's still almost two thousand."

"I know."

"I've been thinking and praying about something, and I think I just got the answer."

"Which is—?"

"We don't snowmobile as much as we used to, and Tom-Tom is into his own stuff. One of our coworkers is interested in buying all three of ours. If he wanted them right away, we would have enough to cover the tickets."

"Danny!" Julie threw her arms around him. "A girl could get used to you!"

"Hey ya'll! You must be from Minnesota or Alaska! We would never swim in water that cold!"

Beachcombers taunted Danny, Julie, and their pasty-looking family. Julie wondered if she were crazy to plan this vacation. The Littles had conveniently forgotten their promise to pay for everyone's food and lodging. The chilly ocean water – although warmer than Lake Michigan – mirrored their attitudes. Wrapping a towel around herself and walking along the beach, Julie figured she was a slow learner. *One of these days I will stop trying to create the family I want. Why do I keep setting myself up for failure? My half-brothers make snide comments about poor people and trailer trash folk; have they forgotten where I came from? They have so much money yet seem so unwilling to use it to make this vacation easier on us. What good is their money? God, why did You let me find them? They don't share my values. They don't seem to care about me.*

The Michigan and West Virginia blended family shared hearty food and laughter for four days; but Julie was unsure of their future together. *There are interesting family dynamics at work here. I thought I fit in in West Virginia, except with Cissy, and now she's the only one reaching out to us.*

"Those people—"

"My *family*—"

"Your *family* better act nicer than they did in Myrtle Beach, or I won't want to be around them again."

It was so unlike Danny to be unkind or ungracious to anyone. Julie knew he was trying to protect her emotions; yet it dug a trench between her loyalty to her husband, children and stepchildren, and her biological family. *When did life get so complicated? This would have been so different had I met the Littles as a teenager.*

"Hon, we all deserve a second change." Julie and Danny were driving to the airport in Grand Rapids to pick up Daddy, Mama Eunice, Tiny, and Lily. It was the last weekend of August, and her parents, half-brother and sister-in-law decided it was time for a Michigan visit. Julie didn't know Arlene's thoughts, or

384

whether she and Andrew would cross paths, or what Mama Eunice thought of it all, or if this visit would redeem the time in Myrtle Beach.

Danny let out a sigh and turned up the air conditioning. "I just don't want you to be hurt again."

"I love you, Danny."

"Love you back."

The sultry Michigan air held its breath under a blazing sun. Most of the countryside was brown and parched. Julie took some comfort in assuming that her southern family was not expecting to pull into their driveway and see lush, green grass sloping gently down to a flowing stream behind their home. She had designed and planted and maintained gardens with pink and blue delphinium, red roses, creeping geraniums, daises, orange day lilies, veronica, purple petunias, majestic lupines, magenta and yellow pansies, and white bellflower.

As they stepped out of the cool minivan into a sauna, Tiny shouted, "Ya'll mow all this stuff?" Danny and Julie stared at each other. This had never been the first comment they heard when friends saw their house and panoramic view.

"Of course." Danny's tone was the only chilly part of the day.

"Man, ya'll are nuts. There must be several acres of grass here. Why do ya'll waste your time mowing?"

"Tiny," explained Julie patiently, "in the Midwest, people value their land more than the size of their homes. We like it that way. We love our grass and gardens, and especially our pole barn."

"Pole *what*?"

"Never mind! Come on, everybody. Dad, you're

going to sweat to death in your suit coat. Let's get in where it's cool!"

"I know it's hot," Julie began as she washed the pancake griddle the next morning, "but I would love for us to go to the Kale Tulip Festival."

"Sounds good to me," said Dad.

"We'll do whatever you want, dear," Mama Eunice chimed in.

"Great! Where did Tiny escape to?"

"He's up on the deck. Said we could call him down whenever."

"I need to finish cleaning up the kitchen, hang out a load of clothes, and then we'll be ready to go."

Julie lugged a heavy basket of wet sheets and towels out to the clothesline as a voice shouted down from the deck. "Ya'll own a clothes dryer?"

"Yes, we have a dryer." *Where is this going?*

"Is it broke?"

"No. It works fine."

"Then for Pete's sake, why are ya'll hanging clothes out?"

"I like the smell of fresh sheets and towels. There's no better drug than climbing into bed and burying my head in line-dried sheets or getting out of the shower and wrapping in an air-dried towel."

"Yeah, when I took a shower this morning, the towel smelled really good," Tiny conceded.

Andrew came out the back door, made his way to the clothesline and helped Julie finish hanging the linens.

"You know, Julie," continued Tiny, "in Charlotte you wouldn't be hanging clothes out."

"Why not?"

386

"Because in Charlotte it would look like—"

"Trailer trash?" Julie finished an unpleasant sentence.

"Well, yeah," replied Tiny sheepishly.

"Tiny, I *was* trailer trash growing up. Even in Midwestern winters, we hung clothes outside on sunny days because we didn't own a dryer. During bitterly cold, subzero days, we slung all the wet clothes over chairs and dressers and tables, and it was my job to iron everything after the clothes dried."

"Uh, yeah," Andrew broke in, "There're certain places in Charlotte where you wouldn't be allowed to have a clothesline, in HOA neighborhoods."

"What's HOA?"

"It stands for Home Owner's Association," said Andrew. "As a matter of fact, you can't paint your house any color you want. You have to go before the city council, and even then, only a few colors are approved. And, you can only have your yard a certain way. Privacy fences are required and need to be repaired at your own expense after a storm, or you are fined—"

With a piercing look, Julie cut in. "Pop, I would never live anywhere I was told I couldn't put up a clothesline ... or had to paint my house a certain color ... or I could only plant certain kinds of trees or plants, and never a vegetable garden. As far as I'm concerned, that's not living."

Andrew and Tiny were both silent.

"Mom, are we ready to go?" Emma was home for another week before classes started at Central Michigan University. "Dusty wondered if we could swing by and get him."

"Let's saddle up!"

CHAPTER 37
THE PRESENT IS NOT A GIFT

Life was a teeter-totter. At the bottom, Julie's southern family stood at one side, cheering her on from a distance. On the other side, Danny stood sentry, arms crossed, mouthing the words, "Get off and let's get out of here." At the top, Julie wondered if she could stay suspended there until she figured out how to balance feelings of guarded joy and ambivalence. She was tired of the up-and-down movement that went nowhere.

Tiny generously mailed a plane ticket for Julie to be in Cissy's November wedding as a Scripture reader. There was only one ticket – none for Danny – which increased the tension in their home. *Maybe when I get back from the wedding, I should pack my clothes and confusion and move to Charlotte permanently. But I would never leave Danny.*

Cissy's wedding was simple and beautiful. Julie was glad and proud to be included in the rehearsal dinner, wedding, and day-after gift opening and family celebration. It felt like the wheel stopped spinning and the arrow pointed to a Caribbean cruise – a valuable prize she won just for being in the right place at the right time. Tiny, Pokey, Cissy and their spouses shared many inside jokes; Julie pushed down any feeling of being left out for the goal of being welcomed unconditionally into the Little clan.

Until she returned home to Michigan.

It was close to their third anniversary, and Julie wasn't sure if, or how, she and Danny would celebrate. Their home was no longer filled with wall-to-wall kids,

kids' friends, and frenetic activity. They were bona fide empty nesters, doing a good imitation of a married couple occupying the same space without sharing the same heart. They had not had a conversation about anything more important than car repairs and broken appliances since Julie's return from West Virginia almost a month earlier.

The last shortened week of school before Christmas break was upon them. Julie tried to sort through her jumbled mess of thoughts, hoping that the ache in her head would lessen. *God, I am tired. I am in a push-me-pull-me between my father's family and my husband – not that either one is fighting for me. They both assume I'm fine with the status quo, but I am miserable.* Julie glanced at the overcast sky, thinking back – again – to Decembers from her childhood, ones filled with sadness and fear. *I should have called in sick this morning ... my head is throbbing and my heart hurts.* Julie got comfortable in her desk chair, turned on her computer, and waited for it to boot up, wishing the school could afford high-speed Internet. Pulling open her desk drawer and reaching for a bottle of ibuprofen, Julie felt a sudden, stabbing pain in her head. *What is that? Did something fall on me?* She grabbed her head with both hands and swiveled the chair as another sharp pain catapulted her out of the chair and on to the floor. "Oh, my God!" screamed Julie, writhing in pain in a fetal position.

"Julie, what's wrong? Did you fall? Are you hurt?"

Julie stared at a pair of shoes, turned her head slightly, looked up at a halo of light, and thought it might be Barb, the teacher from the room across the hall. "My head ... feels ... like ... it's gonna ... blow ...

389

off … need … bathroom … help me up."

"Are you sure?" Barb eased Julie up off the floor.

"If I'm not back … in ten minutes … come and check on me." Julie held on to the wall as she stumbled out of the room and down the hall towards the bathroom. Once inside, the bright lights almost knocked her to the floor again. She leaned over the sink and supported herself as she tried to turn on the faucet. *I'll be okay if I can splash cold water on my face.* Julie could not feel anything in her right hand or arm. Terrorizing panic set in. *This must be a stroke. Barb, come here now!*

The door opened and a voice said, "I don't know what to do. Let's get you back to your desk and I'll get help."

"I can't see anything."

Barb guided Julie to her chair. "I'll be back ASAP!"

I'll call Danny on the room phone. He'll know what to do. It would help if I could see the numbers.

A shadow crossed Julie's peripheral vision. "I decided to come back and call Danny for you. Maybe we should drive you to the ER."

"Barb, I'm either … having … a heckuva migraine … or a stroke."

Within five minutes, Danny was standing in Julie's room talking to Barb about whose car they should drive to the hospital.

"Noooo," slurred Julie. "I want … to go home … bed."

"Really?"

"Yes. No. Call Dr. Beth."

"Is Dr. Beth Steingard there? Tell her it's Danny

Lewis, and it's an emergency." As Danny, Julie, and Barb pulled into the ER door at St. Michael's, Danny fretted over Dr. Barb's last words on the phone – that they needed to be at the ER; that thirty minutes had passed since the initial explosion in Julie's head. Her vision was returning – but she was still numb and frightened.

An hour wait in the cubicle suddenly ended when Julie's face began to droop, and the numbness in her arm turned into paralysis. After a CT scan and the administration of something that made her loopy, Julie spent the night in the hospital wondering how she ever thought previous migraines were the worst pain imaginable. This pain was horrific and relentless.

"What we are dealing with is not good," began Dr. Meyer the next morning, standing somberly next to Julie's bed. "You have a blood clot. I don't know why you should, since you're otherwise young and healthy."

Go on.

Danny stood near Julie's head, rubbing her shoulder, and smoothing her hair. *You asked me to forgive you for being distant, and for trying to force me to choose between you and Andrew. All I can do is blink my eyes. I can't tell you that I absolutely forgive you. And I can't ask you to forgive me for doubting your love. God, please let me talk again.*

"We will need to run further tests over the next few days, but I suspect you have what's called Protein C Deficiency. It predisposes people to blood clots. If that's the case, we can put you on Coumadin."

Three MRIs confirmed Dr. Meyer's diagnosis of a blood clot on the left vena cava, the artery that drains blood from the brain. During the nine days Julie spent in the hospital over Christmas break, she learned that the blood clot affected her speech center – an explanation for her total loss of speech.

The doctors and nurses said I probably had a light stroke. It's a good thing I have conversations in my head. It may be the only way I will ever be able to talk again.

Julie was home, flat on her back, unable to tolerate any light or noise, unable to talk, and unable to process any thoughts except angry ones. *I've had thirteen med changes, including anti-depressants and blood thinners, and nothing has made any difference. How many times, God, did I suffer pain with my back? Didn't you get enough of my attention? I can't walk, and I can't run away from You. I can't turn on my CD player to drown out Your voice. I am totally helpless – You have my attention now.*

Danny's mom, Georgia, walked into Julie's bedroom. "Here, dear, I thought you might like some iced tea. I even found one of those bendable straws in a kitchen drawer.

Julie hoped her eyes showed gratitude.

"Let me help you sit up, and then you can try and take a few sips." Georgia set the glass on the nightstand, pulled Julie to a sitting position and propped pillows behind her back. She brought the glass up to Julie, who took one sip from the straw and motioned to lie down again. Georgia brushed a tear from her eye, set the glass down, made Julie comfortable, kissed her forehead, and left the glass as she walked quickly out of the room.

God, I am so grateful for Georgia; but I don't think I can be with anyone but You right now. I have so much to sort out. I know that I can no longer lay blame for the rottenness of my life at the feet of my adoptive father, my first husband, my mother, my aunt and uncle, or the depraved men in my past. I have not only feasted at the table of bitterness; I also had a hand in cooking the meal.

Julie was wasting away. She could barely walk from the bedroom to the bathroom. She could not lift a fork. Her limited speech was mostly unintelligible. Her thoughts swirled around in her brain like a sandstorm. Her neurologist and the rest of the hospital staff voiced dismay over trying to treat a blood clot resistant to medications, the very ones that should have dissolved it by now. Every other week was "Groundhog Day" for Julie in Dr. Meyer's office.

"Julie, I don't know why you're not getting better."

"Bad."

Danny reached for Julie's hand.

"You're frustrated?" continued Dr. Meyer.

Julie nodded.

"Let's increase the dosage on one of the medications and see if anything has changed by your next appointment."

"Okay."

Is this the dark ages? They've tried everything but leeches with me.

Dr. Meyer walked into the exam room. "Julie, your husband told me that you said the word 'Mayo' last night.

Julie made a partial fist and stuck up her thumb.

"I don't have a problem with you getting a second opinion, but it's likely going to take two to three months for you to get an appointment there."

Julie moaned and put both palms to her forehead.

Dr. Meyer looked at Julie with kind eyes. "Mayo takes patients based on identifiable symptoms, diseases, or illnesses, and you have nothing we can put a name to. Protein C Deficiency isn't enough."

Dr. Bob Carlton, head of the University of Michigan School of Family Practice, was Christina's new father-in-law. *He must know a doctor at the Mayo Clinic in Rochester, Minnesota. I'm desperate. I'll do whatever it takes to get help. Christina could talk to Stu, who could talk to his father, who could plead my case with a neurologist at Mayo. I may only be three degrees of separation from someone who could tell me what's wrong with me. I just need to figure out how to communicate this.*

Julie had the shoulder and arm strength to write out her idea while Christina spent the day with her. While both women were reluctant to take advantage of Dr. Carlton, they knew that this might be the best and last hope Julie had of ever returning to a normal life.

Kind friends regularly checked up on Julie, so a ringing phone was not unusual any time of the day. But she was startled when Georgia brought the phone into her bedroom the day after Christina's visit and announced, "It's Dr. Carlton!"

"Julie, Danny called and told me some of what you've been going through. Why don't you describe your symptoms to me?"

"Dr. Carlton, this is Georgia, Julie's mother-in-law. She still can't talk, so she'll write down the answers to your questions, and I will be her interpreter."

"That sounds good."

The three-way conversation lasted forty-five minutes. When it was over, Julie felt confident that she was heard and understood, but no promises were made about an appointment.

"Julie?" Danny walked into their bedroom carrying a cordless phone.

His beloved wife grabbed her note pad, wrote Dr. Carlton on it, and held it up.

"No. It's a Dr. Binru. He says he's a neurologist at Mayo."

Julie drew a huge exclamation point on her pad.

"Should I find out what he wants?"

Julie nodded vigorously and listened closely to Danny's side of the conversation.

"You want us down there tomorrow? But that's a whole day's drive!"

I don't know if our insurance will cover a visit to Mayo. I haven't had time to check that out yet.

"Julie needs to get copies of her x-rays, CT scans and MRIs?"

That red tape could bog us down for weeks.

"No, she doesn't want to waste any more time, either."

Please, God, make a way when there seems to be no way.

"He will?"

Who *will do* what?

"Just a minute." Danny turned to Julie. "Dr. Binru said that Dr. Meyer promised to write whatever letter necessary to persuade the insurance company to cover his referral to Mayo."

Julie wrote thirty thousand on her notepad.

"I don't care. We will mortgage our house if we have to. We are leaving tomorrow."

Danny held the receiver to his ear. "Dr. Binru, we will be there tomorrow. Thanks for your call."

The May morning, almost five months after Julie's stroke, was delightful. *I'm glad I can walk steadily, feed myself and communicate with my notepad and a few words.* Julie and Danny were in an exam room, waiting for a Dr. Johnson.

"We're finally here, my wife."

I can't believe it!

"Before Dr. Johnson gets here, let's pray together."

Julie nodded her head. "Yeah."

Danny reached for her hand and bowed his head. "God, we spent the last five months looking at the back side of our marriage. Show us Yourself in all of this. Please take away Julie's pain, and trade it for her speech. Show me how to be the husband she needs."

"Amen." Julie carefully lifted her arm and tried to brush the tears from Danny's eyes. She kept missing and poking the bridge of his nose. Danny laughed and wrapped his arms around Julie.

"Have I told you I love you today?"

"Memory loss …"

"Then I will need to keep reminding you!"

There was a quiet knock at the door.

"Come in," said Danny, releasing Julie and wrapping a stray lock of hair behind her ear.

A short, gray-haired man wearing a white coat with an identification badge pinned to the lapel walked into the exam room, shook Danny's hand, and said, "I'm Dr. Johnson."

"Nice to meet you."

He looked at Danny and gestured towards Julie. "I heard she walked in on her own power. What is she doing here?"

"Dr. Binru told us to come," responded Danny.

Dr. Johnson visibly stiffened. "How do you know Dr. Binru?"

"My stepdaughter's father-in-law is a good friend and colleague of his."

I wonder how he would talk about me without hiding behind his obvious authority.

"We don't operate like that," he replied tersely.

Julie reached inside her purse, pulled out her notepad and pen, and wrote, "We're doing what we were told." She tore off the sheet and handed it to Dr. Johnson.

"Well, we'll see about this," Dr. Johnson muttered as he left the room.

Julie stared at Danny as tears sprang to her eyes. She shoved her pad and pen back into her purse, took out a tissue, and cried softly. *I guess it's good that my tear ducts still work. But crying is going to make my head hurt worse.*

A ten-minute eternity passed before there was another knock at the door. Julie looked at Danny and shook her head.

"Yes?"

A tall, fiftyish woman entered the room and headed straight for Julie. "Julie," she smiled and touched her shoulder, "I am Cheryl, the nurse manager. We'll have a room ready for you shortly."

"What about Dr. Johnson?" said Danny.

"Don't worry about him," Cheryl replied cryptically.

397

None of the tests performed on Julie revealed a blood clot. During her four days at Mayo, she learned that she had probably experienced a basal artery migraine – a serious condition which can mimic a stroke and cause facial drooping, paralysis, and loss of vision and speech. The new diagnosis was followed by the administration of Depakote. Within twenty-four hours, Julie's pain decreased from a ten to a five on the pain scale. Forty-eight hours later, she awoke headache-free for the first time since December.

Danny and Julie were almost home. The open windows of the minivan let in bird songs, train whistles, lawnmowers, and chainsaws – all sweet music.

"Hon? Are you awake?"

Julie turned and looked at Danny. "I am."

"I was just thinking …"

"Thanks for the warning."

"Hey! That's my line!"

"Talking too fast for you?"

Danny laughed. "I can only keep up with you when I have the advantage. Soon you will be better, and I will be left behind!"

Julie flashed a crooked smile.

"Seriously – when you had the MRIs at St. Michael's, was your head turned in the wrong position, so that it looked like you had a blood clot?"

"Don't know."

"Or did you really have a blood clot that God miraculously healed?"

"Maybe so."

I wish I could tell you that I think God allowed this illness, or misdiagnosis, or whatever it was, to draw me closer to Him and to you. As far as the Littles go, I don't know what to do. I understand them not being able

398

to talk to me on the phone these past five months, but they never called to talk to you. Cissy e-mailed me once, and Tiny and Pokey a few times. Daddy wrote once. Why did they think that was enough? Whether my head was in the right or wrong position during the MRIs, it's in the right position now – turned toward God and wanting to seek His direction for my life.

"You're not going to believe this!" Danny opened the garage door into the kitchen and found Julie at the table practicing her writing.

"What?" Julie looked at Danny in alarm.

"This!" Danny dropped an official-looking letter on the table. "It's a letter from our insurance company."

"How much ... did they pay?"

"Forty-five thousand! There was such a discrepancy between the original diagnosis at St. Michael's and the accurate diagnosis at Mayo that they are covering the cost, even without the pre-authorization requirement."

"Praise ... God!"

CHAPTER 38
"HONOR THY FATHER
AND MOTHER"

Rose Garden was a perfect name for the long-term care facility five miles east of Allen Park. Someone with a knowledge and love of roses had designed the various gardens around the building for optimum appreciation, including signs throughout the gardens detailing the varieties of roses and when they were discovered. The calligraphic lettering on each sign boasted names like Lavender Princess, Forever Amber, Miami Moon, Chinatown, Matador, and Shocking Blue. The signs were planted in front of roses blooming in spectacular mauves, deep reds and oranges, delicate pinks, rich purples, bright yellows, unusual peaches, and innumerable variegated shades.

The early June afternoon was pleasantly warm. Lavish colors and scents drew Julie to one of the wooden benches placed at the end of a winding concrete sidewalk. She finally conceded defeat to her mom's determination to remain inside, even in the summertime, and to cocoon in her gloom. As Julie tilted her head back, reveling in the bright sunlight, and grateful that it no longer caused headaches, she drained the rest of the water in her Nalgene bottle. The empty bottle was so like Arlene Sandford, who lived in the belief that her bottle, which never had anything but bitter water in it, had long ago been emptied and discarded.

Walking through the front door of the nursing home, Julie was struck by the irony not lost on her. She and her mom had both lost speech and movement within

400

the same month – Julie's through her basal artery migraine, and Arlene's through a second stroke, far more serious than the first one several years earlier. Julie had been highly motivated to do whatever therapy it took to regain the ability to reconnect with family and friends – to walk, to talk, and to feed her own soul by cooking and serving as she had done for so long. Arlene had resisted all pleas from her doctors and nurses and therapists to do any therapy – except the exercises that helped her regain speech. Julie had to admit that she wasn't thrilled about that one remnant of Arlene's former self, especially when her words were pricklier than ever.

Julie knocked on Arlene's partially opened door and walked in.

"Hi, Mom. Whatcha watching?"

"Oprah Winfrey. She has some good shows for a colored lady."

Ignoring the comment, Julie walked over to the window and raised the mini-blind.

"Don't do that! It puts too much glare on the idiot box!"

"It's a beautiful day."

"The sun is too bright."

"But in the winter, you complain that it's too dark."

Arlene pressed a button on the remote until the volume was at full power. "Okay, enough about the outside," said Julie. "I'm sorry."

Arlene hit the off button and put the remote on her lap.

"Would you like something to drink?"

"No. Besides, the coffee is too hot, and the iced tea is too cold."

Is the bed just right? "Do you have everything you need?"

"I guess. I'm used to doing without. It came from years of giving all my money to you for clothes and swimsuits and record albums." *Your memory must have been affected by the stroke.* "Besides, I hated sending you to pay our rent. You probably never knew that."

"No, I didn't." Julie's head began to hurt under the pressure of fighting for control of her thoughts and emotions.

"When that vulgar Cliff Koski complained about missing you … and then he told me he got the rent checks in the mail … I had to go down there myself with the money. He pawed me and practically molested me. I had to put up with it to keep our rent down. You have no idea what I went through."

"Are you kidding me?" Julie tried to relax her facial muscles. "I told you what he did to me, and you accused me of lying!"

"You always thought everything was about you, so I never knew what to believe. Besides, he didn't get you pregnant, and I'm the one who would have looked bad if he had kicked us out of our house."

"Was that more important than protecting me?" Julie whispered.

"Maybe I made some mistakes, but I did the best I could."

Julie looked at her mom's cloudy eyes. "You made one big mistake in your life, and the mistake has a name. Her name is Julie Marie Ness Sandford Dietrich Lewis Little! She was born April first, nineteen fifty-six in the navy hospital in Bremerton, Washington."

"Don't get sassy with me."

"I'm being honest. I think you've always seen me as a mistake."

Bret ... Undeserved Respect ... I always thought that only had to do with Danny Sandford. But it's about my mother, too. God, You have brought me so far. Please don't let Your love in my heart be choked by bitterness.

"The only mistake I ever made was thinking you cared about me." Arlene picked a thread from the sleeve of her green robe.

God, I could rehearse my resentments. I have the right to do that. No one would blame me. "I care."

"You have a funny way of showing it."

"I suppose." *God, I will release my right to rehearse my resentments. I have never forgotten that challenge from one of Pastor Tim's sermons, and I need it now more than ever. You have brought me so far. I haven't arrived yet – but at least I've left the station. This train is barreling down the tracks.*

"Did you want something?" Arlene looked past Julie to the grainy picture of her and Danny, framed and hanging on the wall of the kitchenette.

"No, Mom. I have everything I need." Julie smiled through salty tears, tears of sadness and joy. "I'll come back tomorrow." She got up and squeezed her mom's shoulder.

"If you can spare the time."

Julie walked out and closed the door behind her, resisting the urge to skip as she headed out to her car. The chains that bound her to her mom's approval were beginning to loosen.

CHAPTER 39
POKEY'S STORY

"**D**anny, I'm not sure I want Andrew in my life." Julie tied a bow around Danny's finger as he held the ribbon down on the wrapped Christmas present.

"Julie?" Danny slipped his finger out and touched her cheek. "What's going on?"

"Ever since you proposed to me, I've had Decembers without depression, until now." Julie picked up the present and put it on top of the growing stack of wrapped boxes on the kitchen table. "Can you help me carry these to the tree?" After scattering the gifts under the tree, Julie and Danny backed up and sat on the couch.

"Did I do something wrong?"

"No. But you can't make everything right, either."

"With Andrew?"

"With him, with the rest of the Little family. They still don't seem entirely sure of what to do with me. When they call, words are pleasant, like talking to a cashier at Wal-Mart. I've spent so much time telling them about my past life, and I just get these uncomfortable silences when I ask any of them about their past, especially when I'm curious about Tiny's and Pokey's teen years. And why won't anyone tell me why Pokey wasn't in Tiny's wedding pictures? If he was away on a trip or something, what's the big deal? Why all the secrets?" Julie got up and straightened one of the ornaments on the tree.

Danny stood behind Julie and wrapped his arms

around her shoulders. "What do you think you'll do?" he whispered.

Leaning into his chest, Julie fought back tears. "I don't know. Maybe I should call Pokey before I decide whether to keep him on my dance card."

Turning Julie around, Danny kissed her. "Know what I love about you?"

"Short-term memory loss is returning."

"Just about everything."

"Pokey? It's Julie." Julie turned her body sideways on the couch and tucked her feet under Danny's legs.

"Merry Christmas, Julie!"

"Thanks." Julie took a deep breath. "How are dad and Mama?"

"Great. Everyone's getting ready for Christmas Eve. We always call it the Big Little Party."

"Sounds fun." Julie's voice lacked conviction, her emotions parked in neutral.

"I wish ya'll could be here."

"Me, too."

"Julie—"

"Pokey—"

"You first!" Julie chuckled.

"Naw! Daddy always taught me to let a lady go first."

"Okay, then." *God, be in my words.* "I have an idea for a Christmas present you could give me."

"I already mailed—"

"What I want are answers."

"Like?"

"Like why you aren't in any of your brother's – *our brother's* – wedding pictures? Why does everyone get quiet when I ask about your past?" Julie did not hear anything and thought maybe the connection was lost. "Pokey? Are you there?"

"Yep."

"I'm sorry. I shouldn't have asked."

"I'm the one who's sorry. We should have told you before now. Daddy's been after me to talk to you, but I guess I was waiting for the right time."

"If it's too painful—"

"It was, but not any longer. God brought huge changes into my life."

"I've never heard you talk like this."

"That's because I'm afraid of what people might think of me if they knew the truth."

"After all I've told you about my past? Do you think I'd judge you?"

"No. But you've said so many times that you wish you had found us when you were in high school. And you told us about your cousin who told you about your real dad. You probably dreamed about a perfect family out there, and you would have been disappointed in us."

"I don't know what I would have felt at fifteen, or what I will feel now. I would still like to hear the truth."

When I was fifteen, I started dealing cocaine."

Julie had a lump in her throat. "Oh?"

"I never did any. Just dealt it. By the time I was twenty-two, I was living in a mansion with four Dobermans for security. I always carried a gun, wore a Rolex, and had all the girls and clothes and parties I wanted." Pokey stopped for air. "Are you sure you want to hear the rest of this?"

"Uh-huh."

"I was called a lieutenant, the number three man in the drug ring. It was one of the biggest, toughest rings on the east coast. I was in charge of two-hundred eighty million bucks. I flew to Bogotá and stayed in one of my houses, and when I was back here, I recruited doctors, lawyers, and police for the drug ring."

"Were you ever afraid?"

"Only all the time. I became so paranoid that I slept maybe three hours a night. After years of living like that, the house of cards began to fall in on itself. I met with the number one and two men in the organization, out on abandoned farmland fifty miles from my parents' home. Those two men were as scared and paranoid as I was; number two shot number one. I got out of there before I was next."

"This sounds unbelievable."

"It felt as surreal as you can get. I was way past the point of no return and stayed on the run for the next eight months. The end of the road was a cheap motel in Phoenix. The FBI was trailing me, so I contacted Tiny under the radar."

"What did he do?"

"Nothing he could do. He said he hoped he'd see me alive again someday, and he broke down on the phone. I knew I had to quit running, but I was too afraid, and I didn't think I could trust anyone."

"What happened?"

"I was so desperate that I called my friend James – a guy I had known since first grade. I couldn't get at any of my money without being found by the Fibbies, so I asked James to mail me money at the motel. By the time I hung up the phone, I looked out the window and saw black cars with smoked mirrors pulling up in front of my room. Guys in black suits carrying Uzis spilled out of the doors. I loaded my nine-millimeter, opened the windows, and aimed. 'I can take three guys out from here,' I yelled. Julie, I figured I could kill myself after them. I was only thirty-seven, and I wasn't going to spend the rest of my life in prison.

"One of the guys yelled, 'Mr. Little! We have a search warrant! Put your weapon down!' I didn't know what made me listen to him. Not then, anyway. I know now that God had big plans for my life, and that my folks had spent years praying for protection for me, but that God would allow whatever it took for me to become a broken man. I laid down my gun, and the agents came in, knocked me to the floor, and handcuffed me.

"Long, long story short, Julie, was that I expected to stay broken. As soon as the other guys in prison found out that I was the one-and-only Pokey, I became the only cool white guy they knew. They elevated me to the status I had as a lieutenant in the drug ring, and I slipped into the same prideful attitude that got me in trouble as a kid."

"Did you ever regret what you did?"

"Not until I was transferred to Florida, and then to Tennessee. People stopped caring about who I was. There was a new kid on the block, and I was just another messed up inmate. I resisted calling Daddy for all those years. One morning I woke up and couldn't stand who I was. I remembered reading the story of the prodigal son in Sunday School as a little boy, and I thought maybe my parents would forgive me for making such a mess of my life and for leaving a trail of drug addicts along the way. And, for bringing so much shame on them."

"Did they?"

"Amazingly, they did. They both cried and said they would wait for me however long it took to get out of prison. Through a series of miracles, I was out after only three more years, and that was just a few years before you came into our lives."

Julie was crying freely. "Pokey, I used to wonder how I could fully believe in a God who didn't seem willing or able to protect me from the things my father and other men did to me. After I learned that I had a different dad – a biological dad – I never stopped wondering how different my life would been had I found him sooner."

"Julie, I am really sorry for what your life was like."

"Do you have any idea how much God lead both of our lives? If I had found you when I was a teenager, I would have gone from the frying pan into the fire. God's timing was perfect. Life is different for both of us now. I can appreciate the Littles in a way I never would have before. There was stubbornness in my heart that needed to be dealt with."

"I know we haven't been very open with you, which was mostly my fault. I still battle crushing guilt over what I did to my family. It's hard to talk about it to anyone."

"Pokey, I understand that now. There is no way you're getting rid of me!"

"When I got out of prison, Tiny said that I should get baptized and show everyone that I was a clean, forgiven man. When that day arrived, my pastor baptized me in a lake during a pouring rain. He figured God was doing His job thoroughly!"

"Awesome."

"What about you, Julie?"

"What about me?"

"Have you ever been baptized?"

"No." Julie felt the depression lift from her spirit. "But I think I want to be."

"We have some things to make up to you. You pick a date, and we will all be there, all the Littles, big and little!"

EPILOGUE

Two hands reach down and gently pull Julie up out of the water. The baptismal ceremony lasted less than five minutes, but her mind rewound the tape back to her childhood – through years of alcoholism, abuse, financial poverty, and emotional deprivation. New words of victory are now being recorded.

"We praise God today for a different kind of birth on Julie's forty-fifth birthday," begins Pastor Tim. "We have prayed her through these past several months, and she has regained most of her speech and movement. She stands before you today as a witness to the God who cares about her physical healing. The greater miracle – if there is such a thing as a greater and lesser miracle – is that Julie found her father and his family, who are all here with us today." *My mother could have been here, too. God, please work a miracle of healing in her heart.*

"The greatest miracle – okay, so maybe some miracles *are* greater than others! – is what God did in Julie's heart; what He does in all our hearts when we trust in Him. The book of Isaiah tells us that 'death is swallowed up in victory.' Julie's victory is that she has been cleansed by water in the Word.

"Many of us may wonder – as Julie has over the years – why God chooses not to reverse consequences, some of which are very damaging and can live a lifetime in our spirits. We may never know the answer this side of heaven; but we can be reassured that God redeems all those consequences in a way that strengthens our character and deepens our faith."

Pastor Tim put his arm around Julie's towel-wrapped shoulder. "Julie's desire is to be a wounded healer. She believes God will send people into her life, across her path, who need to hear her story, and to know that He is Abba, Protector, Perfect Father, Preserver of Life.

"I now want to introduce you to Julie Lewis, a new creation!"

Made in the USA
Middletown, DE
30 April 2022

64778669R00246